Fodor's

Bed & Breakfasts, Country Inns and Other Weekend Pleasures

CALIFORNIA

Fodor's Travel Publications, Inc.
New York • Toronto • London •
Sydney • Auckland

First Edition

ISBN 0–679–02263–5

**Fodor's Bed & Breakfasts, Country Inns
and Other Weekend Pleasures: California**

Editor: Edie Jarolim
Contributors: Colleen Bates, Rebecca Bruns, Andrew Collins, Pamela P. Hegarty, Charles Hibbard, Judith Hibbard-Mipaas, Susan LaTempa, Marty Olmstead, Christopher Pennington, Linda K. Schmidt, Terry Trucco, Anne Weinberger, Loralee Wenger, Bobbi Zane
Creative Director: Fabrizio La Rocca
Cartographer: David Lindroth
Illustrators: Alida Beck, Karl Tanner
Cover Photograph: Francis Hammond
Design: Rochelle Udell and Fabrizio La Rocca

Special Sales

Fodor's Travel Publications are available at special discounts for bulk purchases (100 copies or more) for sales promotions or premiums. Special editions, including personalized covers, excerpts of existing guides, and corporate imprints, can be created in large quantities for special needs. For more information write to Special Marketing, Fodor's Travel Publications, 201 East 50th St., New York, NY 10022. Inquiries from Canada should be sent to Random House of Canada, Ltd., Marketing Dept., 1265 Aerowood Dr., Mississauga, Ontario L4W 1B9. Inquiries from the United Kingdom should be sent to Fodor's Travel Publications, 20 Vauxhall Bridge Rd., London, England SW1V 2SA.

Contributors

Colleen Bates, *who contributed to the Central Coast chapter, is the food editor for the* Los Angeles Times *syndicate. A resident of Pasadena, she was formerly the editor of the Gault Millau series of guidebooks and a contributing editor for* L.A. Style.

Rebecca Bruns, *who contributed to the San Francisco chapter, is the author of* Hidden Mexico: Adventurer's Guide to the Beaches and Coasts, *and a frequent contributer to* Travel & Leisure, Caribbean Travel and Life, *and* L.A. Style. *A former staff writer for the* New Orleans Times Picayune, *she won the 1992 Pluma de Plata award from the Mexican government for a story about Mexico and two PATA gold awards for her writing.*

Pamela P. Hegarty, *who lives in the San Francisco Bay Area, has written extensively on travel in northern California and is the author of* San Francisco and Beyond: 101 Affordable Excursions. *Her work has appeared in* Woman's Day, Good Housekeeping, *and other prominent publications. She wrote the San Francisco and Bay Area chapters.*

Judith and Charles Hibbard, *who contributed to the North Coast and Redwood Country chapter, have both worked in the publishing industry for many years. They reside in San Francisco.*

Susan LaTempa, *who wrote the San Bernardino Mountains chapter, is a book packager and playwright, and formerly an editor at L.A. Style. She lives in Culver City.*

Marty Olmstead, *a travel writer and editor who lives in Sonoma, California, wrote the Wine Country chapter and contributed to the Bay Area chapter. She is co-author of* Hidden Florida *and writes for numerous publications about California food, wine, travel, and history.*

Terry Trucco, *who wrote the Sacramento and the Central Valley chapter and the Gold Country chapter, grew up in northern California. Currently living in New York City, she writes on a variety of subjects, including travel, design, and beauty, for the* New York Times, *the* Wall Street Journal, Travel & Leisure, *and other publications.*

Anne Weinberger, *who contributed to the Gold Country and High Sierra chapters, is a freelance writer and translator who lives in San Francisco. She has written about travel for Gault Millau and the* San Francisco Examiner.

Bobbi Zane, *who wrote six California chapters, lives in southern California. The publisher of* Yellow Brick Road, *a monthly newsletter devoted to bed-and-breakfast travel in the western United States, and the annual* California B&B Directory, *she has written for the* Los Angeles Times.

Contents

Foreword

While every care has been taken to ensure the accuracy of the information in this guide, the passage of time will always bring change, and consequently, the publisher cannot accept responsibility for errors that may occur.

All prices and listings are based on information supplied to us at press time. Details may change, however, and the prudent traveler will avoid inconvenience by calling ahead.

Fodor's wants to hear about your travel experiences, both pleasant and unpleasant. When an inn or B&B fails to live up to its billing, let us know and we will investigate the complaint and revise our entries where the facts warrant it.

Send your letters to the editors of Fodor's Travel Publications, 201 E. 50th Street, New York, NY 10022.

Introduction

Fodor's Bed & Breakfasts, Country Inns, and Other Weekend Pleasures *is a complete weekend planner that tells you not just where to stay but how to enjoy yourself when you get there. We describe the B&Bs and country inns, of course, but we also help you organize trips around them, with information on everything from parks to beaches to antiques stores—as well as nightlife and memorable places to dine. We also include names and addresses of B&B reservation services, should properties we recommend be full or should you be inspired to go in search of additional places on your own. Reviews are divided by region.*

All inns are not created equal, and age in itself is no guarantee of good taste, quality, or charm. We therefore avoid the directory approach, preferring instead to discriminate—recommending the very best for travelers with different interests, budgets, and sensibilities.

It's a sad commentary on other B&B guides today that we feel obliged to tell you our reviewers visited every property in person, and that it is they, not the innkeepers, who wrote the reviews. No one paid a fee or promised to sell or promote the book in order to be included in it. Fodor's has no stake in anything but the truth: A dark room with peeling wallpaper is not called quaint or atmospheric, it's called run-down; a gutted 18th-century barn with motel units at either end is called a gutted 18th-century barn with motel units at either end, not a historic inn.

Is there a difference between a B&B and a country inn? Not really, not anymore; the public has blurred the distinction—hence our decision to include both in the title. There was a time when the B&B experience meant an extra room in someone's home, often with paper-thin walls and a shared bathroom full of bobby pins and used cotton balls. But no longer; Laura Ashley has come to town with her matching prints, and some B&Bs are as elegant as the country's most venerable inns. The only distinction that seems to hold is that a B&B was built as a private home and an inn was built for paying guests. Most B&Bs serve breakfast, but not all, and some serve dinner, too; most inns have full-service restaurants. B&Bs tend to be run by their owners, creating a homey, family feeling (which can be anathema to those who relish privacy), while inns are often run by managers; but the reverse is true, too. B&Bs can cost more than inns, or less. B&Bs tend to be smaller, with fewer rooms, but not always. The truth is that many B&Bs are called so only to circumvent local zoning laws.

What all places in this guide—B&Bs or country inns—offer is the promise of a unique experience. Each is one of a kind, and each exudes a sense of time and place. All are destinations in themselves—not just places to put your head at night, but an integral part of a weekend escape.

So trust us, the way you'd trust a knowledgeable, well-traveled friend. And have a wonderful weekend!

***

A word about the service material in this guide:

A mailing address is often included that differs from the actual address of the property. A double room is for two people, regardless of the size or type of beds; if you're looking for twin beds or a king- or queen-size bed, be sure to ask.

Rates are for two in the high season and include breakfast; ask about special packages and off-season discounts. Mandatory state taxes are extra. Most places leave tipping to the discretion of the visitor, but some add a service charge to the bill; if the issue concerns you, inquire when you make your reservation, not when you check out.

What we call a restaurant serves meals other than breakfast and is usually open to the general public. Inns listed as MAP (Modified American Plan) require guests to pay for two meals, usually breakfast and dinner. The requirement is usually enforced during the high season, but an inn may waive it if it is otherwise unable to fill all its rooms.

B&Bs don't have phones or TVs in rooms unless otherwise noted. Pools and bicycles are free; "bike rentals" are not. Properties are open year-round, unless otherwise noted.

Michael Spring
Editorial Director

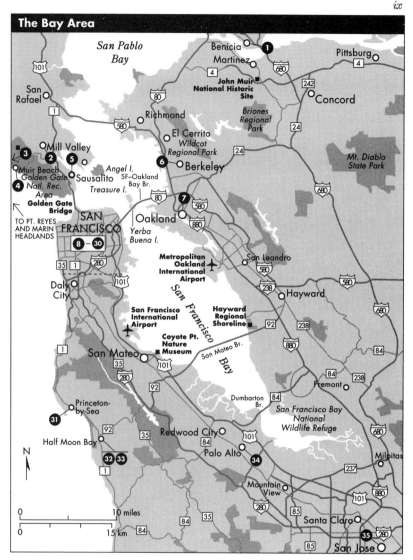

The Bay Area

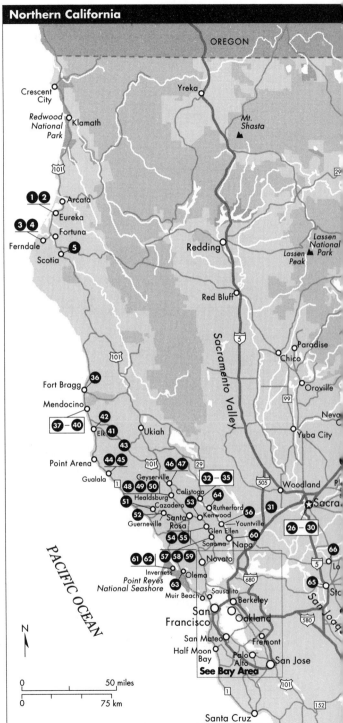

Northern California

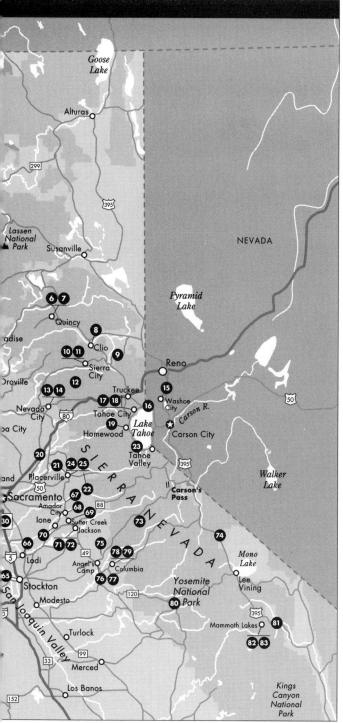

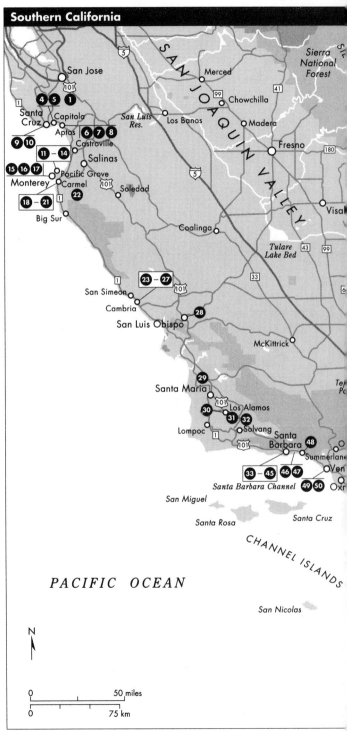

Southern California

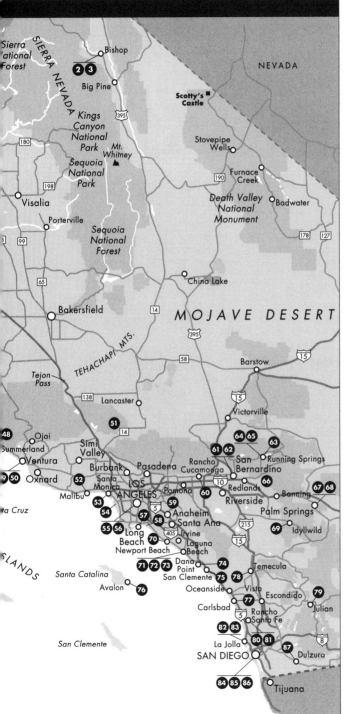

Special Features at a Glance

Name of Property	Accessible for Disabled	Antiques	On the Water	Good Value	Car Not Necessary	Full Meal Service	Historic Building	
SOUTHERN COUNTIES								
Bed and Breakfast Inn at La Jolla	✓	✓					✓	
Brookside Farm						✓		
The Cottage		✓		✓				
Heritage Park Bed & Breakfast Inn	✓	✓					✓	
Hill House								
Ingleside Inn								
Inn at Rancho Santa Fe		✓				✓	✓	
Julian Hotel		✓					✓	
Loma Vista Bed and Breakfast								
Pelican Cove Inn	✓							
Rancho Valencia Resort						✓		
Scripps Inn	✓		✓					
Strawberry Creek Inn	✓	✓						
Villa Royale	✓	✓				✓		
SAN BERNARDINO MOUNTAINS								
The Carriage House		✓						
Gold Mountain Manor		✓					✓	
The Inn at Fawnskin								
The Knickerbocker Mansion		✓						
The Lodge at Green Valley Lake	✓	✓	✓	✓		✓		
Saddleback Inn	✓					✓		
Sky Forest Bed and Breakfast Inn								
LOS ANGELES								
Anaheim Country Inn		✓					✓	

Romantic Hideaway	Luxurious	Pets Allowed	No Smoking Indoors	Good Place for Families	Beach Nearby	Cross-Country Ski Trails	Golf Within 5 Miles	Fitness Facilities	Near Wineries	Good Biking Terrain	Skiing	Tennis	Swimming on Premises	Conference Facilities	Hiking Nearby
	✓		✓		✓		✓								
✓			✓		✓										✓
			✓												
			✓												
			✓												
✓	✓			✓	✓		✓	✓				✓	✓	✓	
			✓							✓				✓	
			✓				✓			✓					
				✓											
✓	✓						✓					✓	✓	✓	
		✓		✓	✓		✓			✓					
✓			✓							✓				✓	
✓	✓						✓			✓			✓		✓
✓			✓							✓					✓
			✓			✓	✓			✓	✓				✓
			✓			✓				✓	✓				✓
✓			✓	✓		✓	✓			✓	✓				✓
✓			✓			✓				✓	✓				✓
				✓										✓	✓
✓			✓							✓					✓
			✓												

Name of Property	Accessible for Disabled	Antiques	On the Water	Good Value	Car Not Necessary	Full Meal Service	Historic Building	
Blue Lantern Inn	✓		✓					
Carriage House		✓						
Casa Tropicana			✓			✓		
Channel Road Inn		✓					✓	
Christmas House		✓					✓	
Eiler's Inn								
Inn at Laguna Beach	✓		✓		✓			
Inn at Mt. Ada					✓	✓	✓	
Lord Mayor's Inn		✓			✓		✓	
Malibu Beach Inn	✓		✓			✓		
Mansion Inn	✓				✓			
Portofino Beach Hotel		✓	✓				✓	
Salisbury House							✓	
Seal Beach Inn and Gardens		✓					✓	
Terrace Manor		✓					✓	
CENTRAL COAST								
Ballard Inn	✓							
Bath Street Inn								
Bayberry Inn								
The Beach House			✓					
Bella Maggiore Inn	✓	✓		✓			✓	
Blue Quail Inn		✓		✓	✓			
The Blue Whale Inn			✓					
The Cheshire Cat		✓			✓			
El Encanto	✓					✓		

Romantic Hideaway	Luxurious	Pets Allowed	No Smoking Indoors	Good Place for Families	Beach Nearby	Cross-Country Ski Trails	Golf Within 5 Miles	Fitness Facilities	Near Wineries	Good Biking Terrain	Skiing	Tennis	Swimming on Premises	Conference Facilities	Hiking Nearby
✓	✓		✓		✓		✓	✓		✓				✓	✓
					✓										
✓			✓		✓					✓					
			✓	✓	✓					✓					✓
✓							✓								
					✓		✓								
	✓				✓								✓	✓	
✓	✓		✓		✓					✓				✓	✓
			✓		✓										
✓	✓				✓										✓
				✓	✓		✓			✓					
					✓					✓					
			✓												
✓					✓								✓	✓	
														✓	
	✓		✓							✓					✓
			✓	✓						✓					✓
✓		✓	✓		✓					✓					✓
				✓	✓	✓			✓	✓					✓
					✓		✓								
✓			✓	✓	✓		✓		✓	✓					
	✓		✓		✓					✓					
✓			✓		✓		✓		✓	✓				✓	
✓	✓			✓	✓		✓		✓	✓		✓	✓	✓	

Name of Property	Accessible for Disabled	Antiques	On the Water	Good Value	Car Not Necessary	Full Meal Service	Historic Building	
Garden Street Inn	✓	✓						
Harbour Carriage House	✓	✓						
Inn at Summer Hill	✓							
J. Patrick House	✓							
La Mer		✓						
Los Olivos Grand Hotel	✓	✓			✓	✓		
Montecito Inn				✓	✓	✓	✓	
Olallieberry Inn	✓	✓		✓				
Old Yacht Club Inn		✓						
The Olive House		✓						
The Parsonage		✓					✓	
Pickford House	✓	✓		✓				
Rose Victorian Inn	✓	✓					✓	
San Ysidro Ranch	✓				✓	✓	✓	
Simpson House Inn		✓						
Tiffany Inn		✓			✓			
Union Hotel/Victorian Mansion		✓					✓	
The Upham					✓		✓	
Villa Rosa					✓			
MONTEREY BAY								
Apple Lane Inn		✓					✓	
Babbling Brook Inn	✓	✓					✓	
Bayview Hotel		✓					✓	
Blue Spruce Inn	✓	✓						
Cliff Crest Bed and Breakfast Inn		✓						

Romantic Hideaway	Luxurious	Pets Allowed	No Smoking Indoors	Good Place for Families	Beach Nearby	Cross-Country Ski Trails	Golf Within 5 Miles	Fitness Facilities	Near Wineries	Good Biking Terrain	Skiing	Tennis	Swimming on Premises	Conference Facilities	Hiking Nearby
			✓												
✓			✓		✓		✓		✓	✓					
	✓		✓		✓										
			✓												
			✓		✓										
✓	✓								✓	✓			✓	✓	✓
				✓	✓		✓	✓		✓			✓	✓	
✓			✓		✓					✓					✓
			✓		✓			✓		✓					✓
✓			✓		✓		✓		✓	✓					
✓			✓		✓					✓					✓
				✓	✓					✓					
✓			✓		✓		✓								
✓	✓			✓	✓		✓		✓	✓			✓		✓
	✓		✓							✓					✓
✓			✓		✓		✓		✓	✓					
✓	✓														
				✓			✓		✓	✓				✓	
✓					✓		✓		✓	✓			✓	✓	
				✓	✓		✓			✓					✓
				✓	✓	✓	✓			✓					
				✓	✓				✓	✓					✓
				✓	✓		✓		✓	✓					
				✓	✓		✓			✓					

Name of Property	Accessible for Disabled	Antiques	On the Water	Good Value	Car Not Necessary	Full Meal Service	Historic Building	
Country Rose Inn		✓						
Gatehouse Inn	✓	✓	✓				✓	
Gosby House		✓						
Green Gables Inn		✓						
Happy Landing Inn			✓					
Inn at Depot Hill		✓					✓	
The Jabberwock		✓			✓			
Mangels House		✓					✓	
Martine Inn	✓	✓	✓				✓	
Old Monterey Inn		✓						
Sandpiper Inn		✓						
Sea View Inn								
Seven Gables Inn		✓	✓				✓	
Stonehouse Inn							✓	
Stonepine		✓				✓		
SAN FRANCISCO								
The Alamo Square Inn					✓		✓	
Albion House Inn		✓		✓			✓	
Archbishops Mansion		✓		✓	✓		✓	
The Bed and Breakfast Inn					✓			
Chateau Tivoli		✓			✓		✓	
Golden Gate Hotel		✓		✓	✓		✓	
Hotel Griffon	✓		✓	✓		✓	✓	
Hotel Triton	✓			✓		✓		
Inn at the Opera	✓	✓				✓	✓	

Romantic Hideaway	Luxurious	Pets Allowed	No Smoking Indoors	Good Place for Families	Beach Nearby	Cross-Country Ski Trails	Golf Within 5 Miles	Fitness Facilities	Near Wineries	Good Biking Terrain	Skiing	Tennis	Swimming on Premises	Conference Facilities	Hiking Nearby
✓			✓						✓						
			✓		✓					✓					
						✓				✓				✓	
						✓				✓					
			✓	✓	✓	✓									
✓	✓		✓												
			✓		✓		✓			✓				✓	
			✓		✓					✓					✓
	✓				✓		✓			✓				✓	
✓	✓		✓		✓		✓			✓				✓	
							✓			✓					
			✓		✓		✓			✓					
			✓		✓		✓			✓					
			✓		✓		✓			✓					
✓	✓						✓	✓		✓		✓	✓		✓
✓			✓	✓			✓							✓	
✓		✓	✓	✓											
✓	✓						✓							✓	
✓			✓												
✓	✓	✓	✓	✓			✓								
		✓	✓	✓											
✓	✓	✓						✓						✓	
✓	✓		✓	✓										✓	
✓	✓	✓	✓	✓						✓				✓	

Name of Property	Accessible for Disabled	Antiques	On the Water	Good Value	Car Not Necessary	Full Meal Service	Historic Building	
Inn San Francisco		✓			✓		✓	
Inn at Union Square	✓	✓		✓	✓		✓	
Jackson Court		✓		✓			✓	
The Mansions Hotel		✓		✓	✓	✓	✓	
The Monte Cristo		✓		✓			✓	
Petite Auberge		✓		✓	✓		✓	
The Queen Anne	✓	✓		✓			✓	
Savoy Hotel	✓			✓	✓	✓		
The Sherman House		✓				✓	✓	
Spencer House		✓		✓	✓		✓	
Union Street Inn		✓			✓		✓	
Victorian Inn on the Park		✓		✓	✓		✓	
Washington Square Inn		✓		✓	✓			
White Swan Inn		✓		✓	✓		✓	
BAY AREA								
Blackthorne Inn								
Captain Dillingham's Inn		✓	✓				✓	
Casa del Mar				✓				
Casa Madrona Hotel			✓		✓	✓		
Claremont Resort and Spa	✓					✓	✓	
Cowper Inn							✓	
Gramma's Inn							✓	
The Hensley House		✓					✓	
The Mill Rose Inn								
Mountain Home Inn					✓			

Romantic Hideaway	Luxurious	Pets Allowed	No Smoking Indoors	Good Place for Families	Beach Nearby	Cross-Country Ski Trails	Golf Within 5 Miles	Fitness Facilities	Near Wineries	Good Biking Terrain	Skiing	Tennis	Swimming on Premises	Conference Facilities	Hiking Nearby
✓		✓		✓											
✓	✓		✓	✓											
✓	✓		✓							✓				✓	
✓	✓	✓		✓										✓	
✓			✓												
✓	✓			✓											
✓	✓		✓	✓						✓				✓	
✓	✓			✓										✓	
✓	✓		✓							✓				✓	
✓	✓		✓			✓	✓			✓					✓
✓			✓	✓											
✓	✓		✓			✓	✓			✓					✓
✓	✓		✓	✓											
✓	✓													✓	
✓			✓		✓										✓
			✓		✓					✓					✓
✓	✓													✓	✓
✓	✓		✓	✓			✓	✓		✓		✓	✓	✓	
			✓											✓	
			✓												
			✓		✓									✓	
✓			✓		✓								✓	✓	
✓										✓				✓	

Name of Property	Accessible for Disabled	Antiques	On the Water	Good Value	Car Not Necessary	Full Meal Service	Historic Building	
Old Thyme Inn							✓	
The Pelican Inn		✓				✓		
Pillar Point Inn	✓		✓	✓				
Roundstone Farm		✓						
Ten Inverness Way				✓				
WINE COUNTRY								
Auberge du Soleil	✓					✓		
Beltane Ranch		✓		✓			✓	
The Boonville Hotel				✓		✓	✓	
Brannan Cottage Inn					✓		✓	
Camellia Inn	✓	✓			✓		✓	
Campbell Ranch Inn	✓							
Cross Roads Inn								
El Dorado Hotel	✓				✓	✓	✓	
The Gaige House	✓							
Healdsburg Inn on the Plaza		✓			✓		✓	
Highland Ranch				✓		✓		
Hope-Merrill House	✓	✓					✓	
Kenwood Inn								
Larkmead		✓						
Madrona Manor	✓	✓		✓		✓	✓	
Magnolia Hotel		✓		✓	✓		✓	
Mount View Hotel		✓			✓	✓	✓	
Quail Mountain				✓				
Sonoma Hotel		✓				✓	✓	

Romantic Hideaway	Luxurious	Pets Allowed	No Smoking Indoors	Good Place for Families	Beach Nearby	Cross-Country Ski Trails	Golf Within 5 Miles	Fitness Facilities	Near Wineries	Good Biking Terrain	Skiing	Tennis	Swimming on Premises	Conference Facilities	Hiking Nearby
			✓					✓							
✓					✓					✓				✓	
✓					✓		✓								
			✓		✓									✓	
			✓		✓					✓					✓
✓	✓			✓			✓	✓	✓	✓		✓	✓	✓	✓
			✓			✓	✓		✓	✓		✓			✓
			✓						✓	✓					✓
✓			✓						✓	✓					✓
✓	✓								✓	✓					✓
			✓		✓				✓	✓					✓
			✓			✓			✓	✓					✓
									✓	✓					✓
✓			✓						✓	✓			✓		✓
			✓						✓						✓
				✓					✓			✓	✓	✓	✓
			✓	✓					✓	✓			✓		✓
✓	✓		✓						✓	✓			✓		✓
									✓	✓					✓
✓		✓	✓	✓					✓	✓			✓		✓
			✓						✓	✓			✓		✓
									✓	✓			✓		✓
			✓	✓					✓				✓		✓
									✓	✓					✓

Name of Property	Accessible for Disabled	Antiques	On the Water	Good Value	Car Not Necessary	Full Meal Service	Historic Building	
Thistle Dew Inn	✓	✓						
Vintners Inn	✓			✓		✓		
NORTH COAST AND REDWOOD COUNTRY								
Applewood: An Estate Inn							✓	
Carter House		✓						
"An Elegant Victorian Mansion"		✓					✓	
Gingerbread Mansion		✓						
Grey Whale Inn	✓						✓	
Harbor House			✓			✓	✓	
The Headlands Inn	✓	✓						
Joshua Grindle Inn		✓					✓	
Rachel's Inn	✓							
Scotia Inn						✓		
The Shaw House Inn		✓					✓	
St. Orres				✓		✓		
The Stanford Inn by the Sea	✓	✓	✓		✓			
Timberhill Ranch	✓					✓		
The Whale Watch Inn by the Sea			✓					
SACRAMENTO AND THE CENTRAL VALLEY								
Amber House		✓					✓	
Aunt Abigail's		✓					✓	
Davis Inn				✓				
The Driver Mansion Inn		✓					✓	
Hartley House		✓					✓	
The Old Victorian Inn		✓		✓			✓	

Romantic Hideaway	Luxurious	Pets Allowed	No Smoking Indoors	Good Place for Families	Beach Nearby	Cross-Country Ski Trails	Golf Within 5 Miles	Fitness Facilities	Near Wineries	Good Biking Terrain	Skiing	Tennis	Swimming on Premises	Conference Facilities	Hiking Nearby
			✓						✓	✓					✓
✓				✓					✓	✓				✓	✓
✓	✓		✓										✓		✓
	✓		✓											✓	
			✓												
	✓		✓		✓										
			✓	✓										✓	
✓			✓		✓									✓	✓
			✓				✓								
			✓												
✓	✓			✓	✓		✓								✓
														✓	
	✓		✓				✓			✓					✓
✓	✓				✓										✓
✓	✓	✓	✓		✓		✓	✓		✓			✓		✓
✓	✓		✓			✓	✓				✓	✓	✓	✓	✓
✓	✓		✓		✓					✓				✓	✓
✓	✓		✓		✓		✓			✓				✓	✓
✓			✓		✓		✓			✓		✓		✓	
			✓	✓			✓			✓					✓
✓	✓		✓		✓		✓			✓		✓		✓	
✓	✓		✓		✓		✓			✓				✓	✓
✓	✓		✓				✓			✓				✓	

Name of Property	Accessible for Disabled	Antiques	On the Water	Good Value	Car Not Necessary	Full Meal Service	Historic Building	
The Sterling Hotel						✓	✓	
Victorian Manor		✓		✓			✓	
Wine & Roses Country Inn	✓	✓					✓	
GOLD COUNTRY								
Camino Hotel		✓		✓			✓	
The Chichester House		✓		✓			✓	
City Hotel		✓		✓		✓	✓	
The Coloma Country Inn		✓	✓				✓	
Combellack-Blair House		✓					✓	
Cooper House		✓					✓	
The Court Street Inn		✓					✓	
Culbert House Inn		✓					✓	
Dunbar House, 1880		✓					✓	
Fallon Hotel	✓	✓		✓			✓	
The Foxes Bed and Breakfast Inn		✓					✓	
Grandmère's		✓					✓	
The Heirloom	✓	✓		✓			✓	
Indian Creek		✓					✓	
Red Castle Inn		✓					✓	
The Ryan House	✓	✓		✓			✓	
Windrose Inn		✓					✓	
HIGH SIERRA								
Busch and Heringlake Country Inn		✓				✓	✓	
The Cain House							✓	
The Captain's Alpenhaus		✓				✓	✓	

Romantic Hideaway	Luxurious	Pets Allowed	No Smoking Indoors	Good Place for Families	Beach Nearby	Cross-Country Ski Trails	Golf Within 5 Miles	Fitness Facilities	Near Wineries	Good Biking Terrain	Skiing	Tennis	Swimming on Premises	Conference Facilities	Hiking Nearby
✓	✓		✓		✓		✓			✓				✓	✓
			✓				✓			✓					✓
✓	✓		✓	✓	✓		✓			✓		✓		✓	
			✓				✓		✓	✓					✓
			✓						✓						✓
			✓	✓			✓			✓		✓			✓
✓			✓						✓	✓					✓
			✓						✓						✓
✓			✓	✓		✓				✓	✓	✓		✓	✓
			✓						✓	✓		✓			✓
✓	✓		✓	✓					✓	✓		✓			✓
✓	✓		✓			✓	✓		✓	✓					✓
✓			✓	✓	✓	✓		✓		✓		✓			✓
✓	✓		✓						✓	✓		✓			✓
			✓				✓			✓		✓			✓
✓			✓		✓				✓	✓				✓	✓
			✓						✓	✓			✓		✓
✓	✓		✓				✓			✓		✓			✓
			✓				✓		✓	✓		✓			✓
			✓						✓	✓		✓			✓
	✓		✓			✓				✓	✓				✓
	✓		✓			✓									✓
		✓	✓	✓	✓	✓				✓	✓		✓		✓

Name of Property	Accessible for Disabled	Antiques	On the Water	Good Value	Car Not Necessary	Full Meal Service	Historic Building	
Chalfant House		✓		✓			✓	
Clover Valley Mill House		✓					✓	
Cottage Inn at Lake Tahoe			✓					
The Feather Bed							✓	
Haus Bavaria								
High Country Inn		✓						
The Matlick House		✓		✓			✓	
Mayfield House							✓	
New England Ranch		✓					✓	
Rainbow Tarns		✓					✓	
Rockwood Lodge		✓						
Sorensen's						✓	✓	
White Horse Inn		✓						
White Sulphur Springs		✓					✓	
Wildassin House		✓						
Winters Creek Ranch		✓						
The Yosemite Peregrine								

Romantic Hideaway	Luxurious	Pets Allowed	No Smoking Indoors	Good Place for Families	Beach Nearby	Cross-Country Ski Trails	Golf Within 5 Miles	Fitness Facilities	Near Wineries	Good Biking Terrain	Skiing	Tennis	Swimming on Premises	Conference Facilities	Hiking Nearby
			✓			✓	✓			✓		✓			✓
✓			✓			✓				✓					✓
			✓	✓	✓	✓				✓	✓				✓
			✓			✓				✓					✓
			✓		✓	✓	✓			✓	✓	✓			✓
			✓			✓			✓	✓			✓		✓
			✓			✓	✓			✓		✓			✓
			✓		✓	✓	✓			✓	✓	✓			✓
✓			✓			✓	✓			✓		✓			✓
✓			✓			✓				✓	✓				✓
✓	✓		✓		✓	✓				✓	✓				✓
		✓		✓		✓				✓	✓			✓	✓
	✓		✓			✓	✓	✓		✓	✓	✓			✓
			✓	✓		✓	✓			✓	✓		✓		✓
			✓			✓	✓	✓		✓	✓	✓			✓
			✓			✓				✓					✓
✓			✓			✓					✓				✓

Southern Counties

Southern Counties
Including San Diego and Palm Springs

*"From the desert to the sea . . ." is the signature of
longtime southern California TV newsman Jerry Dunphy.
These are the natural boundaries of the vast area known as
the Southern Counties: San Diego, Riverside, Imperial.
Each has its own charms.*

*San Diego hugs the sea, stretching inland 4,255 square
miles over mile-high mountains to the desert at sea level.
Beyond is vast Riverside, the desert resorts of Palm Springs
and Palm Desert, and the date-growing areas surrounding
Indio. To the north are a dozen wineries in the historic
Temecula countryside and a pair of mountains more than
10,000 feet high, San Jacinto and San Gorgonio. Imperial,
ranging along the Mexican border, is the source of most of
the tomatoes, lettuce, and grapefruit consumed by
Americans.*

*The Southern Counties also contain the oldest and newest
communities in California. San Diego is the birthplace of
California; Portuguese explorer Juan Rodríguez Cabrillo
landed here and claimed the area for Spain in 1542. The
burgeoning suburban communities of Riverside County
represent the youngest and fastest-growing in the state.*

*History and geography aside, this is a land of recreation.
Hiking on wooded mountain trails. Sailing the deep-green
Pacific or blue inland lakes. Playing golf at one of dozens
of championship courses. Tennis. Bicycling. Ballooning.
Wine tasting. Discovering the lushness of a flower-carpeted
desert in spring. Delving into history at southern
California's only gold-rush town. Encountering wild
animals at the San Diego Zoo and Wild Animal Park.
Cavorting with the whales at Sea World. Exploring the vast
1,400-acre Balboa Park. Watching thoroughbred racing*

from the grandstand or elegant clubhouse at Del Mar. Basking on a long white beach.

Culture abounds here, too. San Diego's Old Globe Theatre is world-famous for its performances of classics, contemporary drama, experimental works, and, of course, its summer Shakespeare Festival. The San Diego Opera draws audiences from all over southern California. Art galleries flourish in seaside La Jolla. Balboa Park's art, anthropological, natural history, and other museums lure Sunday-afternoon visitors.

While this is an area of many splendid resorts, the Southern Counties also offer the intimacy, individuality, and personal contact that only bed-and-breakfast lodging can provide.

Places to Go, Sights to See

Balboa Park (tel. 619/239–0512). In addition to the *San Diego Zoo*, the 1,074-acre urban park contains 13 museums, including the *San Diego Museum of Art* (tel. 619/232–7931), *Reuben H. Fleet Space Theater and Science Center* (tel. 619/238–1233), *Museum of Man* (tel. 619/239–2001), *Museum of Photographic Art* (tel. 619/239–5262), and *Centro Cultural de la Raza* (tel. 619/235–6135). The *Simon Edison Centre for the Performing Arts* houses three stages, including the famed *Old Globe Theatre* (tel. 619/239–2255), the oldest professional theater in California, which presents a full season of Shakespearean, classic, and contemporary plays. On weekends the park fairly sings with fun as street performers, mimes, and musicians work the crowd on the Prado.

Cabrillo National Monument (tel. 619/557–5450), atop the tip of Point Loma, commemorates Juan Rodríguez Cabrillo's 1542 exploration of San Diego, offering exhibits, films, and lectures at the visitor center about the monument, tidal pools, and gray whales migrating offshore. Descriptive signs line the cliffside walks leading to a promontory that affords stunning views over the bay as far south as Mexico. You can explore the old Point Loma lighthouse, replaced in 1891 by one closer to shore.

The Desert. *Indian Canyons* (S. Palm Canyon Dr., tel. 619/325–5673), ancestral home of the Agua Caliente Indians, begins 5 miles south of downtown Palm Springs. Inside this Indian-owned sanctuary, visitors can see relics of ancient American history while wandering through landscapes of palms and wildflowers, towering rockfaces, and dense growths of sycamores, willows, and mesquite. *Joshua Tree National Monument* (north of I–10 via

Hwy. 62, 29 Palms, tel. 619/367–7511), about a one-hour drive from Palm
Springs, is a colorful preserve illustrating desert life and history, with hiking
trails, picnic areas, and naturalist-led walks. This meeting place of the
Mojave and Colorado deserts includes such sights as Hidden Valley,
a legendary cattle rustlers' hideout, the Oasis of Mara, and Key's View, an
outstanding scenic point commanding a superb sweep of valley, mountain,
and desert. The southern part of the park is especially beautiful in spring,
when wildflowers bloom. *Living Desert Reserve* (17–900 Portola Ave., tel.
619/346–5694) in Palm Desert is a 1,200-acre wildlife park and botanical
garden with bighorn sheep, coyotes, birds of prey, reptiles, and other desert
wildlife roaming in natural settings. *Palm Springs Aerial Tramway* (1
Tramway Rd., tel. 619/325–1391) is a 2½-mile gondola ride from the desert to
an observation area at the 8,516-foot level of Mt. San Jacinto, where there
are 54 hiking trails, camping and picnic areas, and a restaurant and lounge.
The Desert Museum (101 Museum Dr., tel. 619/325–7186) in Palm Springs
offers art exhibitions, often western in flavor, and natural history and science
sections illuminating aspects of the surrounding desert. The *Annenberg
Theater* there features top-name popular entertainers.

Gaslamp Quarter National Historic District (tel. 619/233–5227). The 16-
block area in downtown San Diego, centered around 4th and 5th avenues
from Broadway to Market Street, contains most of the city's Victorian
commercial architecture, now housing antiques shops, cafés and restaurants,
lively nightspots, and the San Diego Repertory Theater. Walking tours of the
district are conducted on Saturdays at 10 AM and 1 PM starting at the
Gaslamp Quarter Association headquarters (410 Island Ave., tel. 619/233–
5227). Also located in the area is the Center City East Arts Association (600–
1300 G St.), a large concentration of galleries, art studios, boutiques, and
coffeehouses.

Hot-Air Ballooning. *Sunrise Balloons* (tel. 800/548–9912) offers 45- to 60-
minute balloon flights in the Palm Springs and Temecula areas, with
packages that include picnics and ground transportation in antique cars.

Julian (tel. 619/765–1857). East of San Diego and reached by Highway 78–
79, this is the site of the only gold rush to take place in southern California.
The historic mountain town, now known for its apples, has a gold mine that
can be visited, *Eagle Mine* (tel. 619/765–0036); an old-fashioned soda fountain
in an 1880s drugstore; a historical museum in an old brewery (tel. 619/765–
0227); antiques shops; and restaurants, many of which serve a mean apple
pie.

Old Town State Historic Park (tel. 619/237–6770), just north of downtown
San Diego at Juan Street, near the intersection of I-5 and I-8, was the
center of San Diego when it was incorporated in 1850. The historic buildings,
clustered around California Plaza, include original and reproduction adobe
and log houses in a subdued Mexican colonial style. Bazaar del Mundo is
a shopping and dining enclave built to resemble a colonial Mexican square.

Mission Bay, a 4,600-acre aquatic playground, is the largest of its kind in the
world and is devoted to boating, waterskiing, swimming, board sailing, and

other forms of recreation, such as cycling and kite flying. There are 27 miles of bayfront beaches with six designated swimming areas and numerous picnic grounds. *Giant Dipper*, a 65-year-old wooden roller coaster at Belmont Park—an abandoned amusement park turned shopping and dining center— has recently been restored and is running again. *Sea World* (1720 S. Shores Rd., tel. 619/226–3901) is a 150-acre, ocean-oriented amusement park featuring trained, performing killer whales, seals, and dolphins. The Penguin Encounter has a moving sidewalk passing by a glass-enclosed arctic environment, where hundreds of emperor penguins slide over glaciers into icy waters.

San Diego Zoo (Balboa Park, tel. 619/234–3153) is widely recognized as one of the world's best zoos. More than 3,900 animals of 800 species reside in 100 acres of expertly crafted habitats, including the African Rain Forest, Gorilla Tropics, Sun Bear River, and Tiger River. The zoo is also an enormous botanical garden, with one of the world's largest collections of subtropical plants.

San Diego Wild Animal Park (15500 San Pasqual Valley Rd., Escondido, tel. 619/747–8702) is a 1,800-acre wildlife preserve containing more than 2,500 wild animals that roam free over hillsides resembling their native habitats in Asia and Africa.

Scripps Institution of Oceanography (8602 La Jolla Shores Dr., tel. 619/534–6933) in La Jolla has a fine aquarium filled with saltwater fish, and an outdoor tidal-pool exhibit with live starfish, anemones, and other shoreline creatures.

Temecula, 60 miles northeast of San Diego off Highway 15, has an Old Town with a number of historic buildings dating from the 1890s, when Temecula was a frontier cow town. Most of the action is on Front Street, where you'll find an ever-changing array of antiques and gift shops. A favorite local restaurant is the *Bank of Mexican Food* (tel. 714/676–6160), housed in a former Bank of America building, dating from 1913 to 1914. The vault has been converted into a small dining room. Thirteen wineries can be found scattered along Rancho California Road, about 5 miles from Old Town. Tours and tastings are offered on weekends. Most prominent is *Callaway Vineyard and Winery* (tel. 714/676–4001), which offers a calendar of tastings, seminars, picnics, chefs' dinners, and festivals. Another popular spot is the *Culbertson Winery,* which has a champagne bar, gift shop, and the Champagne Restaurant (tel. 714/699–0088).

Beaches

The long beaches of San Diego are one of the county's principal attractions. The turquoise Pacific invites swimming, surfing, and sunbathing while whales, seals, and dolphins frolic. **Imperial Beach,** a classic southern California beach, is the site of the U.S. Open Sandcastle Competition every July. With the famous Hotel Del Coronado as a backdrop, the **Coronado Beach** is one of the largest in the county and is surprisingly uncrowded on most days. **Sunset Cliffs,** beneath the jagged cliffs on the west side of Point Loma peninsula, is one of the more secluded beaches in the area, popular primarily with surfers and locals. It's not Atlantic City, but the boardwalk stretching along **Mission Beach** is a magnet for strollers, roller skaters, and bicyclists. The south end attracts surfers, swimmers, and volleyball players. **La Jolla Cove** is one of the prettiest spots in the world: A beautifully palm-tree-lined park sits atop cliffs formed by the incessant pounding of the waves. The beach below the cove is almost nonexistent at high tide, but the cove is still a must-see. One of the most overcrowded beaches in the county, **La Jolla Shores** lures bathers with a wide sandy beach, relatively calm surf, and a concrete boardwalk paralleling the beach. Admission to **Mission Bay's** 27 miles of bayfront beaches and 17 miles of ocean frontage is free.

Restaurants

San Diego's gastronomic reputation rests primarily on its seafood. At **Cafe Pacifica** (tel. 619/291–6666), the approach to fish is moderately nouvelle, with light, interesting sauces and imaginative garnishes. With its extravagant view of La Jolla Cove, **Top O' the Cove** (tel. 619/454–7779) is more or less synonymous with romance, but it also boasts competently prepared luxury fare—beef, fowl, veal, and seafood—dressed with creamy, well-seasoned sauces. Also in La Jolla, **Cindy Black's** (tel. 619/456–6299) has attained a national reputation for southern French fare. So many L.A. natives have second homes "down in the Springs" that local restaurateurs try to match the Big City's standards—and more and more are succeeding. **Bono** (tel. 619/322–6200), owned by former Palm Springs mayor Sonny Bono, serves southern Italian cuisine to show-biz folk and the curious. **Las Casuelas Original** (tel. 619/325–3213) is a longtime favorite among natives when it comes to great margaritas and average Mexican dishes. It gets very, very crowded during the winter months. Hearty eaters will enjoy **Di Amico's Steak House** (tel. 619/325–9191), an early California-style restaurant featuring such dishes as prime Eastern corn-fed beef, liver steak vaquero, and son-of-a-gun stew.

Tourist Information

Julian Chamber of Commerce (Box 413, Julian, CA 92036, tel. 619/765–1857); **Palm Springs Desert Resorts Convention and Visitors Bureau** (69930 Hwy. 111, Suite 201, Rancho Mirage, CA 92270, tel. 619/770–9000); **San Diego Convention and Visitors Bureau** (1200 3rd Ave., Suite 824, San Diego, CA 92101–4190, tel. 619/232–3101); **Temecula Valley Chamber of Commerce** (40945 County Center Dr., Suite C, Temecula, CA 92591, tel. 714/676–5090).

Referral Services

Bed and Breakfast Innkeepers of Southern California (Box 15425, Los Angeles, CA 90015–0385, no tel.).

Bed and Breakfast Inn at La Jolla

L a Jolla is Spanish for "the jewel," the perfect description of this seaside village in northern San Diego. Located across from the Museum of Contemporary Art and just a three-minute walk from the ocean is the Bed and Breakfast Inn at La Jolla. The building, an outstanding example of the stripped-down architecture locals call cubist, was designed by Irving Gill. "We should build our houses simple, plain and substantial as a boulder, then leave the ornamentation to nature," Gill wrote.

The inn, built as a home for George Kautz in 1913, follows those tenets. A simple white stucco box with the occasional arched window or doorway, it has huge, diamond-pane windows opening like shutters onto Pacific views. Additional, natural "ornamentation" (helped along by famous horticulturist Kate Sessions) takes the form of a crimson bougainvillea-filled garden with fountain and Japanese pine.

Set in a quiet neighborhood near the town's commercial district, the inn was masterminded by Betty Albee and her daughter, Ardath, who saved the house from demolition, renovated and restored it, and added a sympathetic annex in the rear, which now houses six guest rooms. The inn is managed by Pierrette Timmerman, who has hired an appealing young staff of university students.

Each room is individually decorated, from rattan-and-white-iron bedsteads to American-country pine, and stocked with fresh fruit and sherry. The lion's share of the antiques are in the old part of the house. The pricier rooms have the most sought-after views. The most spacious rooms are the Holiday Room and the Irving Gill Penthouse, a duplex with its own deck.

Pierrette has added Gallic specialties to the Continental breakfast: French pear cake, *gâteau marbré*, and other traditional French cakes. (And, yes, there are always croissants.) In fine weather, guests may opt to dine outside on the raised garden deck or on the terrace off the sitting room.

Address: *7753 Draper Ave., La Jolla, CA 92037, tel. 619/456–2066.*
Accommodations: *14 double rooms with bath, 1 double room with public bath, 1 suite.*
Amenities: *Robe in room, phone available, hair dryers in several rooms, fireplace in 3 rooms, refrigerator in 8 rooms, TV in suite and sitting room; afternoon refreshments, picnic baskets available, off-street parking.*
Rates: *$85–$225; Continental breakfast. MC, V.*
Restrictions: *Smoking outside only, no pets; 2-night minimum on weekends and holidays.*

Brookside Farm

Edd and Sally Guishard have created a mountain retreat out of an old dairy farm in the tiny hamlet of Dulzura, a 30-minute drive from downtown San Diego. Set on 4 tree-shaded acres bisected by the seasonal brook for which the inn is named, the farm is surrounded by colorful gardens planted with geraniums, poppies, roses, and sweet peas.

Rooms, scattered throughout the property—in the main house, built in 1928, in the old stone dairy barn, and in two cottages—have farm motifs. The Carpenter's Shop, a long, narrow room in the dairy barn with garden and brook view, contains an extensive collection of antique carpenters' tools, a potbellied stove facing the brass bed, and a screened porch. The bright-green Sun Porch room in the main house has wooden car-siding walls, wraparound windows, and a small garden patio; you can hear doves cooing and a fountain gurgling nearby. One of two very private cottages, the Hunter's Cabin hangs right over the brook. Originally the pump house, it is decorated in an Old West style and has a wood-burning stove standing in front of an iron bed and a screened-porch entry.

While no longer a commercial farm, Brookside still has animals—chickens and geese, a pair of Nubian goats, and a pig—and gardens planted with corn, tomatoes, berries, lettuce, zucchini, and herbs. These ingredients are used in the excellent four-course dinners prepared by Edd, a professional chef, on weekends. Featured entrées might be chicken mirabella, poulet Louis in tarragon sauce, or grilled chicken with rosemary. Accompanied by soup, salad and dessert, meals are a bargain at $15 per person.

While Edd enjoys cooking, Sally likes to party. You're likely to find yourself part of a celebration: tacky-crafts party, honeymoon in June, tricycle-race weekend. Guests tend to return time and again. "We have a sort of extended family here," Edd explains. "Brookside Farm is everybody's second home."

Address: *1373 Marron Valley Rd., Dulzura, CA 91917, tel. 619/468–3043.*
Accommodations: *8 double rooms with bath, 1 suite.*
Amenities: *Fireplace in 4 rooms; library, guest refrigerator, outdoor hot tub, badminton, horseshoes, croquet.*
Rates: *$60–$80; full breakfast, dinner Fri.–Sun. MC, V.*
Restrictions: *Smoking outside only, no pets; 2-night minimum on weekends.*

Heritage Park Bed & Breakfast Inn

This turreted Victorian in a historic park is the ideal headquarters for touring San Diego's Old Town, a shopping-restaurant complex across the street. It's also convenient for exploring San Diego's other attractions via the Old Town Trolley, which stops at the zoo, Seaport Village, Coronado, Balboa Park, and Horton Plaza.

A beautiful 1889 Queen Anne, the inn has a wraparound veranda decorated with spindlework, a variety of chimneys, stained-glass windows, and very ornate millwork on its banisters and wainscoting. Furnishings include an unusual double Eastlake panel bed with carved sunflowers, four-poster canopy beds, an antique fainting couch, and antique quilts.

Rooms range from smallish to ample; most are bright and cheery. Those upstairs have views of the park and Mission Bay beyond. One of the most popular rooms is the Turret, which has a sitting room in the inn's two-story tower that offers city and park views. From Queen Anne, a spacious room on the second floor, you can gaze out to the water through a squared bay window. Downstairs, the Garden Room, which looks out on the sunny Victorian garden, is a guest favorite.

When they purchased the inn in early 1992, longtime San Diegans Charles and Nancy Helsper brought a new vitality to the Heritage Park and developed a number of packages to entertain guests. Five-course, catered candlelight dinners are now served in the dining room, on the veranda, and in the Turret room. The Helspers will also make arrangements for picnics at the waterfront Sunday pops concerts, balloon excursions, and Sunday-morning breakfasts at Tiffany's, with a ride in the antique Bentley that Queen Elizabeth II rode to her coronation.

Breakfast is served in a formal dining room with burgundy flowered wallpaper. Nancy, formerly director of catering at a San Diego resort hotel, puts out her best antique Spode china and stemware and offers a varied menu that includes entrées such as banana walnut pancakes and eggs Benedict.

Address: *2470 Heritage Park Row, San Diego, CA 92110, tel. 619/299–6832.*
Accommodations: *4 double rooms with bath, 4 double rooms share 2 baths.*
Amenities: *Fireplace in 3 rooms; robes, afternoon refreshments, off-street parking.*
Rates: *$80–$120; full breakfast. MC, V.*
Restrictions: *Smoking outside only, no pets; 2-night minimum on weekends in July and Aug.*

Inn at Rancho Santa Fe

One of California's most elegant hideaways, this family-operated inn dates to 1924, when architect Lillian Rice designed what was known as the Inn at La Morada. Originally used by the Santa Fe Railroad to house prospective purchasers of land the company was developing northeast of San Diego, the inn became a gathering place in the 1930s for movie stars such as Errol Flynn, Bette Davis, and Jimmy Stewart. A celebrity staying here today would enjoy the same pampering and tranquillity that attracted earlier stars.

Steve Royce, a former pitcher with the New York Giants, purchased the inn in 1958; the family has operated it ever since. Duncan Royce Hadden, a grandson, is the current innkeeper. Family memorabilia decorates much of the house. Team photos of Steve Royce taken in 1914 line corridors; embroidery and needlepoint canvases done by Duncan's grandmother adorn guest-room walls; and Chinese paintings collected by family members hang in the living room.

Accommodations are located in the original structure and in a series of red-tile-roofed cottages scattered around 20 acres of manicured, eucalyptus-shaded grounds. Those in the main building tend to be smallish, while newer rooms in the cottages are very spacious, some with large living rooms and private bricked and flower-decked patios. Decor is traditional, but colors tend to be bright: reds, greens, blues.

Over the years the inn's dining rooms have become popular gathering places for Rancho Santa Fe's wealthy residents, who enjoy Sunday brunch in the Garden Room or the book-filled Library. The fare is as traditional as the inn itself.

Just a few miles away at the beach at Del Mar, the inn maintains a cottage for guest use. The inn also owns box seats at the famed Del Mar racetrack and makes seats available to guests during the summer thoroughbred season.

Address: *5951 Linia del Cielo, Box 869, Rancho Santa Fe, CA 92067, tel. 619/756–1131 or 800/654–2928, fax 619/759–1604.*
Accommodations: *70 double rooms with bath, 8 cottage suites.*
Amenities: *TV, phone, air-conditioning, refrigerator in rooms, fireplace in 30 rooms, wet bar in 40 rooms, Jacuzzi in 7 suites; swimming pool, 3 tennis courts, croquet, fitness facilities, room service during meal hours, 4 dining rooms.*
Rates: *$80–$185, suites $420. AE, DC, MC, V.*
Restrictions: *No pets; 2-night minimum on selected holiday weekends.*

Julian Hotel

When Steve and Gig Ballinger moved to Julian in 1976 to take over the Julian Hotel, they had a major undertaking ahead of them: restoring the oldest continuously operating hotel in southern California to its former glory. Set at the top of the mountains east of San Diego, Julian was the site of a major gold rush during the 1870s. When the mines played out, the argonauts moved on, leaving a few farmers who planted apple trees. Now Julian, with its gently rolling, oak tree–studded hills, is a popular weekend getaway for southern Californians.

The hotel was founded in 1897 by a freed Georgia slave, Albert Robinson, and his wife, Margaret. Purists, Steve and Gig refused to compromise with history as they undertook the process of restoring the "modernized" hotel to its original Victorian appearance. Rooms were small then; they have not been enlarged. In this mining town few luxuries were available, and thus the rooms are simply furnished; some pieces, most of them oak, are original to the hotel from its earliest days, and other furnishings date to the same period. Beds are of brass, iron and brass, or wood with applied decoration. Each room has an oak dresser with a beveled-glass mirror. The bathrooms are called Necessary Rooms, in deference to Victorian modesty, and three have claw-foot tubs. Two cottages can be rented:

one a suite with a lady's vanity room, the other a single bedroom with bath and its own porch.

The Victorian theme starts in the hotel's comfortable lobby, furnished with a settee, black leather armchairs with carved lions' heads, a boldly patterned rose-print carpet, and a Kayton tiger-oak piano dating from 1910. It's a busy place in the late afternoon, when guests return from touring the town's historic sites. In cool weather a fire crackles in the wood stove, lending a warmth to the entire room. Guests can also relax in a wicker-filled sun room or in the parlor, which also has a stove.

If you're interested in local history, ask to see the ancient guest register with its many famous signatures, including those of British prime minister David Lloyd George, Admiral Chester Nimitz, members of the Copley and Scripps publishing families, and Ulysses S. Grant, Jr.

Address: *2032 Main St., Box 1856, Julian, CA 92036, tel. 619/765–0201 or 800/734–5854.*
Accommodations: *4 double rooms with bath, 12 double rooms and 1 single room share 4 baths, 1 suite.*
Amenities: *Afternoon tea; private veranda off 1 room, fireplace and dressing room in suite.*
Rates: *$82–$94, suites $145; full breakfast. AE, MC, V.*
Restrictions: *No pets; 2-night minimum on weekends.*

Loma Vista
Bed and Breakfast

The first bed-and-breakfast accommodations in California were the 21 missions built during the 18th century by the Spanish padres, providing lodging and food along El Camino Real. The missions are also the inspiration for the design—and the hospitality—of the Loma Vista Bed and Breakfast.

The inn, which sits like a terra-cotta crown atop a hill in the Temecula wine country, about an hour's drive north of San Diego, is the creation of Betty Ryan, who designed it from the ground up. The look is more like a hacienda than a mission. Carefully tended rose gardens border red-tiled patios. A fountain gurgles. Hummingbirds poke their long beaks into the hearts of fragrant flowers.

Inside, the inn is cool and inviting, with ceiling beams and other oak details. Objects collected from years of world travel, from African brasswork to Thai silk-screen hangings, are displayed throughout the house. Large picture windows in the common rooms reveal gardens and vineyard-covered hillsides. The views from the bedrooms upstairs are more dramatic, unfolding in a broad panorama of citrus groves, distant mountains, and even Mt. Palomar observatory.

The guest rooms are named for varietal wines, but the connection ceases there. Zinfandel is swathed in green and peach, with Colonial reproduc-

tions that include a handsome Chippendale-style secretary bookcase with bonnet top. Chardonnay is furnished in oak and has a Laura Ashley look. Art deco describes Champagne, with a black lacquer bed, tubular steel chairs, and photographs of Marilyn Monroe and Fred Astaire on the walls. Each room is stocked with fresh fruit and port.

Whatever room you select, the setting is lovely. Don't miss the chance to spend some time sitting on the veranda sipping local wine, enjoying the fresh, cooling breezes, colorful gardens, or setting sun.

Champagne at breakfast, served family-style in the inn's large dining room, makes it a festive meal. Betty has a large repertoire of southwestern favorites, such as *huevos rancheros.*

Address: *33350 La Serena Way, Temecula, CA 92591, tel. 909/676–7047.*
Accommodations: *6 double rooms with bath.*
Amenities: *Air-conditioning, afternoon refreshments, fire pit.*
Rates: *$95–$125; full breakfast. D, MC, V.*
Restrictions: *Smoking outside only, no pets; 2-night minimum on holiday weekends.*

The Cottage

Two accommodations are available in this garden-graced, tree-shaded 1913 homestead, located in a quiet neighborhood containing an eclectic mix of small businesses, lovely old homes and bungalows, and some of the best inexpensive restaurants in San Diego. The cottage, a small house located behind Carol and Bob Emrick's home, contains a bedroom, living room, and kitchen-dining room; furnishings include an antique pump organ, a 1920s Austrian sideboard full of books, and a wood stove. A smallish room done in white and green florals is available in the main house. It has a private garden entrance, an antique sideboard filled with books, and a lift-top desk.

Guests have the use of the inn's antiques-filled parlor and dining room, which reflect the Emricks' interest in music: The rooms contain old opera posters—"from Puccini's garage," according to Carol—a player piano, and a player organ.

Address: *3829 Albatross St., San Diego, CA 92103, tel. 619/299-1564.*
Accommodations: *1 double room with bath, 1 cottage suite.*
Amenities: *Fireplace and phone in cottage, TV and refrigerator in 2 rooms.*
Rates: *$49-$65; Continental breakfast. AE, MC, V.*
Restrictions: *No smoking indoors, no pets; 2-night minimum.*

Hill House

This 1904 gambrel-roofed Dutch colonial is in San Diego's Golden Hill Historic District. "It's named Golden Hill because of the way the setting sun reflects on the windows of the homes here," explains innkeeper Russ Atwater.

Rooms are located in each of the corners of the big, square second floor and in a third-floor loft. The second-floor rooms, done in burgundy, mauve, and soft pink, are furnished simply, with a smattering of antiques, some from Russ's family: Jenny Lind spindle beds, a four-poster rice bed, a 50-year-old rocking chair, a cathedral-window quilt. The Loft, by contrast, is completely modern, decorated in shades of pink and gray. Fully equipped for housekeeping, it has a great view of the San Diego skyline.

Russ, who once served as a private chef for a prominent San Diego family, gives breakfast a special flair with a selection of home-baked breads, quiches, and frittatas.

Address: *2504 A St., San Diego, CA 92102, tel. 619/239-4738.*
Accommodations: *4 double rooms share 2½ baths, 1 suite.*
Amenities: *TV, phone, kitchen in suite; fireplace in 1 room, TV in 1 room; robes, afternoon refreshments, picnic baskets.*
Rates: *$55-$85; full breakfast. MC, V.*
Restrictions: *Smoking outside, no pets; 2-night minimum on weekends.*

Ingleside Inn

Garbo slept here—so did Elizabeth Taylor, Marlon Brando, and diva Lily Pons. Ingleside Inn has been a Palm Springs hideaway for celebrities, Hollywood and otherwise, since the 1930s. The reasons become obvious when you step inside this unpretentious hacienda-style inn and meet innkeeper Babs Rosen, who has watched over the property like a mother hen for many years. Located on a quiet street just a few blocks from Palm Canyon Drive, the inn is a tranquil and private enclave surrounded by lush gardens and a high adobe wall. Individually and elegantly decorated villas and cottages are scattered around the property. All rooms have whirlpool tubs and steam showers. Some are furnished with valuable antiques; the suite occupied by Pons for 13 years features her Louis XV bedroom set.

Address: *2000 W. Ramon Rd., Palm Springs, CA 92264, tel. 619/325–0046 or 800/772–6655, fax 619/325–0710.*
Accommodations: *27 double rooms with bath, 2 double suites.*
Amenities: *Air-conditioning, TV with VCR, phone, stocked refrigerator, whirlpool bath, and steam shower in rooms, fireplace in 10 rooms, room service; restaurant, lounge, limousine pickup at local airport, meeting facilities, outdoor swimming pool and whirlpool tub.*
Rates: *$85–$375, suites $450–$550; Continental breakfast. AE, D, MC, V.*
Restrictions: *2-night minimum on weekends Oct.–May.*

Pelican Cove Inn

The beachfront town of Carlsbad has long been a popular summer destination for southern Californians seeking sand and sun. Those are the lures of Pelican Cove Inn, which is located just two short blocks from the beach. This contemporary inn, vaguely Cape Cod in style, was built by Celeste Hale and her late husband, Robert.

Guest rooms, all with private outside entrances, are furnished with a mix of antiques, period reproductions, and modern pieces. The most striking is the La Jolla Room, where tall, arched bay windows, two-story cathedral ceiling, and elegant champagne color scheme can best be appreciated from the turn-of-the-century French fainting couch. Guests can have breakfast in the parlor, or take a tray outside to the garden gazebo, sun deck, or wraparound porches. Beach chairs, towels, and picnic baskets waiting to be filled are provided for those heading for the surf.

Address: *320 Walnut Ave., Carlsbad, CA 92008, tel. 619/434–5995.*
Accommodations: *8 double rooms with bath.*
Amenities: *TV and fireplace in rooms, phone available, whirlpool tub in 2 rooms; afternoon refreshments, railroad station pickup.*
Rates: *$85–$150; Continental breakfast. AE, MC, V.*
Restrictions: *No pets; 2-night minimum on weekends.*

Rancho Valencia Resort

This beautiful, modern resort tucked among the rolling hills of north San Diego County offers rooms in 20 red-tile-roofed, Mediterranean-style casitas scattered around 40 lushly landscaped acres. It also offers broad walkways, sparkling fountains, orange trees, bougainvillea, expansive terra-cotta terraces, and sweeping hillside views.

Guest accommodations are uncommonly large, with sunken sitting-dining areas or separate bedrooms; they feature terra-cotta-tiled floors, sand-colored walls, hand-painted decorator tiles, adobe fireplaces, and open-beam ceilings. Spacious bathrooms have marble countertops, walk-in closets, and separate dressing areas. Guests can have breakfast brought to the casitas or eat in the dining room.

Address: *5921 Valencia Circle, Box 9126, Rancho Santa Fe, CA 92067, tel. 619/756–1123 or 800/548–3664, fax 619/756–0165.*
Accommodations: *43 suites.*
Amenities: *TV, phone, fireplace, stocked minibar, safe, coffee maker, robes, hair dryer, private entrance, patio in rooms, room service during meal hours; 2 pools, 3 Jacuzzis, 18 tennis courts, health and fitness facilities, pro shop, gift shop, 2 restaurants, lounge, conference facilities.*
Rates: *$275–$415; full breakfast. AE, DC, MC, V.*
Restrictions: *No pets.*

Scripps Inn

This comfortable, reasonably priced inn offers spacious, attractively decorated rooms and a stunning seaside location. Resembling a classic three-level motel, it was built in 1937 to provide accommodations for families and patients at the adjacent Scripps Clinic. Now the inn is in the process of upgrading under the direction of innkeeper Charlene Browne.

Rooms are simply furnished with overstuffed chairs, sofas covered in wine-colored plaids, and stenciled white chests, dressers, and tables. Some rooms have Shaker accent pieces. If you want a sweeping view of La Jolla Cove, request one of the front rooms; number 14, for example, has windows on three sides.

While the inn has no real common area, outdoor tables are set up on a second-level garden patio; guests can linger here with breakfast or watch the sun set in the evening.

Address: *555 Coast Blvd. S, La Jolla, CA 92037, tel. 619/454–3391, fax 619/459–6758.*
Accommodations: *9 double rooms with bath, 4 suites.*
Amenities: *TV, phone, refrigerator, safe, hair dryer in rooms, fireplace in 2 rooms, kitchenette in 5 rooms; off-street parking.*
Rates: *$80–$165; Continental breakfast. AE, DC, MC, V.*
Restrictions: *2-night minimum on weekends.*

Strawberry Creek Inn

Idyllwild is a tiny hamlet high on Mt. San Jacinto, where hiking and exploring hundreds of miles of forested trails are the main activities. Jim Goff and Diana Dugan, former San Diego city planners, had been visiting the mountains for years when they discovered that the rambling shingled house located on the banks of Strawberry Creek was for sale. They purchased it and by 1985 had turned it into the Strawberry Creek Inn.

The heart of the inn is a big, comfortable living room with a fieldstone fireplace filling one wall, and a glass-enclosed dining porch. Guests can select from antiques-filled rooms in the main house, many displaying quilts; one of the four skylighted theme rooms added later; and the recently completed Cottage on Strawberry Creek, which has a sitting area, kitchen, whirlpool tub, and a Murphy bed in the living room for overflows.

Address: *26370 Banning-Idyllwild Hwy., Box 1818, Idyllwild, CA 92549, tel. 909/659–3202, 800/262–8969.*
Accommodations: *9 double rooms with bath, 1 housekeeping suite.*
Amenities: *Evening refreshments; fireplace and refrigerator in 5 rooms, TV with VCR in suite.*
Rates: *$90–$130; full breakfast (except in suite). MC, V.*
Restrictions: *No smoking, no pets; 2-night minimum on weekends, 3-night minimum on holidays.*

Villa Royale

A European-style country inn in the desert, Villa Royale in Palm Springs is a walled, flower-filled oasis with pilasters, glazed terra-cotta walls, marble and tile floors, open-beam ceilings, French doors, canopied and painted beds, heavy carved-wood furnishings, and delicate flowered upholstery. All are set beneath the red-tiled roofs of eight buildings on 3½ acres of grounds.

Rooms surround a series of three gardens of bougainvillea, where guests lounge around one of two swimming pools or the outdoor hot tub. The inn has a noted garden restaurant, the Europa, which serves dinner; nightly specials have different European themes.

Address: *1620 Indian Trail, Palm Springs, CA 92264, tel. 619/327–2314 or 800/245–2314, fax 619/322–4151.*
Accommodations: *23 double rooms with bath, 10 housekeeping suites, 3 double housekeeping suites.*
Amenities: *Restaurant, cocktail lounge, air-conditioning; TV and phone in rooms, fireplace in 16 rooms, whirlpool tub in 8 rooms, kitchen in 10 double rooms, VCR and tape rental; massage and facials available, room service during restaurant hours, 2 outdoor swimming pools, outdoor hot tub, bicycles.*
Rates: *$85–$285; Continental breakfast. AE, MC, V.*
Restrictions: *No pets; 2-night minimum on weekends, 3-night minimum on holidays.*

The San Bernardino Mountains

The San Bernardino Mountains
From Lake Arrowhead to Big Bear Lake

*Not for every Los Angeleno the sunny life of sea and surf.
Thousands instead opt to spend their leisure time in the
mountains, shedding the smog and fast track for lakeside
walks and lift lines. When time doesn't permit the long
trek to Lake Tahoe or Mammoth, southern Californians
head up to the nearby San Bernardino Mountains, usually
to Big Bear Lake, Lake Arrowhead, or such tiny
neighboring hamlets as Fawnskin, Arrowbear and Running
Springs.*

*Set within the more than 600,000 acres of the San
Bernardino National Forest (home of the tallest peaks in
southern California), these towns are perched above San
Bernardino, a small, smoggy city about 60 miles east of
Pasadena and 50 miles west of Palm Springs. If you're not
fighting the Friday-night crowds, the drive can be pleasant,
up Highway 330 to Highway 18, dubbed the Rim of the
World because of its dramatic views of the urban valley
below.*

*If the snow is good, winters draw skiers and lovers of other
cold-weather sports. Summers bring visitors for waterskiing
on the lakes, fishing, and hiking. But off-season visitors
won't be disappointed. On closer inspection, the somewhat
barren-looking spring hills prove to be filled with
wildflowers, and the creeks flow with the runoff of melting
snow, and the dogwood trees bloom in April and May.
Autumn brings an Octoberfest and cold, crisp nights—
perfect for sitting around a fireplace.*

*Since it's closest to urban areas (only about a half hour up
the mountain from San Bernardino), Lake Arrowhead is
the preferred site for quick visits. The "cabins"—often four-
bedroom luxury homes—surrounding crystalline Lake
Arrowhead have been hideaways for L.A.'s famous, well-to-*

do, and socially connected since the 1910s. Arrowhead isn't for everyone: It can be almost impossible for visitors to use the lake (with the exception of an hour-long boat tour), since most of it is fronted by private property, and the ski areas aren't conveniently close.

The Big Bear area, about 20 miles farther east on Highway 18 from Arrowhead, is considerably more eclectic, home of charming inn and tacky motel alike. With plenty of public beaches, docks, and waterfront walking areas, huge Big Bear Lake is also more easily accessible to visitors than Lake Arrowhead. Three distinct communities—Big Bear Lake, Big Bear City, and Fawnskin—grew up around the lake. Big Bear Lake is a weekend base for skiers bound for Snow Summit, a good-size, often crowded but well-run ski area a few miles to the south; the smaller ski areas of Bear Mountain and Snow Forest are a few minutes from town. In summer, visitors head for the local golf course, public swimming beach, or lake, where boat rentals are available. Year-round, the less athletic wander the rustic boutiques in town or stop in for a beer and burger at one of the local joints; Big Bear Lake is down-home and inelegant, a place to shed big-city pretensions. On the North Shore, where Fawnskin is located, there are picnic parks and campgrounds right at the water's edge. Big Bear City is a bit off the lake, a quiet community where year-rounders congregate.

Although the San Bernardino Mountains have long been one of L.A.'s favorite nearby resorts, the mountain communities have only recently joined the bed-and-breakfast bandwagon. Before the late '80s, overnight visitors to the area had to choose among sparsely furnished cabins, impersonal condos servicing mostly skiers, and an abundance of shabby post–World War II–era motels. If these mountains have come lately to the idea of bed-and-breakfast inns, they have come with enthusiasm. Innkeepers seeking a new life for themselves have discovered beautiful properties ranging from rustic '20s-era hunting lodges to contemporary wood-and-glass light-flooded aeries.

Places to Go, Sights to See

Alpine Slide and Water Slide (Big Bear Blvd. before town, between Forest and Lakeview, tel. 714/866–4626). In the summer, attractions include a waterslide and a chair lift to a summit from which one descends on a cart via a "slic-trac"; in winter, there's a snow-play area.

Boat Rentals (Pine Knot Marina, at the foot of Big Bear Village, tel. 714/866–BOAT). Pontoons, canoes, sailboats, speedboats, rowboats, and fishing gear can be rented, and waterskiing and windsurfing lessons are available.

Boat Tours. The *Arrowhead Queen* (tel. 714/336–6992), moored on the waterfront in Lake Arrowhead Village, leaves hourly from 10 AM to 5 PM; offering a look at the area's luxurious private homes, it's great for real estate enthusiasts. In Big Bear, the *Sierra* and the *Queen* operate from Pine Knot Landing (tel. 714/866–BOAT, 714/866–3218), afternoons during the week, all day on weekends.

Gold Fever Trail. At the Forest Service Ranger Station in North Shore (tel. 714/866–3437), you can pick up a free map for a self-guided tour through Holcomb Valley; it'll take you past an old log saloon, mill, gold-digging areas, cabins, mines, and grave sites.

Green Valley Lake (tel. 714/337–3715). About halfway between Arrowhead and Big Bear, tiny Green Valley Lake offers paddle-boat rentals, rowing, and fishing. It's an old-fashioned spot, congenial to families and easygoing types. A ski area, Ski Green Valley, is nearby.

Heap's Peak Arboretum (Hwy. 18 between Skyforest and Running Springs, no tel.). An interpretive nature trail, perhaps the best in the area, goes for $7/10$ of a mile on easy terrain through a variety of landscapes—bracken fern, vanilla-smelling Jeffrey pine, beautiful blooming dogwood.

Lake Arrowhead Children's Museum (lower Lake Arrowhead Village, end of the peninsula, tel. 714/336–1332). Terrific for very small children, this museum has hands-on nature and science exhibits, a toddler area, and a puppet theater.

Magic Mountain Stables (Big Bear Blvd. before town, between Forest and Lakeview, tel. 714/866–7715). In season, these stables offer pony rides for little ones (parents lead kids on ponies for independent walks) and escorted one-hour trail rides for older children and grown-ups.

Moonridge Wild Animal Park (Moonridge Dr. at the end of Goldmine Golf Course, tel. 714/585–3656). This unique, tiny facility houses and cares for wild animals of the area—coyotes, bears, eagles, foxes, and deer, among others—that have been hurt, illegally kept as pets, or otherwise rendered unable to fend for themselves in the wild. Open daily May–Oct.

Santa's Village (Hwy. 18, Skyforest, tel. 714/337–2481). At this very mom-and-pop amusement park, visitors can watch local dance groups perform on the outdoor stage, ride little trains and a Buzzy-Bee monorail, eat gingerbread and rock candy, pet reindeer, and talk to Santa. Open Memorial Day–June, Labor Day–Veterans Day, Jan., and Feb., weekends; June–Labor Day and Veterans Day–Dec., daily. Closed Christmas Day.

Skiing: *Downhill.* Snow Summit (tel. 714/866–5766); Bear Mountain (tel. 714/585–2519); Snow Forest (tel. 714/585–3848); Ski Green Valley (tel. 714/867–2338). *Cross-country:* Maps available at Forest Service Ranger Station in North Shore (tel. 714/866–3437).

Restaurants

Don't expect L.A.-quality restaurants in the San Bernardino Mountains; eateries here are rustic and casual, and there isn't a bit of California cuisine for miles around. In Arrowhead, many fast-food and casual restaurants can be found in the village area. It says a lot about Arrowhead Village that the best lake views are offered by the local McDonald's. **The Chef's Inn and Tavern** (tel. 714/336–4487) serves good Continental and American cuisine in an 1840 building in Cedar Glen; **Antler's Inn** (tel. 714/337–4020), in another converted historic building (established 1925) in Twin Peaks, is fine for steak and barbecue. A good, family-owned Italian restaurant is **Paoli's Italian Country Kitchen,** which has branches in both Arrowhead and Big Bear Lake (tel. 714/866–2020). In Big Bear Lake, the casual patio of **Boo Bear's Den** (tel. 714/866–2932), right in the village, is often bustling; out by the ski areas, **La Montana** (tel. 714/866–2606) offers decent Mexican food and margaritas. In Fawnskin, the **Longhorn Cafe and Grill** (tel. 714/866–3136) uses homemade ingredients for hearty mountain meals.

Tourist Information

Big Bear Lake Chamber of Commerce (40588 Big Bear Blvd., Big Bear Lake, tel. 714/866–4601); **Lake Arrowhead Chamber of Commerce** (Vineyard Bank Building, at entrance to Lake Arrowhead Village, tel. 714/337–3715).

The Knickerbocker Mansion

A four-story log cabin of gracious proportions situated on a hillside overlooking the treetops and Big Bear Lake, the Knickerbocker Mansion looks like the kind of place that would have housed a large, rollicking family—and, indeed, it was built in the 1920s for the Knickerbockers and their five children. Now innkeeper Phyllis Knight and assistant Linda Ford keep the mansion furnished with comforts most homes don't have. Stacks of books and magazines can be found in every corner of the pine-paneled living room, and if you curl up in one of the big leather chairs or on the vintage sofas, the cat, Sissy, is apt to curl up with you. Two verandas stretch the length of the lake-view side on the second and third floors. There's always hot coffee, tea, and cookies and cinnamon crisps in the kitchen. The Knickerbocker has, in fact, been carefully designed as a place to gather one's energies. A former marriage and family counselor, Phyllis Knight intended to create a true haven here. Her own soothing personality permeates the place.

The two acres of inn property back up to the San Bernardino National Forest. An outdoor spa with a magnificent view of rolling pine hills and a sun deck with tables link the main house with the renovated former barn. This is the Rainbow Sun Lodge, with four loft rooms looking out over the forest above.

The most spectacular view is found in the third-floor suite of the main house; its potbellied stove and windows on three sides have made it a popular movie set.

The Knickerbocker is furnished with antiques and vintage furniture, and although it has an appropriately countrified look the house is blessedly unfrilly, which is in keeping with such features as the hewn-log staircase and the Teddy Roosevelt–type verandas.

Come morning, breakfast is hearty and beautifully presented—blueberry pancakes, a savory "California crepe," fresh fruits, and juices. You can eat in the formal dining room or take a tray out on the big veranda.

Address: *869 S. Knickerbocker Rd., Box 3661, Big Bear Lake, CA 92315, tel. 714/866-8221.*
Accommodations: *4 double rooms with private bath, 1 double room with half-bath, 4 double rooms share 2 baths, 1 suite.*
Amenities: *TV in rooms; fireplace in lounge, outdoor spa, croquet; snacks available.*
Rates: *$95–$165; full breakfast. MC, V.*
Restrictions: *Smoking outside only; no pets; 2-night minimum on weekends, 3-night minimum on some holidays.*

The Lodge at Green Valley Lake

With its wood front porch, hitching post, and remote end-of-the-road location north of Lake Arrowhead, the picturesque, bright-yellow-and-blue Lodge at Green Valley Lake looks like a turn-of-the-century stagecoach stop. The western-saloon ambience of its restaurant only adds to that impression. But, in fact, the lodge was built as a hostel in 1947.

Margo Deshler, who owns the place, brought contemporary ideas of comfort to the retreat (all rooms have private baths, and some have separate entrances) but kept the rooms homey. The overall look is country-cottage, achieved in part with an appealing mix of flea-market antiques.

If you're a couple or a family who wants togetherness and quiet time alone, this is a good place to come. Kids can walk a few hundred yards from the lodge to the lake and fish for trout; older ones can paddleboat or canoe or row. They will likely enjoy the company of Thunder, the resident Saint Bernard.

There are plenty of adult-oriented activities, too: hiking in the adjacent San Bernardino National Forest or, in winter, cross-country skiing on one of the many trails. For downhill skiers, the shuttle to Ski Green Valley stops at the Lodge's front door. The less energetic can fritter their winter mornings away with a champagne brunch in the restaurant or curl up with a murder mystery in the parlor; wine and cheese are served there in the afternoon.

Four of the accommodations are compact two-room suites, one a separate cottage suite with its own deck; the others have window seats and sofa beds. A set of two suites and one twin-bedded room are connected, making it possible for a family or group of six to have their own wing.

The Lodge at Green Valley Lake is far from nightlife, but its restaurant, which serves steak and seafood, keeps one from feeling isolated at night. The restaurant also serves breakfast and Sunday brunch.

Address: *33655 Green Valley Lake Rd., Box 8275, Green Valley Lake, CA 92341, tel. 714/867–4281.*
Accommodations: *1 double room with private bath, 3 two-room suites, 1 cottage suite.*
Amenities: *Fresh flowers and sherry in rooms, sink and refrigerator in cottage; TV in parlor lounge, afternoon wine and cheese in parlor; restaurant.*
Rates: *$65–$95 for two, $10 each extra person; extended Continental breakfast weekdays, full breakfast Sat., champagne brunch Sun. MC, V.*
Restrictions: *No smoking, no pets.*

The Carriage House

Those seeking a romantic weekend with relaxing walks around a lake should consider this New England–style gray-clapboard house in a residential Lake Arrowhead neighborhood. The Karstens built this house to be their weekend home; they so enjoyed the process that they've since built another house for themselves next door, turning this one into an inn in 1988.

The Carriage House was designed to take advantage of the fabulous views of pine trees all around. The summer parlor backs onto a large, sunny breakfast deck, and the winter parlor has a large fireplace. The accommodations all have lake views; one room has a private balcony. Furnishings are a tasteful combination of antiques, whitewashed pine, and vintage finds: hand-stenciled wardrobes, lace-trimmed window seats, and needlepoint chair covers. Other features of the inn are a private lakeside path to the village, and a talking parrot who whistles the theme from *Andy Griffith.*

Address: *472 Emerald Dr., Box 982, Lake Arrowhead, CA 92352, tel. 714/336–1400.*
Accommodations: *3 double rooms with bath.*
Amenities: *TV in rooms; afternoon hors d'oeuvres.*
Rates: *$85–$115; full breakfast. D, MC, V.*
Restrictions: *No smoking, no pets; 2-night minimum on weekends, 3-night minimum on some holidays.*

Gold Mountain Manor

So picturesque that it's been used as a backdrop for Ralph Lauren and Eddie Bauer ads, Gold Mountain Manor is the largest surviving building by famous '20s builder Guy Maltby. Close to skiing, the manor was a summer retreat for a wealthy Angeleno, as evidenced by such luxurious details as bird's-eye maple floors, beamed ceilings, and a wine cellar. The common rooms are spacious, and there's a proper front porch.

The nicest guest room is the pine-paneled Presidential Suite, in its own wing with a massive river-rock fireplace. The most romantic is the Honeymoon Room, which has a canopy bed, wicker furniture, and a brick fireplace. The more masculine Clark Gable Room is done in forest green with a potbellied stove (reputed to be from Gable's old cabin).

Address: *1117 Anita Dr., Box 2027, Big Bear City, CA 92314, tel. 714/585–6997.*
Accommodations: *1 double room with bath, 1 double room with half-bath, 4 double rooms share 2 baths, 1 double suite.*
Amenities: *TV, robes in rooms, Jacuzzi in 1 room, fireplace or wood-burning stove in 5 rooms and suite; afternoon hors d'oeuvres, self-serve coffee and tea in kitchen, billiard table, player piano.*
Rates: *$75–$180; full breakfast. MC, V.*
Restrictions: *Smoking outside only, no pets; 2-night minimum on weekends.*

The Inn at Fawnskin

Innkeepers G. B. and Susan Sneed did a lot of entertaining in Orange County when G. B. was in the savings-and-loan business, and they say that experience helps them determine when their guests would enjoy some company and when they'd like to be left alone. Their log-cabin inn is one of the few noncamping accommodations on the north shore of Big Bear Lake, which offers walks and woods and access to good boating.

The Sneeds offer a fun murder-mystery weekend, designed for four couples who know one another. The less socially oriented can request the romantic suite, with a high-beamed ceiling and private balcony. Three common lounging areas include one with a sofa and fireplace and another with a pool table and a big-screen TV with VCR. In the third, guests gather at the fireside table to eat a hearty breakfast, beginning with fresh breads.

Address: *880 Canyon Rd., Box 378, Fawnskin, CA 92333, tel. 714/866-3200.*
Accommodations: *1 double room with bath, 2 double rooms share a bath, 1 suite.*
Amenities: *TV, robes in rooms, fireplace in 1 room, balcony in suite; piano, library, basketball court, afternoon refreshments.*
Rates: *$75–$155; full breakfast. MC, V.*
Restrictions: *No smoking, no pets; 2-night minimum on weekends.*

Saddleback Inn

Although it calls itself a "unique bed-and-breakfast inn," the Saddleback doesn't have an innkeeper in evidence—it's owned by a corporation, and a hired staff serves breakfast. It seems more like a small hotel, but it's a very pleasant one. Sited at the entrance to Arrowhead Village, the inn bears the burdens and advantages of its location: traffic and car exhaust instead of pine-scented air during the summer season, and plowed roads and ease of access during the snow season.

The Saddleback Inn consists of a historic main building, a mountain lodge–style structure with a stone chimney, and a cluster of cabins ranging in size from single-room doubles to three-bedroom suites. The rooms in the main building are decorated in pine and prim, Laura Ashley–style wallpaper. Some of the cottages have four rooms or suites; some of the suites are duplex. A coffee shop is on the ground floor.

Address: *300 S. Hwy. 173, Box 1890, Lake Arrowhead, CA 92352, tel. 714/336-3571 or 800/858-3334.*
Accommodations: *17 double rooms with bath, 9 suites, 8 cottages.*
Amenities: *Fireplace, refrigerator, whirlpool tub in most rooms; air-conditioning in main building; conference facility, gazebo for meetings.*
Rates: *$110–$165; suites $180–$425; Continental breakfast weekdays, full breakfast weekends. AE, D, DC, MC, V.*
Restrictions: *No pets.*

Sky Forest Bed and Breakfast Inn

In California country inns, ceramic squirrels and pine paneling often stand in for real squirrels and real trees. No chance of that at Sky Forest, a contemporary chalet with cathedral ceilings punctuated by skylights. Huge windows and a narrow deck face the hillside behind, so guests can sit inside or out and enjoy the view. Innkeeper Meta Morgan has spotted all kinds of creatures, but, she says, no bears.

Close to a café and some boutiques, Sky Forest is in a wooded canyon. Guests gather in a dramatic two-story room with a huge stone fireplace and a loft. The decor is modern and spare, softened with lace. There are beamed ceilings throughout. The rooms are warm and woody, some with delicate floral wallpaper and sloping attic roofs, others with skylights or log walls. Such hearty fare as eggs Benedict and homemade muffins is served in three breakfast nooks.

Address: *760 Kuffel Canyon Rd., Box 482, Sky Forest, CA 92385, tel. 714/337-4680 or 800/339-3368.*
Accommodations: *2 double rooms with bath, 2 double rooms share a bath, 1 suite.*
Amenities: *Whirlpool tub in suite; TV in common room, air-conditioning, afternoon refreshments.*
Rates: *$90–$150; full breakfast. No credit cards.*
Restrictions: *Smoking outside on decks only, no pets; 2-night minimum on weekends, 3-night minimum on holidays.*

Los Angeles

Los Angeles
With Orange County

Set off from the rest of the continent by mountains and desert, and from the rest of the world by an ocean, this incredible corner of creation has evolved its own identity, which conjures envy, fascination, ridicule, and scorn—often all at once.

Los Angeles is a city of ephemerals, of transience, and above all, of illusion. Nothing here is quite real, and that's the reality of it all. The lure that "anything can happen"—and it often does—is what keeps thousands moving to this promised land each year and millions more vacationing here. They come not just from the East or Midwest, but from the Far East, Down Under, Europe, and South America. It's this influx of cultures that's been the lifeblood of Los Angeles since its Hispanic beginning.

The first immigrants were the Spanish padres who, following a dream of finding wealth in California, founded their Pueblo de la Reina de Los Angeles in 1781. Oil and oranges helped the town shed its image as a dusty outpost, but the golden key to success came on the silver screen: the movies.

In 1911, the same sunshine that draws today's visitors and new residents drew Cecil B. DeMille and Jesse Lasky, who were searching for a new place to make movies outside of New York City. The silent-film era made Hollywood's name synonymous with fantasy, glamour, and, as the first citizens would snicker in disgust, with sin. Outrageous partying, extravagant homes, eccentric clothing, and money, money, money have been symbols of life in Los Angeles ever since. Even the more conservative oil, aerospace, computer, banking, and import-export industries on the booming Pacific Rim have enjoyed the prosperity that often leads to excess. But even without piles of money, many people have found Los Angeles conducive to their colorful lifestyles, be they spiritually, socially, or sexually unusual.

No city embraces the romance of the automobile as does Los Angeles. Cars announce the wealth, politics, and taste of their drivers. Vanity license plates, a California innovation, condense the meaning of one's life into seven letters (MUZKBIZ). Sun roofs, ski racks, and cardboard windshield visors sell better here than anywhere else. You are what you drive—a thought worth remembering when you rent a car. Yes, Lamborghinis are available—even by the hour.

The distance between places in Los Angeles explains the ethnic enclaves that do not merge, regardless of the melting-pot appearance of the city. The tensions between racial and ethnic groups learning to share Los Angeles have been well publicized. More notable for visitors, however, is the rich cultural and culinary diversity this mix of peoples creates.

You can laze on a beach or soak up some of the world's greatest art collections. You can tour the movie studios and stars' homes or take the kids to Disneyland, Magic Mountain, or Knott's Berry Farm. You can shop luxurious Beverly Hills' Rodeo Drive or browse for novelties on boutique-lined Melrose Avenue. The possibilities are endless—rent a boat to Catalina Island, watch the floats in Pasadena's Rose Parade, or dine on tacos, sushi, goat cheese pizza, or just plain hamburgers, hot dogs, and chili. You can experience the best in theater, music, and dance; world-class spectator sports; and a great outdoors that beckons nearly 365 days a year.

Places to Go, Sights to See

Catalina Island, the island of song and legend, lies a bit more than 20 miles across the sea from Los Angeles. The island is known for the clear-blue waters surrounding it, warm sunny beaches, and the crescent-shaped harbor of Avalon. Inland there's hiking and mountain-bike riding over virtually unspoiled mountains and canyons, coves, and beaches. You reach the island via a two-hour cruise. Contact *Catalina Express* (tel. 310/519–1212) for departure schedules from San Pedro, Long Beach, and Redondo Beach.

Disneyland (Harbor Blvd. exit, I–5, tel. 714/999–4565), Walt Disney's land of fantasy, is even grander than it was when it opened in Anaheim in 1955. New rides, adventures, and attractions are added every year. From Fantasyland to Tomorrowland, Disneyland has many different shops, restaurants, and entertainment areas, but lines for rides can be long; to reduce the wait, plan to arrive early or late, midweek or off-season. A highlight for many visitors is the Electrical Parade and fireworks display presented on summer evenings.

Ethnic Los Angeles. As a major port of entry to the United States, Los Angeles boasts more ethnic diversity than any other city in the country. While every aspect of life here is colored by the culture brought by the newcomers—Hispanics from various Latin American countries, Filipinos, Japanese, Chinese, Vietnamese, Koreans—some communities are more accessible than others. Olivera Street, in the heart of downtown Los Angeles, boasts a colorful Mexican marketplace, restaurants, and several historic buildings—including Old Plaza Church, Old Plaza Firehouse, and Avila Adobe. Little Tokyo, between 1st and San Pedro streets, is the cultural and commercial center for the Japanese community, with restaurants, sushi bars, shops, and Buddhist temples. Koreatown, Chinatown, Monterey Park (another Chinese community), Fairfax (the Jewish neighborhood), and East Los Angeles (one of the Latino neighborhoods) all have a wide variety of ethnic restaurants, shops, and cultural events.

Hollywood. It may not be the glitter town it once was, but even the name still evokes a bygone era of glamour and legendary movie stars. The corner of Hollywood and Vine *does* exist. The Walk of Fame lines both sides of Hollywood Boulevard from Gower to Sycamore and on Vine from Yucca to Sunset; the walk glitters with terrazzo and brass stars engraved with the names of more than 1,800 entertainment personalities. *Mann's Chinese Theater* (6925 Hollywood Blvd.), originally Grauman's, is where you'll find the names, foot, hand, hoof, or leg prints of famous stars eternalized in concrete in the entryway. To see how movies are made, there are two opportunities: *Paramount Pictures* (860 N. Gower St., Los Angeles, tel. 213/956–1777) offers two-hour weekday guided tours of production facilities and has a limited number of free tickets to shows being produced there. *Warner Bros. Studios* (4000 Warner Blvd., Burbank, tel. 818/954–1744) offers personalized VIP tours during the week, permitting visitors to watch live shooting wherever possible.

Horse Racing. Thoroughbred horse racing takes place at two local tracks: *Santa Anita* (tel. 818/574–7223) and *Hollywood Park* (tel. 310/419–1500).

Knott's Berry Farm (8039 Beach Blvd., tel. 714/220–5200), in Buena Park, is one of the West's most popular attractions, with more than 165 rides, shops, and shows. Don't miss Mrs. Knott's Chicken Dinner Restaurant—it's as popular now as it was during the 1930s, when Walter Knott built the original "ghost town" to entertain diners waiting for a table.

Melrose Avenue between Highland Avenue and Doheny Drive is the best street for people-watching in Los Angeles. The hippest of the hip hang out here in one-of-a-kind boutiques, chic restaurants, theaters, and exclusive clubs.

Rodeo Drive is the famed Beverly Hills shopping street. You'll find international stores such as Chanel, Gucci, Giorgio, and Alfred Dunhill, among many other luxury boutiques. *South Coast Plaza* (Bristol and Sunflower Sts., Costa Mesa, tel. 714/241–1700), in Orange County, has one of the largest concentrations of upscale retail stores in the world.

Universal Studios Hollywood (100 Universal Pl., Universal City, tel. 818/508–9600) stretches across 400 acres, many of which are crossed in the enthusiastically narrated tram tour that takes visitors through a re-creation of the largest television and movie studio's backlots. Meet King Kong, the shark from *Jaws*, and E.T., or experience an earthquake or the parting of the Red Sea.

Museums

Craft and Folk Art Museum (6067 Wilshire Blvd., Los Angeles, tel. 213/937–5544) features changing exhibitions of contemporary crafts and traditional folk art from around the world. Six to eight major shows are planned each year.

George C. Page Museum of La Brea Discoveries (5801 Wilshire Blvd., Los Angeles, tel. 213/936–2230) contains fossils and bones recovered from the La Brea Tar Pits, the world's richest source of Ice Age mammal and bird fossils. The glass-enclosed Paleontological Laboratory permits observation of the ongoing cleaning, identification, and cataloguing of fossils excavated from the nearby asphalt deposits.

Hollyhock House (4800 Hollywood Blvd., Hollywood, tel. 213/485–4581), built in 1921, was the first of a number of houses that Frank Lloyd Wright designed in the Los Angeles area. Now owned by the city (as is Barnsdall Park, where it is located), it has been restored and furnished with originals and reproductions of Wright's furniture.

Huntington Library, Art Collections, and Botanical Gardens (1151 Oxford Rd., San Marino, tel. 818/405–2100) displays 18th- and 19th-century British art, including Gainsborough's *Blue Boy*. The library exhibits rare books, prints, and manuscripts. There are more than 14,000 varities of plants on the beautiful grounds.

J. Paul Getty Museum (17985 Pacific Coast Hwy., Malibu, tel. 310/458–2003) is a re-creation of a 1st-century Roman villa, with formal gardens, major collections of Greek and Roman antiquities, paintings ranging from the 13th

century to the late-19th century, and decorative arts. Parking reservations
are required.

Los Angeles County Museum of Art (5905 Wilshire Blvd., Los Angeles, tel.
213/857–6000) is a complex of five buildings on the site of the La Brea Tar
Pits that houses fine collections of paintings, sculpture, textiles, costumes,
and decorative arts. Of particular interest to movie fans is the classic film
series presented in the Leo S. Bing Theater.

Museum of Contemporary Art (250 S. Grand Ave., Los Angeles, tel.
213/626–6222) is a unique below-ground-level museum, designed by Arata
Isozaki, featuring modern art from 1940 to the present. Originally designed
by Frank Gehry as a temporary home for MOCA, the *Temporary
Contemporary* (152 N. Central Ave., tel. 213/626–6222), in Little Tokyo, is
now a permanent part of MOCA. A free shuttle bus runs between the two
buildings.

Norton Simon Museum of Art (411 W. Colorado Blvd., Pasadena, tel.
818/449–6840) houses many famous Old Master artworks, including paintings
by Rembrandt, Rubens, Raphael, and Goya. Highlights of the modern art
collection include bronze ballet dancers and horses by Degas and works by
Cézanne, Toulouse-Lautrec, Renoir, and Van Gogh.

Southwest Museum (234 Museum Dr., Los Angeles, tel. 213/221–2163)
contains extensive collections of Native American art and artifacts housed in
a 1914 Mission Revival building. Exhibits include Navajo blankets, an
incredible array of baskets, and a full-size Blackfoot tepee.

Performing Arts

Hollywood Bowl (2301 H Highland Ave., Los Angeles, tel. 213/850–2000),
a 17,680-seat amphitheater, offers a summer season of outdoor concerts
ranging from pop and jazz to classical. Elegant picnics are part of the
experience here; bring your own or purchase one when you get here.

Music Center of Los Angeles (135 N. Grand Ave., Los Angeles, tel. 213/972–
7211) is a three-theater complex. The large Dorothy Chandler Pavilion
presents classical concerts, ballet, and opera; resident companies include the
Los Angeles Philharmonic Orchestra, the Los Angeles Music Center Opera,
the Joffrey Ballet Los Angeles/New York, and the Los Angeles Master
Chorale. The Mark Taper Forum, an intimate theater, features regional
productions, some of which land on Broadway. The Ahmanson Theater stages
large musical productions.

Orange County Performing Arts Center (600 Town Center Dr., Costa Mesa,
tel. 714/556–ARTS) presents musical theater, opera, dance, and classical and
jazz concerts.

Tourist Information

Anaheim Area Visitor and Convention Bureau (800 W. Katella Ave., Box 4270, Anaheim, CA 92802, tel. 714/999–8999); **Long Beach Area Convention and Visitors Council** (3387 Long Beach Blvd., Long Beach, CA 90807, tel. 310/426–6773 or 800/4-LBSTAY); **Los Angeles Visitor and Convention Bureau** (515 S. Figueroa St., Los Angeles, CA 90071, tel. 213/624–7300).

Reservation Services

Bed & Breakfast Innkeepers of Southern California (Box 15425, Los Angeles, CA 90015, no tel.); **Bed & Breakfast Los Angeles** (32074 Waterside La., Westlake, CA 91361, tel. 818/889–8870); **CoHost America's B & B** (Box 9302, Whittier, CA 90608, tel. 213/699–8427); **Eye Openers** (Box 694, Altadena, CA 91003, tel. 213/684–4428 or 818/797–2055).

Blue Lantern Inn

The Blue Lantern Inn hasn't been open long, but it already has quite a following. This Cape Cod–style hotel is perched on a bluff above the Dana Point Marina in southern Orange County. One of the only inns around, it offers sweeping marina and ocean views from almost every room. You can watch as the more than 2,000 small boats move in and out of their slips, or keep an eye on the children as they explore a replica of the tall ship *Pilgrim,* immortalized by Richard Henry Dana in his book *Two Years Before the Mast.*

The Blue Lantern is operated by Four Sisters, which owns a number of inns and small hotels, mostly in northern California. Each guest room contains an unusually spacious bathroom; most have double sinks, showers, and whirlpool baths. The decor is contemporary; light mauve with accents in soft green and cream is a favorite color scheme. There's a tall mahogany four-poster bed in the Tower Suite; other rooms have brass, sleigh, or rattan beds. Wicker side chairs, small boudoir chairs, and Queen Anne–style desks can be found in nearly every room, as well as armoires that conceal TV sets, and refrigerators stocked with complimentary soft drinks.

The lobby is set up with tables for two and four for the buffet-style breakfast. French doors lead to an outdoor sitting area, where many guests take coffee and the morning paper. The library, which contains a collection of books you might actually want to read, is where guests gather in the afternoons for wine and hors d'oeuvres.

Although visitors might be tempted to spend an entire weekend enjoying the beauty and comfort of the inn, the marina complex offers a number of activities. Bicycles are available for exploring the many trails that crisscross the surrounding hills. The innkeepers will make arrangements for sail- or powerboat charters or whale-watching excursions in season. They will also prepare a picnic basket for guests to enjoy at one of the two parks within walking distance of the inn. In addition, guests can visit the mission and the chic boutiques, art galleries, and antiques stores at San Juan Capistrano, just a 10-minute drive away.

Address: *34343 St. of the Blue Lantern, Dana Point, CA 92629, tel. 714/661–1304, fax 714/496–1483.*
Accommodations: *29 double rooms with bath.*
Amenities: *Robes, whirlpool tub, refrigerator, TV, and phone in rooms; afternoon refreshments, fitness center, conference facilities, bicycles.*
Rates: *$135–$350; full breakfast. AE, MC, V.*
Restrictions: *No smoking, no pets.*

Casa Tropicana

Rick Anderson, a young building contractor, had a dream: to turn the somewhat seedy oceanfront of San Clemente into a showplace. The centerpiece would be his unique bed-and-breakfast inn. Casa Tropicana, the inn and restaurant he created and opened in 1990, has a young, beach-bum-casual ambience—the kind of place where guests are more likely to be parking their boogie boards than their BMWs.

The five-story, whitewashed Mediterranean-style inn sits on a narrow hillside across the street from the historic San Clemente pier. On a clear day, the view from some rooms goes all the way to Catalina Island. Right across the street is a prime surfing beach where most of the year surfers can be seen riding the breakers to shore. The Tropicana Grill occupies the ground floor, and guest rooms are located on the second, third, and fifth floors (Rick is on the fourth). Each level has its own deck overlooking the ocean.

Every room offers the fulfillment of a different tropical fantasy. Out of Africa is the most popular. The oversize room holds a step-up four-poster bed topped with faux mosquito netting, and guests can soak in the double whirlpool tub while watching TV or enjoying the view through a peekaboo window. Other rooms are equally fantastic. Coral Reef has a bed with a peach rattan-clamshell headboard. Emerald Forest is cool and green with vines hanging from the ceiling. The Penthouse has a three-sided fireplace and a deck with outdoor Jacuzzi. Only the rooms facing the ocean have a view or much outside light; if you tend to be claustrophobic, take one of these.

The laid-back atmosphere carries through to the Tropicana Grill, whose bar is tucked under a thatched roof. The reasonably priced menu offers Cabo swordfish tacos, chicken fajita salad, and Ragin' Cajun garlic ribs. Room service is available to guests from the restaurant beginning at 7:30 in the morning. Guests can select breakfast from the restaurant menu, have it delivered to their rooms or outdoor deck, or join early-morning diners in the café.

Address: *610 Avenida Victoria, San Clemente, CA 92672, tel. 714/492-1234.*
Accommodations: *7 double rooms with bath, 2 housekeeping suites.*
Amenities: *TV, refrigerator, and phone in rooms, double whirlpool tub in 8 rooms, fireplace in 8 rooms; complimentary champagne, room service, restaurant.*
Rates: *$120–$180, suites $240, penthouse $350; full breakfast. AE, MC, V.*
Restrictions: *Smoking outside only, no pets; 2-night minimum on weekends.*

Channel Road Inn

O riginally the home of Thomas McCall, a pioneering Santa Monica businessman, this house was moved from a hilltop site to its current location tucked in a hillside of Santa Monica Canyon, one block from the beach. With the help of the local historical society, innkeeper Susan Zolla saved the Colonial Revival building from demolition and turned it into a gracious inn.

The house is sheathed in blue shingles, a rarity in Los Angeles and for a Colonial Revival house. The architectural details are pure Craftsman. Windows are very large and abundant to take advantage of cool ocean breezes and bright sunlight. The honey-colored woodwork in the living room is unusually elegant, with moldings and baseboards carefully milled. Other woodwork has been painted white, which Susan says is historically accurate.

The decor covers a variety of styles, with a common thread of wicker throughout, including the dining room, library, and several of the guest rooms. Beds are the focal point: four-poster beds, pencil-post canopy beds, or sleigh beds. Special attention has been paid to the needs of guests, particularly business travelers who require phones or writing surfaces. Not all rooms, however, have comfortable chairs for extended sitting.

Several rooms have access to balconies or decks with views of the flowering hillside and a glimpse of the ocean. There's an attractive garden sitting area for people who want to relax at the inn, as well as robes and oversize towels for beachgoers or spa users.

The broad white-sand beach is just across Pacific Coast Highway; it's bordered on one side by a 30-mile-long bicycle path that stretches north to Malibu and south to Venice beach. The Venice portion of the path is a colorful carnival on weekends as crazily clad street musicians beat out tunes, vendors sell everything from food to art, and skaters zip by. The J. Paul Getty Museum, with its lovely gardens and superb collection specializing in ancient and French 18th-century art, is only a five-minute drive away.

Address: *219 Channel Rd., Santa Monica, CA 90402, tel. 310/459–1920, fax 310/454–9920.*
Accommodations: *12 double rooms with bath, 2 suites.*
Amenities: *Cable TV and phone in rooms, refrigerator in 2 rooms, VCR in 6 rooms; afternoon refreshments, outdoor hot tub, bicycles, off-street parking.*
Rates: *$95–$170, suites $165–$195; full breakfast. AE, MC, V.*
Restrictions: *Smoking outside only, no pets.*

Christmas House

Built by wealthy ranchers in 1904, this late Queen Anne mansion was known locally as the Christmas House because of the many lavish holiday parties thrown here. Indeed, when Jay and Janice Ilsley opened the inn in 1985, they held to custom and had a Christmas party of their own. Holiday celebrations have been a tradition at the inn ever since.

Set amid an acre of grapefruit and tangerine trees, this inviting house has turrets, gables, stained-glass windows, sweeping verandas, seven working fireplaces, dark wood wainscoting, and a grand staircase leading to the second floor. Colors are cool deep greens and burgundies. Among the inn's fine group of antiques are a 150-year-old brass bed and a family collection of framed handkerchiefs.

Guest rooms are located on the first and second floors of the main house and in a carriage house behind. Accommodations in the latter are unique: Decorated with an English floral theme, Elizabeth has a black iron bed and green wicker furnishings; a big bath suite with French doors leads to a private plant-filled atrium containing a massive outdoor shower. The adjacent Carriage Room has a more masculine feel, with its fireplace, burgundy sofa, and dark antiques, including a sleigh bed; it offers a private garden with a whirlpool tub set into a gazebo.

In the main house, all the ground-floor rooms have private courtyards. In the front of the mansion, the Celebration Suite, a huge double room with bed chamber and parlor divided by an enormous pocket door, is a popular choice of honeymooners. It has fireplaces in the corners of both rooms; a dining table set up in the corner turret, where breakfast is served; and a lace-draped antique canopy bed.

Convenient to the companies of the nearby city of Ontario and to Ontario International Airport, the Christmas House has become a favorite address of business travelers, but it continues to attract leisure visitors, too. Festivities include a monthly murder-mystery weekend, a follow-the-actors production of *A Christmas Carol*, and a Dressed to Kill New Year's Eve Murder Mystery Gala.

Address: *9240 Archibald Ave., Rancho Cucamonga, CA 91730, tel. 714/980–6450.*
Accommodations: *3 double rooms with bath, 3 double rooms share 1 bath, 1 suite.*
Amenities: *Air-conditioning, robes; fireplace in 4 rooms, TV with VCR in 1 room; hot tub in 2 rooms, TVs available, afternoon refreshments.*
Rates: *$60–$145; full breakfast. AE, D, MC, V.*
Restrictions: *Smoking outside only; no pets.*

Lord Mayor's Inn

I n 1987, Reuben and Laura Brasser, anticipating retirement, were ready to chuck their ranch house and move into something smaller. Instead the couple discovered a historic house that needed to be rescued.

Thus was born Lord Mayor's Inn, located in the heart of Long Beach and within walking distance of the convention center, Terrace Theater, World Trade Center, and most offices. Built in 1904 by Charles Windham, the first mayor of Long Beach, the house is a classic example of Edwardian architecture—a streamlined evolution of fussy Victorian. Although it's big and boxy, with bay windows, deep porches, and generous amounts of woodwork throughout, the ornaments are straight-lined and angled rather than curved.

Reuben, formerly a music teacher, says he learned to tell Victorian from Edwardian during the renovation, which took three years. Reuben was meticulous in his attention to detail: light fixtures, brass hardware, windows, even the old sliding barn doors on the Tack House. He preserved the unusual hand-hewn Vermont granite fireplace, though a 1933 earthquake rendered its chimney unusable.

The five spacious guest rooms, all on the second floor, open onto a small sitting parlor. They contain an impressive collection of antiques, one

of the most notable of which is a carved bed with Hawaiian motif in which Andy Warhol is said to have slept. The Eastlake Room contains an early folding chair dating to 1870 and a fainting couch. A pair of carved 18th-century mahogany twin beds from Austria with opposing crowns on the headboards grace Margarita's Room.

Common rooms downstairs are unusually cozy. Original wainscoting and built-in cabinets in the living room, dining room, and foyer are gleaming golden oak. Furnishings are comfortably Victorian: a sofa, cherry-wood breakfront, Stickley chairs in the foyer. A library is modern, however, with Danish lounge chairs set in front of the guest TV.

Gregarious hosts, Reuben and Laura are longtime Long Beach residents with roots deep in the community. Thus they can be particularly helpful to guests wanting to explore Shoreline Village or cruise to Catalina.

Address: *435 Cedar Ave., Long Beach, CA 90802, tel. 310/436-0324.*
Accommodations: *5 double rooms with bath.*
Amenities: *Phone in rooms; TV in library, computer available, afternoon refreshments; off-street parking.*
Rates: *$85-$95; full breakfast. AE, MC, V.*
Restrictions: *Smoking on porches and balconies only; no pets.*

Malibu Beach Inn

The Malibu Beach is one of the few southern California inns situated right on the shore. Its location, ocean views, and high level of service and amenities draw the occasional famous guest. This inn is the creation of Skip and Lu Miser, local developers who previously owned a restaurant and small motel on the property. When a storm in 1983 destroyed the restaurant, Skip decided he liked being an innkeeper better than being a restaurateur and opted to construct new lodgings instead of a new eatery.

The pink-stucco, Mediterranean-style inn has what is coming to be called the "Malibu look": red-tiled roof, terra-cotta floors, soft pink and blue accents on hand-painted tiles in the lobby and bathrooms. All the rooms have an ocean theme, with images of sea horses, scallop shells, and sea snails stenciled on warm, white walls. Rattan headboards and dresser modules were specially made in the Philippines for the inn. All rooms have private balconies, workspaces, sofa beds, and bathrooms with separate dressing areas. A deep-tiled deck extending the length of the building on the ocean side is an ideal spot to sit and watch the surfers work the waves off Malibu Point, to enjoy breakfast and the morning sun—or wine and the evening sunset.

You can serve yourself from the huge bowls of fruit and baskets of muffins and croissants set up for breakfast in the inn's lobby, or you can have your breakfast brought to your room. The innkeeper has also made arrangements with Alice's Restaurant, located on the Malibu Pier just a few steps away, to cater lunch and dinner for guests.

The inn is convenient to such Malibu attractions as the J. Paul Getty Museum; guests can also explore historic Malibu pier or shop with the rich and famous at the Malibu Colony Plaza. Outdoor activities include hikes in the hills at nearby Malibu Creek State Park or snorkeling, sailboarding, and jetskiing at the beach.

Address: *22878 Pacific Coast Hwy., Malibu, CA 90265, tel. 310/456–6444 or 800/255–1007, fax 310/456–1499.*
Accommodations: *44 double rooms with bath, 3 suites.*
Amenities: *Air-conditioning; TV with VCR, phone, refrigerator, honor bar, wet bar, coffee maker, hair dryer in rooms; fireplace in 43 rooms; room service 7:30 AM–9 PM, beach towels and lounge chairs, picnic baskets, gift shop, off-street parking.*
Rates: *$125–$290; Continental breakfast. AE, DC, MC, V.*
Restrictions: *No pets; 2-night minimum on weekends, 3-night minimum on holidays.*

Seal Beach Inn and Gardens

Marjorie Bettenhausen has a romantic spirit. It's what drove her to purchase a 70-year-old hotel that had once been headquarters for rumrunners in Seal Beach—a 1920s-era seaside resort just south of Long Beach—and turn it into an antiques-filled, flower-decked bed-and-breakfast inn. Opened in 1977, it's one of the first B&Bs in southern California.

Marjorie's romantic spirit also took her to Europe, where she became enchanted with the "exquisite furnishings, lush gardens, and striking colors of the inns along the Mediterranean coast of France." She brought back the antique treasures you'll find at the inn: a 2,000-pound iron fountain from Paris; a red phone booth from Britain; Mediterranean tile murals; flower-filled Napoleonic jardinieres; stately 1920s streetlights; and classic wood-inlaid beds—including one from John Barrymore's estate.

The delightful French Mediterranean–style inn that Majorie created includes one- and two-story buildings adorned by ornate white-iron balustrades, geranium-filled window boxes, and classic blue awnings surrounding a colorful, flower-decked courtyard. Another building faces a quiet residential street.

The largest and most attractive rooms are those in the main buildings that look out onto the courtyard. Most are suites with kitchens as well as sitting rooms; furnishings include four-poster beds, stained-glass windows, and floral wallpapers and bedspreads. Some ground-level rooms have private outdoor sitting areas.

Guests gather for afternoon refreshments in a library warmed by a fireplace, lit with brass chandeliers, and filled with Marjorie's personal book collection. Breakfast is served in the adjacent lace-curtained Tea Room, with a view of the swimming pool. A number of packages are offered to guests, including a chocolate "love-inn" and a gondola getaway cruise through the canals of Naples (the nearby California town, that is).

Address: *212 5th St., Seal Beach, CA 90740, tel. 310/493–2416, fax 310/799–0483.*
Accommodations: *9 double rooms with bath, 14 housekeeping suites.*
Amenities: *TV, phone, and refrigerator in rooms, fireplace in 1 room, Jacuzzi in 1 room; afternoon refreshments, picnic baskets, library, gift shop, swimming pool.*
Rates: *$98–$155; full breakfast. AE, DC, MC, V.*
Restrictions: *Smoking outside only, no pets.*

Anaheim Country Inn

This 1910 "Princess" Anne, located on a quiet residential street, is convenient to Disneyland and the Anaheim Convention Center. It's the only inn in Anaheim, offering an intimate alternative to the hotels in the area. Innkeepers Marilyn Watson and Lois Ramont are longtime Anaheim residents who operated a restaurant here before opening the inn in 1983.

The architecture of the Princess Anne is less ornate than that of the earlier Queen Anne, so the innkeepers have kept the decor very simple. Furnishings are country style, with some oak pieces dating from the turn of the century. A spool bed, an old-fashioned sewing machine, a brass bed, and Oriental rugs on the floors help sustain the comfortable country atmosphere. The rooms upstairs connect with each other, so combinations are possible for families or couples traveling together. The inn is surrounded by a spacious garden, planted with roses and other flowers.

Address: *856 S. Walnut, Anaheim, CA 92802, tel. 714/778-0150 or 800/755-7801.*
Accommodations: *6 double rooms with bath, 4 double rooms share 2 baths.*
Amenities: *Afternoon refreshments; air-conditioning in 1 room; phone available in 3 rooms; hot tub, croquet, parking.*
Rates: *$55-$100; full breakfast. AE, D, MC, V.*
Restrictions: *Smoking outside only, no pets.*

Carriage House

Like many other bed-and-breakfast inns, the Carriage House was something else first—in this case, an apartment building. When innkeepers Dee, Vernon, and Tom Taylor rescued the 1920s-era, two-story clapboard structure, located on a quiet side street a few blocks from the heart of Laguna, they converted the former parking area into a brick-floored tropical courtyard garden, installing a canopy of banana and carrotwood trees, a fish pond, bowers of hibiscus and geraniums, and an aviary.

The bright rooms reflect the building's apartment-house past: All are unusually spacious suites, with fully equipped kitchens and dining and sitting areas. Furnishings and decorative items come from the Taylor family: a silk quilt cover in a log-cabin pattern, an antique pump organ. Dee serves breakfast at a long, lace-covered table in what she calls Grandma Bean's Dining Room, but on nice days guests usually head out to the flower-filled courtyard.

Address: *1322 Catalina St., Laguna Beach, CA 92651, tel. 714/494-8945.*
Accommodations: *1 suite, 5 double housekeeping suites.*
Amenities: *TV in rooms; beach towels, parking.*
Rates: *$95-$150; Continental breakfast. No credit cards.*
Restrictions: *No pets; 2-night minimum on weekends, 3-night minimum on holidays.*

Eiler's Inn

Henk Wirtz and his family came to the United States from Germany 13 years ago expressly to open one of the first bed-and-breakfast inns in southern California, in the artsy town of Laguna Beach. He chose a building that had a checkered life dating from the 1930s, when families visiting the beach used its small rooms as headquarters for the day. Later, during the '60s and '70s, it became a rooming house for hippies— including Timothy Leary.

Henk made a lot of changes, creating a very proper European-style inn, complete with lace curtains and a flower-filled courtyard where breakfast is served. The rooms, surrounding the courtyard on two levels, are small, simply furnished and decorated, usually with a double bed and a chair or two; there's an occasional carved armoire or dresser. The bathrooms are small and functional.

Henk came, he said, for the same reasons that guests continue to come—because of the town's lovely beachside setting, and because it's a good place to nourish a creative spirit.

Address: *741 S. Coast Hwy., Laguna Beach, CA 92651, tel. 714/494-3004.*
Accommodations: *11 double rooms with bath, 1 housekeeping suite.*
Amenities: *TV in suite; afternoon refreshments.*
Rates: *$100–$175; Continental breakfast. AE, MC, V.*
Restrictions: *No pets; 2-night minimum on weekends.*

Inn at Laguna Beach

This luxurious, new Mediterranean-style inn perched on a bluff offers direct access to Main Beach. Rooms front either ocean or village; the latter, although right on the highway, are surprisingly quiet. Many rooms are spacious, containing sitting areas and flower-fringed balconies. The decor is contemporary, with walls painted in desert colors. The inn offers wheelchair-accessible rooms, TDDY telephones, close-captioned TV sets, and a security system designed to alert hearing- and vision-impaired guests in an emergency.

Convenient for those wishing to explore the Laguna Beach art scene, the inn is near the art museum and many of Laguna's galleries; in summer, there's a shuttle to the Laguna Art Festival grounds.

Address: *211 N. Coast Hwy., Laguna Beach, CA 92651, tel. 714/497-9722 or 800/544-4479, fax 714/497-9972.*
Accommodations: *70 double rooms with bath.*
Amenities: *Air-conditioning, TV with VCR, phone, refrigerator, honor bar, robes, hair dryer in rooms, microwave in 30 rooms; video rentals, laundry service, conference facilities, swimming pool, off-street parking.*
Rates: *$99–$299; Continental breakfast. AE, MC, V.*
Restrictions: *No pets; 2-night minimum weekends in July and Aug., 3-night minimum on holidays.*

Inn on Mt. Ada

Chewing-gum magnate William Wrigley, Jr., built this impressive Georgian Colonial mansion in 1921 as his Catalina Island summer home. It has a stunning view of Avalon Harbor, the coastline, and the mountains beyond from nearly every room.

Though the home is grand, Wrigley furnished it so his family and guests would feel comfortable. Susie Griffin and Marlene McAdam, who transformed the millionaire's mansion into an inn in 1986, maintained that feeling. Furnishings are comfortable rather than elegant: overstuffed sofas and wing chairs in the living room, natural wicker in the downstairs den. The rooms range from spacious to small, but all offer a sea view. Full meal service is included.

The inn offers not only a stunning location but also the sort of pampering that a millionaire would require: privacy and discreet attention to detail. Since no private cars are permitted on the island, guests are provided with golf carts for transportation.

Address: *398 Wrigley Rd., Box 2560, Avalon, CA 90704, tel. 310/510–2030.*
Accommodations: *4 double rooms with bath, 2 suites.*
Amenities: *Fireplace in 4 rooms; robes, TV available, conference facilities.*
Rates: *$290–$490, suites $490–$580; AP. AE, MC, V.*
Restrictions: *Smoking outside only, no pets; 2-night minimum on weekends and holidays.*

Mansion Inn

This inn, offering economical accommodations in pricey Marina del Rey, is popular with visitors from Europe, who take advantage of its proximity to the largest small-boat marina on the West Coast, the nonstop festival at Venice Beach, and shopping and dining at nearby Santa Monica. Some rooms are quite small; larger rooms have sofa beds and dining tables, and suites have loft bedrooms. Most rooms are on the dark side, but the best are those facing the interior courtyard. Simple furnishings throughout include pine beds and armoires; colors are soft blues and mauves.

Breakfast is served in a small café adjoining the interior courtyard. Guests tend to sit out on the patio, flooded with light at midday, to enjoy the gurgling fountain, mountains of greenery, and bowers of flowers that fill the area.

Address: *327 Washington Blvd., Marina del Rey, CA 90291, tel. 310/821–2557 or 800/828–0688, fax 310/827–0289.*
Accommodations: *25 double rooms with bath, 5 suites.*
Amenities: *Air-conditioning, TV, phone, refrigerator, honor bar, hair dryer in rooms; off-street parking, brunch and dinner-dance yacht cruises available.*
Rates: *$79–$125, children under 12 free; Continental breakfast. AE, D, DC, MC, V.*
Restrictions: *No pets; 2-night minimum on weekends.*

Portofino Beach Hotel

This Old World–style inn, just a few steps from the surf in a busy section of Newport Beach, is a good spot from which to watch the teenagers on skateboards, lovers strolling, and dory fishermen hawking their catch. The hotel's restaurant, Renato, is popular for its good northern Italian fare.

The decor in the common areas has an Italian accent: bouffant balloon curtains, faux-marble columns, lace antimacassars, brocade-covered wing chairs, curved-back settees, and etched-glass windows. Guest rooms are located on the second floor of the main hotel and in a wing in back; most have some ocean view, but the best are from the Portofino suites. Antique furnishings in the rooms include brass beds, carved headboards, and French side chairs; many of the appealing marble bathrooms have skylights, and some have step-down double whirlpool tubs.

Address: *2306 W. Oceanfront, Newport Beach, CA 92663, tel. 714/673–7030, fax 714/723–4370.*
Accommodations: *15 double rooms with bath.*
Amenities: *Air-conditioning, TV, phone in rooms, whirlpool tub in 9 rooms, private sun deck in 3 rooms; restaurant, room service during dinner hour, lounge, conference facilities, off-street parking.*
Rates: *$100–$235; Continental breakfast. AE, DC, MC, V.*
Restrictions: *No pets; 3-night minimum on holiday weekends.*

Salisbury House

For their new home, Jay and Sue German chose a 1901 Craftsman with some Victorian touches: a curved bay window in the dining room and an abundance of stained-glass windows. There are lots of fir-wood moldings, a built-in china closet in the dining room, dark polished floors, and wainscoting.

All the guest rooms are quite large and comfortable. There is a white iron bed in the Blue Room and a brass bed and braided rugs in the Attic Suite, which is finished with redwood siding. It also has a claw-foot tub positioned so that the bather can look out over the bird-filled trees. The inn's common areas include a living room, where a fire crackles most of the year, and a striking formal dining room, where Sue serves an imaginative breakfast featuring zucchini pancakes or potato frittatas. A self-described foodie, she says that the local Chinese, Korean, Mexican, Vietnamese, and Italian restaurants inspire her in the kitchen.

Address: *2273 W. 20th St., Los Angeles, CA 90018, tel. 213/737–7817.*
Accommodations: *2 double rooms with bath, 2 double rooms share bath.*
Amenities: *Phone, TV with VCR, and air-conditioning in attic room, refrigerator in rooms; TVs available, afternoon refreshments.*
Rates: *$70–$95; full breakfast. AE, MC, V.*
Restrictions: *Smoking outside only, no pets.*

Terrace Manor

L ocated in the Alvarado Terrace Historic District near the downtown high rises, this inn has a history that's intertwined with that of Los Angeles and Hollywood. Home, in the 1920s, of Los Angeles mayor John C. Porter and later of actress Susan Seaforth, the house is currently owned by actor Gene Kidwell, who has appeared in numerous commercials. A striking Tudor, perched on a hill opposite a Victorian park, it boasts such Craftsman touches as burnished-wood wainscoting; heavy-beamed ceilings; and built-in, glass-fronted cabinets. The tranquil colors of the common areas—deep shades of green, red, and pink—are carried out in the second-floor bedrooms, which have white-iron, carved-wood, and sleigh beds; bathrooms are unusually spacious.

Innkeeper Joyce Elder and husband John, a chef at a Hollywood studio, bring a lively Scottish brogue to the inn, preparing high teas and British breakfasts for the guests.

Address: *1353 Alvarado Terr., Los Angeles, CA 90005, tel. 213/381–1478.*
Accommodations: *4 double rooms with bath, 1 suite.*
Amenities: *Air-conditioning in 1 room; private parking, passes to Magic Castle, afternoon refreshments.*
Rates: *$70–$100; full breakfast. AE, DC, MC, V.*
Restrictions: *Smoking outside only, no pets.*

Central Coast

Central Coast
From Santa Barbara to San Simeon

The drive along California's Central Coast is one of the most rewarding in the state and is the scenic California that most visitors have come to see. Except for a few smallish cities—Ventura and Santa Barbara in the south and San Luis Obispo in the north—this is a rural excursion of nearly 200 miles of rolling, golden oak-studded hills and wave-washed beaches.

Highway 101, one of the state's great north–south thoroughfares, is also one of its most historic. The route follows the original El Camino Real (Kings Road) forged by the Spanish padres that leads from one mission to another and is now marked by a series of roadside bells.

Starting in the south, the highway passes through Ventura, gateway to the Channel Islands National Park. It hugs the coast as it moves north toward Santa Barbara. With its Spanish-style architecture, fine restaurants, and collection of outstanding bed-and-breakfast inns, Santa Barbara has become a popular weekend destination for work-weary Angelenos. Santa Barbara strives to preserve its Mediterranean ambience, as a walk among the red-tile-roofed shops along State Street reveals.

From Santa Barbara the highway heads north along the coast, skirting a number of lovely beaches at El Capitan, Refugio, and Gaviota. Moving inland at San Marcos, it passes through the lovely Santa Ynez Valley, where wine tasting and bike riding on tranquil country lanes are two popular pursuits. This is also home of ultratouristy Solvang, which has a Danish theme and an array of bakeries and gift shops.

The highway touches the coast again at a place locals call the Five Cities. Here visitors can explore miles of wide, hard-packed beaches and fluffy white sand dunes; these beach communities are popular with clam diggers, skin divers, and anglers.

San Luis Obispo, just a few miles up the coast, offers a number of surprises. A laid-back university town, it's the home of California Polytechnic University and has an attractive old-fashioned downtown that reveals its Spanish heritage. Like the area north of Santa Barbara, this is wine country.

Cambria, a few miles north along the coast, is the gateway to Hearst Castle and has long been a stopover for visitors to La Cuesta Encantada. *It has also developed as an artists' colony, with many local artists specializing in creating luminous glass objects. Cambria also boasts a number of bed-and-breakfast inns as well as a collection of good restaurants.*

No trip to the Central Coast would be complete without a visit to William Randolph Hearst's castle on the hill at San Simeon. With money from his vast publishing empire, Hearst devoted more than 30 years to building the Italian-Spanish-Moorish-French-style castle with its acres of paintings, sculptures, and other European artwork; gardens; marble swimming pools; lavish dining room; and guest houses that are almost as opulent.

Places to Go, Sights to See

Channel Islands National Park (1901 Spinnaker Dr., Ventura 93001, tel. 805/658–5730) consists of five islands and a visitor center at Ventura Harbor. *Island Packers* (tel. 805/642–1393) offers day-long boat trips to the islands.

Hearst San Simeon Historical Monument (San Simeon State Park, 750 Hearst Castle Rd., San Simeon 93452, tel. 805/927–2020; for tour reservations, tel. 800/444–7275) consists of the famed castle on the hill, 123 acres of pools, gardens, terraces, and guest houses built over three decades by William Randolph Hearst. Half- and three-hour tours are available year-round; the garden tour is offered April through October.

Missions. *La Purisima Mission* (2295 Purisima Rd., Lompoc 93436, tel. 805/733–3713) is the most completely restored mission in the state, illustrating secular as well as religious life at the missions. In this remote setting, which vividly evokes the lives of early settlers, costumed docents demonstrate crafts, including weaving and bread and candle making. *Mission Santa Barbara* (Laguna and Los Olivos Sts., Santa Barbara 93105, tel. 805/682–4149) is known as the Queen of the Missions for its Spanish Renaissance architecture, serene gardens, quiet courtyard, and exhibits of embroidered vestments and illuminated manuscripts.

Santa Barbara County Courthouse (Anacapa and Anapamu Sts., Santa Barbara 93101, tel. 805/962–6464) is a Spanish-Moorish palace with murals, painted ceilings, massive doors, balconies, and Tunisian tiles. Tours are given Tuesday through Saturday.

Santa Barbara Wine Country (Santa Barbara County Vintner's Association, Box 1558, Santa Ynez 93460–1558, tel. 805/688–0881) is actually located in the rolling hillsides of the Santa Ynez Valley. More than 20 wineries are found along Highways 154 and 176, and many offer tours and tastings; many also have picnic facilities and schedule special dinners.

Restaurants

Ian's (tel. 805/927–8649) in Cambria offers elegant dining and an eclectic menu featuring light California cuisine. Santa Barbara's **La Super-Rica Taco** (tel. 805/963–4940) is an unsigned corner taco stand where the line always stretches out the door. Also in Santa Barbara, **Citronelle** (tel. 805/963–0111) combines a great ocean view and bistro decor with outstanding California cuisine. **Oysters** (tel. 805/962–9888), an easy walk from the inns near State Street, serves elegant fresh seafood in a casual setting. In the Santa Ynez wine country, locals love the modern American fare at the charming **Ballard Store & Wine Bar** (tel. 805/688–5319), and history buffs frequent **Mattei's Tavern** (tel. 805/688–4820), an old stop along the stagecoach route. **Pane E Vino** (tel. 805/969–9274) in Montecito has generated a following for sophisticated Italian cuisine, especially pasta. **Paoli's Italian Country Kitchen** (tel. 805/688–9966) in Solvang serves pasta, pizza, chicken, and seafood.

Tourist Information

San Luis Obispo County Visitors and Convention Bureau (1041 Chorro St., Suite E, San Luis Obispo 93401, tel. 800/634–1414); **Santa Barbara Conference and Visitors Bureau** (510A State St., Santa Barbara 93101, tel. 800/927–4688).

Reservation Services

Bed and Breakfast Innkeepers of Southern California (Box 15425, Los Angeles 90015–0385, tel. 800/284–INNS); **Santa Barbara Bed and Breakfast Innkeepers Guild** (Box 90734, Santa Barbara 93190–0734, tel. 800/776–9176).

Blue Quail Inn

here aren't a lot of luxuries at the Blue Quail—no hot tub, no VCRs, only one fireplace—but it doesn't need these extras to be one of Santa Barbara's better bed-and-breakfasts. Born into a B&B family, owner Jeanise Suding Eaton clearly learned early on how to create a welcoming inn. She took over the Blue Quail as a very young woman in 1982 and lived here until her growing family (husband, toddler daughter, and two dogs) required more space.

The antithesis of Santa Barbara's typical grand Victorian B&B, this collection of five little shingled bungalows is low-key and quiet, with an overall decor that will appeal more to lovers of American-country style than of Victorian formality. The main cottage houses a homey, carpeted living room; a dining room with hardwood floors, tan striped wallpaper, country-pine antiques, and an inviting window seat; a tiled country kitchen, where someone friendly is often baking something cinnamony; and two of the more modest guest rooms.

In the rear of the property is the inn's best quarters, the Wood Thrush cottage. There are luxurious white-on-white French linens on the king bed, pickled-pine shutters at the windows, and large, comfortable wicker armchairs in the living room. Those who prefer a Ralph Lauren look should try the Cardinal Suite, with

its veranda, wicker bed, botanical prints, and rich fabrics in paisleys and stripes. American-country fans will love the smaller Mockingbird, with its cheerful yellow floral fabrics and blue-and-white quilt on the wall.

Outside, the cool gardens are thick with ferns and fragrant with jasmine; in fair weather (almost always), breakfast is served on the patio. The many good restaurants, shops, and sights of State Street are a comfortable stroll or quick bike ride away; beachgoers will probably want to drive.

Families take note: This is one of the very few Santa Barbara B&Bs that happily welcome young children, as long as they stay in one of the more private suites.

Address: *1908 Bath St., Santa Barbara, CA 93101, tel. 805/687–2300 or 800/676–1622.*
Accommodations: *5 double rooms with bath, 2 suites with bath, 2 suites share a bath.*
Amenities: *Fireplace in 1 suite, TV in main house; afternoon and evening wine and refreshments; bicycles.*
Rates: *$82–$95, suites $95–$165; full breakfast. AE, MC, V.*
Restrictions: *Smoking outside only, no pets; 2-night minimum on weekends.*

The Blue Whale Inn

Like many southern Californians, Fred Ushijima had been visiting the town of Cambria regularly for years, attracted by the laid-back beachfront atmosphere, good restaurants, and the shops and galleries of a growing artists' colony. Cambria's proximity to the Hearst Castle at San Simeon has always meant large numbers of visitors, but the village hasn't become touristy or overdeveloped.

Fred decided to sink roots in Cambria, and he found the perfect location on a triangular point of land jutting out to the sea along Moonstone Beach Drive. A visual delight, the Blue Whale consists of six guest rooms stepped back from the ocean at such an angle that each captures a bit of the view (the best views, surprisingly, are from the rooms farthest back). At the front of the inn is a spacious living room furnished with overstuffed sofas and chairs and a wood-burning stove; it adjoins the dining area, and the two together create a great room with a wall of windows revealing the everchanging ocean vista.

A tiny Japanese-style garden, created by Fred, separates the guest rooms from the parking lot. Planted with a colorful selection of native plants—including lupine, coreapsis, thyme, and westringa—the garden is punctuated by a series of stepping-stones that lead from the parking area to the decks in front of the guest rooms. Guests often contemplate the beauty of nature while sitting on the garden's wooden bench or watching its tumbling waterfall.

In sharp contrast to the expansive views of sea and sky outside, the inn's interior is a riot of wallpapers and flowered fabrics, mostly in shades of blue. Appointments are comfortable: step-up canopy beds, love seats, desks, a coffee table and side chair in each room. Skylights punctuate each vaulted ceiling. Bathrooms, also skylit, have adjacent dressing areas complete with a sink set into a long vanity.

Although Fred is often at the inn sharing his dining suggestions with guests ("a walking menu," one guest observed), John and Nancy Young are the day-to-day innkeepers. John has earned quite a reputation for his breakfasts, particularly the gingerbread pancakes with lemon sauce.

Address: *6736 Moonstone Beach Dr., Cambria, CA 93428, tel. 805/927-4647.*
Accommodations: *6 double rooms with bath.*
Amenities: *Fireplace, refrigerator, hair dryer, TV, phone in rooms; afternoon refreshments, gift shop.*
Rates: *$125–$165; full breakfast. MC, V.*
Restrictions: *Smoking outside only, no pets; 2-night minimum on weekends and holidays.*

The Cheshire Cat

Two words sum up these adjacent gray-and-white Victorian-era houses linked by a brick patio: "Laura" and "Ashley." If you like the late designer's delicate floral fabrics, bedding, and wallpapers, then you'll be in heaven here. Owner Christine Dunstan, who spends six months a year in Scotland (where she owns another inn), gave her B&B a thoroughly British look, from the picket-fenced flower gardens to the formal entry and fireplace-warmed sitting area. Some masculine English antiques offset the frilly prettiness of the public rooms, most notably the huge refectory-style table and weighty sideboard in the dining room.

Since she's not often in attendance, Dunstan hired Midge Goeden and a small crew of friendly collegiate types to cook the substantial full breakfast and tend to the guests and the property. There's a fair amount to tend to: the main house, all Victorian turrets and bays; the neighboring house, a Georgian-style box with shutters and bay windows; the Tweedledum & Tweedledee house, a simple clapboard cottage, in back; and the various garden areas, including a large brick patio where a first-rate breakfast is served.

Larger and more upscale than most other B&Bs in town, the Cheshire Cat is popular with small groups for retreats or meetings, but most of its customers are couples seeking romance. They generally find it, particularly if they splurge on the Eberle Suite, which has a brick fireplace and a whirlpool tub for two; the White Rabbit Suite, whose private patio overlooks the gardens; and the swank Tweedledum Suite in the newly built back house, complete with living room, dining room, kitchenette, fireplace, TV, king-size bed, and whirlpool tub.

The west-facing rooms in the main house can be a bit noisy, since they're the closest to busy Chapala Street. On the plus side, the inn is a short walk from the shops and restaurants of State Street.

Address: *36 W. Valerio St., Santa Barbara, CA 93101, tel. 805/569–1610.*
Accommodations: *6 double rooms with bath, 1 housekeeping room with bath, 6 suites, 1 housekeeping suite.*
Amenities: *Phone, chocolates, liqueurs in rooms, fireplace in 4 rooms, whirlpool tub in 4 rooms, TV in 2 rooms; meeting room for 8 to 12 with fireplace, afternoon wine, mountain bicycles, spa in gazebo.*
Rates: *$119–$169, suites $169–$290; full breakfast. MC, V.*
Restrictions: *Smoking outside only, no pets; 2-night minimum on weekends.*

El Encanto

Like its rival high-end country inn, the San Ysidro Ranch, El Encanto has had its ups and downs over the years. It's definitely on the ascendance these days, now that an extensive renovation has dealt with the shabbiness that had crept up on the place in the '80s. Fortunately, just a bit of genteel shabbiness remains—too much slickness would most definitely not suit this tumble of cottages in the hills above the Santa Barbara Mission.

The sort of country inns that pepper New England are scarce in California, home of the grand hotel, the tiny B&B, and the faceless motel—which makes this almost-in-the-country inn so welcome. Although red-tile-roofed Spanish villas dominate in the surrounding areas, most of El Encanto's buildings are board-and-batten cottages.

What makes El Encanto as enchanting as its name promises are the view of ocean, trees, and red-tiled roofs from the restaurant's huge patio; the extensive grounds (lush gardens, banana palms, towering eucalyptus, thick lawns, even a lily pond); and the larger cottage suites and villas, done up in a pleasant, generally informal mishmash of French-country fabrics, English-style florals, and updated American-country furniture with a Shaker feeling. Most of the cottages have porches and French doors; some have private patios.

The standard rooms, which can be fairly small, lean more toward the updated American-country look, with Berber carpets, crisp tile bathrooms, and a predominant hunter green and tan color scheme.

The terrace restaurant's lovely views, not to mention its good California–contemporary American cuisine, have made it one of Santa Barbara's most popular brunch spots, so reserve early; it tends to sell out on summer weekends. To work off the food, guests play tennis, swim laps, or walk the hilly streets. Or they snooze in one of the yellow-striped swings dotting the grounds. The beach is a five-minute drive away, and the State Street shops are even closer.

Address: *1900 Lasuen Rd., Santa Barbara, CA 93103, tel. 805/687–5000 or 800/346–7039; fax 805/687–3903.*
Accommodations: *34 double rooms with bath, 45 suites and villas.*
Amenities: *Phone and cable TV in rooms, fireplace and private patio or deck in many rooms; restaurant, bar, lounge, 9 meeting and banquet rooms, room service 7 AM–9 PM; pool, tennis court, walking paths.*
Rates: *$119–$169, suites and villas $169–$290. AE, DC, MC, V.*
Restrictions: *No pets; 2-night minimum on weekends.*

Los Olivos Grand Hotel

onald Reagan and Michael Jackson have ranches hereabouts, as do lots of less famous but similarly moneyed folks. Which explains this country inn's haute-bourgeoise style and high prices. Those who value rusticity should look elsewhere; those looking for creature comforts (and who don't mind paying for them) are likely to have a memorable stay.

About 45 minutes up a lovely, sharply winding mountain road from Santa Barbara, Los Olivos is tucked into the oak-dotted ochre hills of the Santa Ynez Valley. Vineyards and ranch land occupy most of the valley, and the town isn't much more than a dozen art galleries, a wine shop, a gas station, a saddlery, a couple of restaurants, and this inn. Amusements in these parts are genteel: wine tasting, horseback riding, hiking, dining, gallery hopping, and taking in the night air from the confines of a steaming Jacuzzi.

The Grand Hotel hews to the polished (as opposed to the rustic) French-country style. Classical music wafts through the lobby, with its stone fireplace, gleaming piano, French doors, and various clusters of sofas, wing chairs, and Queen Anne furniture. At one end is Remington's, a good Continental-American restaurant named for the western artist; downstairs, the Wine Cellar, a pri-

vate dining room, is great for larger parties.

Each of the large suites (set in two low-lying Victorian buildings) is individually styled; vaulted, beamed ceilings, Pierre Deux–style fabrics, iron or brass beds, hand-painted tile fireplaces, and Impressionist paintings are the norm. The Monet Suite, with its bay window, restful blues, and comfy chaise, is particularly lovely, but there isn't a loser in the bunch. Luxurious touches abound, from wet bars to down comforters.

Though the inn lacks the homey, personal feeling of owner-operated B&Bs, the staff exudes friendly professionalism and will tend to most any request, from arranging a private tour of a winery to delivering a freshly brewed cup of tea to your room at 3 AM.

Address: *2860 Grand Ave., Los Olivos, CA 93441, tel. 805/688-7788 or 800/446-2455.*
Accommodations: *22 suites with bath.*
Amenities: *Fireplace, phone, cable TV, wet bar, refrigerator, wine in rooms; whirlpool tub in many rooms; restaurant, lounge, meeting and banquet rooms, room service; pool, spa; bicycles, picnics and backpacks extra.*
Rates: *$160–$325; Continental breakfast. AE, D, DC, MC, V.*
Restrictions: *No pets; 2-night minimum on weekends.*

Old Yacht Club Inn

When former school administrators Nancy Donaldson and Lu Caruso and teacher Sandy Hunt opened Santa Barbara's first bed-and-breakfast in 1980, they set out to provide a homey atmosphere in which guests would feel comfortable putting their feet up—and so pampered that they'd want to return again and again. In addition, there would be the outstanding food prepared by Nancy, a member of the American Wine and Food Institute.

Initially the inn consisted of only the historic 1912 Craftsman house with its broad porches, tiny balcony across the front, redbrick fireplace, and colorful gardens. Just a block from the beach, it had been built as a private home, and during the 1920s served as the headquarters for the Santa Barbara Yacht Club. In 1983 the innkeepers acquired the more spacious house next door, which they transformed into the Hitchcock House.

The Hitchcock is a monument to the families of the innkeepers, with its four rooms named and decorated to honor parents and grandparents. The Julia Metelmann is decorated with life-size photographs of the mother of a former inn partner. The photographs depict Julia as a young pioneer in South Dakota, and furnishings include a red lacquer Chinese chest that once belonged to her.

There are five rooms in the main house, four on the second floor, and one downstairs. The upstairs rooms offer a light and airy ambience. In the two front-facing rooms French doors open onto a balcony where guests can sip wine while taking in the afternoon sun. Downstairs, the sunny Captain's Corner opens onto a private patio.

Breakfast and Saturday-night dinners are served in the inn's dining-living room. Nancy uses fresh local ingredients in her five-course gourmet dinners: shrimp from the bay, artichokes from nearby fields, and sorrel grown in the backyard. Breakfast, usually prepared by Sandy, features the lightest of light omelets, home-baked breads, and fresh fruit.

Address: *431 Corona del Mar Dr., Santa Barbara, CA 93103, tel. 805/962–1277.*
Accommodations: *8 rooms with bath, 1 suite.*
Amenities: *Phone in rooms, TV on request, evening refreshments, whirlpool tub in 1 room; dinner served to guests on Sat. nights (about $25), golf privileges at local country club, bicycles, beach towels, chairs.*
Rates: *$75–$135; full breakfast. AE, D, MC, V.*
Restrictions: *No smoking in guest rooms, no pets; 2-night minimum on weekends.*

The Parsonage

In 1981, Hilde Michelmore transformed a dreary school for problem children (formerly the home of the parson of nearby Trinity Episcopal Church) into an excellent bed-and-breakfast, immediately becoming a leader of Santa Barbara's just-developing B&B scene. Now she has retired and passed the baton to Holli and Tom Harmon, who fled Redondo Beach in search of, in Holli's words, "a new lifestyle."

Thus far their new lifestyle is off to a great start. Terry is still working as a firefighter for Los Angeles County, but Holli has shifted gears from being a financial planner to being an innkeeper—and new mother. Terry's folks, Dick and Audrey Harmon, live at the inn, contributing their years of experience running a small Catalina Island hotel.

The Harmons have dreams and schemes for this big, boxy hillside Queen Anne Victorian (built circa 1892); the light, airy three-story house offers all sorts of possibilities. They're thinking, for a starter, of adding some of Holli's inherited antiques into the furnishings mix. But for now the Parsonage looks exactly as Hilde left it. Her French and English antiques are scattered throughout, from the Louis XVI dresser and mirror in the Versailles Room to the Victorian settee in the Las Flores Room and the Oriental rugs in nearly every room.

The Honeymoon Suite may be one of the most romantic accommodations in town. A huge three-room suite that wraps around a front corner of the house, it offers stunning views of ocean, city, and mountains; it also has a separate solarium. Good sea views can also be had from the bay windows of Las Flores, and the other two second-story rooms offer mountain views. On the ground floor is the large, bright living room, filled with some of Hilde's favorite antiques.

Weather permitting—which is most of the time—breakfast is served on bone china on the outdoor deck or in the gazebo. Audrey makes all her own breads and muffins; a typical breakfast might include omelets, Amish bread, fruit, and fresh orange juice. Home-baked cookies are often set out on the kitchen counter, along with pitchers of iced tea or lemonade. And sometimes Audrey puts out the espresso machine for those in need of an afternoon pick-me-up.

Address: *1600 Olive St., Santa Barbara, CA 93101, tel. 805/962–9336.*
Accommodations: *5 rooms with bath, 1 suite.*
Amenities: *Afternoon refreshments.*
Rates: *$85–$115, suites $160; full breakfast. AE, MC, V.*
Restrictions: *Smoking outside only, no pets; 2-night minimum on weekends, 3-night minimum on holidays.*

San Ysidro Ranch

San Ysidro's current luxurious-
ness belies its humble roots as
one of the Santa Barbara Mission's working ranches. It became
a guest ranch in the late 1800s after
cottages were added to the 1825
adobe, which still stands, and
reached international fame in the
1930s, when owners Ronald Colman
(the actor) and Alvin Weingand (a
state senator) attracted stars, writers, and royalty. Here Vivian Leigh
and Laurence Olivier married, John
and Jackie Kennedy honeymooned,
and Winston Churchill wrote some
of his memoirs.

Nestled in the hills above Montecito,
one of the country's wealthiest small
towns, the Ranch, as it is known to
faithfuls, had become shabby by the
'60s. New owners restored the cottages and added some luxurious new
ones, and Hollywood was once again
in residence. In 1987, Claude Rouas,
owner of Napa Valley's luxe Auberge du Soleil, took over and set out to
make the atmospheric stone restaurant, the ranch's old packing house,
up to France's country-inn standards, a goal he achieved. But chef
Marc Ehrler left recently, and Stonehouse has suffered a considerable
drop in quality.

The inn itself, however, is still swell,
even if there seem to be a few more
weeds in the gardens. Winding paths
connect the various board-and-batten
cottages, which house everything
from smallish double rooms to huge

two-bedroom suites with soaring
beamed ceilings. The decor is generally American-country style,
achieved with a mix of clean-lined
antiques, country-print upholstery,
quilts, and a lavish use of pine.

Some highly stressed guests (including many of the very famous) just
hide out by their fireplaces and
order room service. Others stroll the
gardens and orchards, hike through
the 550 acres, swim, play tennis, ride
horses, play chess in the games
room, have a drink or snack in the
cozy Plow & Angel bar, or venture
into downtown Montecito or nearby
Santa Barbara. Nearly all get what
they came for: clean air, charm, comfort, pampering, romance, and
enough peace and quiet to finish
writing that script.

Address: *900 San Ysidro La., Montecito, CA 93108, tel. 805/969-5046
or 800/368-6788, fax 805/565-1995.*
Accommodations: *26 double rooms
with bath, 18 suites and cottages.*
Amenities: *Fireplace or wood stove,
phone, cable TV, private deck, wet
bar, refrigerator in rooms, whirlpool tub in many rooms; restaurant, bar, room service, pool, spa;
horses and picnics extra.*
Rates: *$195–$325, suites $350–$625;
full breakfast during the week, no
breakfast included on weekends.
AE, MC, V.*
Restrictions: *2-night minimum on
weekends.*

Union Hotel/ Victorian Mansion

In the tiny Old West outpost of Los Alamos, some 50 miles north of Santa Barbara, these two inns present a study in fantasy fulfillment. The Union Hotel, a onetime Wells Fargo stagecoach station dating from 1880, was renovated by Dick Langdon in 1970 and turned into one of the first bed-and-breakfasts in California. The whimsical Old West atmosphere, which begins in the lobby peopled with mannequins costumed in frontier finery, is carried into the saloon with its mahogany Ping-Pong table supported by marble statues and continues in the bedrooms with their French and patriotic wallpapers.

In the neighboring yellow three-story 1864 Mansion, mere whimsy gives way to flat-out fantasy. Dick has created a sort of Disneyland for adults here. Take the Egyptian Room, designed to make a couple feel like Antony and Cleopatra camping out in the desert. A step-up white bed, canopied with gauze, stands in the middle of the room facing a wall-size mural of a desert. Walls are draped with Near East–motif fabrics, there's a step-up hot tub, and a marble-faced fireplace flanked by floor cushions. The bathroom door is a life-size statue of King Tut, opened by tugging his beard, and the bathroom itself resembles the inside of a pyramid. Dick supplies hooded desert robes, backgammon, computer-controlled background music, video-

tapes of *Lawrence of Arabia* and *The Wind and the Lion.*

Other rooms are equally fantastic: Roman, Gypsy, Pirate, '50s Drive-In, and French—each with fitting murals, bed, theme robes, music, movies, games, and menus. Breakfast is delivered to the theme rooms through lockers concealed in the walls.

Dick, who moved to Los Alamos 21 years ago, has built a community of artists and artisans who continue to give life to his fantasy. Many live at the inn while working on new projects: a hedge-maze connecting the two inns; a dry-docked, 67-foot Danish yawl; and a tree house.

Address: *362 Bell St., Box 616, Los Alamos, CA 93440, tel. 805/344–2744.*
Accommodations: *Hotel: 3 rooms with bath, 10 rooms with sinks share 2 baths; mansion: 6 rooms with bath.*
Amenities: *Mansion: TV with VCR, tapes, phone, hot tub, fireplace, robes, refrigerator in rooms; restaurant, saloon, shuffleboard, Ping-Pong, swimming pool; spa in gazebo; maze.*
Rates: *Hotel $80–$100, mansion $200; full breakfast. AE, MC, V.*
Restrictions: *No pets; hotel and restaurant open Fri., Sat., Sun. only.*

Ballard Inn

This gray and white updated Cape Cod–style inn looks out of place in the Santa Ynez Valley, home of sprawling horse ranches and the up-and-coming wineries of Santa Barbara County. Standing on a corner in the tiny town of Ballard, the Ballard Inn was built in 1985 by a group of Hollywood celebrities and is now owned by Santa Barbara restaurateur Steve Hyslop and partner Larry Stone.

Each room is decorated to illustrate different aspects of local lore. One room feels like a frontiersman's mountain cabin, with a rough stone fireplace and rustic wooden furnishings; another recalls stagecoach days, with a collection of cowboy hats and early photographs of local cattle ranches; another room honors a pair of sister schoolteachers, with a platform rocker, wing chair, and brass chandelier. The common rooms feature comfortable, overstuffed sofas in the living room; and Old West ambience prevails in the Stagecoach room.

Address: *2436 Baseline Ave., Ballard, CA 93463, tel. 805/688-7770 or 800/638-2466.*
Accommodations: *15 double rooms with bath.*
Amenities: *Air-conditioning, fireplace in 7 rooms; afternoon wine tasting; bicycle rentals, carriage rides extra.*
Rates: *$155–$185; full breakfast. MC, V.*
Restrictions: *Smoking outside only, no pets; 2-night minimum on weekends.*

Bath Street Inn

At first glance, the Bath Street Inn, an 1870s Victorian cottage on a quiet street a few blocks off Santa Barbara's main drag, looks deceptively small. There's no clue that it's so much larger than it appears, thanks to a recent renovation and expansion.

Guest rooms are located upstairs, with those on the third floor filling odd-shaped spaces created by the steep pitch of the roof and its many eaves and gables. The decor throughout is predominantly Victorian, with comfortable, overstuffed sofas, wing chairs, canopy beds, reading nooks, and cabbage-rose wallpaper patterns. "People say it reminds them of their mother's house," remarks Bath Street's creator, Susan Brown, one of Santa Barbara's first innkeepers.

Guests have the use of the entire house, including the garden out back. As pleasant as it is to linger in, this inn makes a convenient home base for excursions to the beach or for exploring the chic shops that line nearby State Street.

Address: *1720 Bath St., Santa Barbara, CA 93101, tel. 805/682-9680 or 800/788-BATH, 800/549-BATH in CA.*
Accommodations: *8 rooms with bath.*
Amenities: *Afternoon refreshments, bicycles.*
Rates: *$90–$115; full breakfast. AE, MC, V.*
Restrictions: *Smoking outside only, no pets; 2-night minimum on weekends.*

Bayberry Inn

Carlton Wagner, a renowned interior designer, color consultant, and one of the owners of the Bayberry, has created an inn reminiscent of the gilded age just after World War I within this shingle-covered, late-19th-century building in Santa Barbara. Throughout you'll find an abundance of silk, crystal, and porcelains. The dining room ceiling is draped in yard after yard of soft pink silk with folds brought together in the center by a crystal chandelier. The walls in the dining room are covered by beveled mirrors. Beds are canopied in heavy fabric, with a crystal chandelier in the center of the canopy. The rooms tend to be cozy, with the dramatic bed as the main feature; lighting in most rooms is subdued, creating a romantic mood.

Wagner and his partner Keith Pomeroy specialize in pampering guests. Pomeroy, whose background is in catering, prepares breakfasts as pretty as they are tasty, served on fine china in the opulent dining room.

Address: *111 W. Valerio St., Santa Barbara, CA 93101, tel. 805/682-3199.*
Accommodations: *8 double rooms with bath.*
Amenities: *Robes, fireplace in 4 rooms, whirlpool tub in 1 room, phone in 4 rooms; afternoon refreshments, guest refrigerator, TV on request, bicycles, croquet, badminton; small dogs allowed.*
Rates: *$85–$135; full breakfast.*
Restrictions: *No smoking; 2-night minimum on weekends.*

The Beach House

The outstanding feature of this aptly named B&B is its location across the street from Cambria's gorgeous dark-sand beach. Trails meander along the bluff above the sand; you can surf crisp waves at one end, explore tidal pools at the other, or lose yourself in a book in one of the many sunny coves.

The inn, if less impressive than the beach, is not without comforts. Resembling any number of beach houses lining southern California's shores, it's a typical '60s contemporary, all wood and glass, with a steeply pitched roof and huge second-floor concrete deck. Common areas range from a cramped ground-floor sitting area to an airy second-floor room. Bedrooms are fairly nondescript—wall-to-wall carpeting in

greens and browns, knotty-pine ceilings, wicker furniture, new quilts. The two downstairs rooms have fireplaces but are rather dark; more impressive is the high-ceiling king-bedded room upstairs, boasting ocean views and a private deck.

Address: *6360 Moonstone Beach Dr., Cambria, CA 93441, tel. 805/927-3136.*
Accommodations: *7 rooms with bath.*
Amenities: *Cable TV in rooms, fireplace in 2 rooms; evening wine and cheese; mountain bikes.*
Rates: *$100–$135; full breakfast. MC, V.*
Restrictions: *Smoking outside only, no pets.*

Bella Maggiore Inn

Designed by famed Los Angeles architect A. C. Martin, this 1925 hotel in Ventura's historic district is a lovely example of the Italianate style, a cool Mediterranean building with an ornamental plaster facade, awnings, and a high-ceilinged, earthtone lobby dotted with comfortably worn sofas and chairs. Toward the rear is a hushed walled courtyard, complete with fountain and iron-and-glass patio furniture.

Though breakfast is served, the Bella Maggiore is more a small hotel than a B&B. Rooms vary in size, but they're similar in appearance, done in a spare Mediterranean style, with simple wood furnishings and shuttered windows. They're notable more for quiet, comfort, and good value than luxury. Just around the corner is Ventura's "old" shopping street, home to lots of good, cheap antiques stores and junk shops. The mission, grand old courthouse, and beach are all nearby.

Address: *67 S. California St., Ventura, CA 93001, tel. 805/652–0277 or 800/523–8479.*
Accommodations: *21 rooms with bath, 3 suites.*
Amenities: *Cable TV, phone, ceiling fans in rooms; fireplace in 6 rooms, air-conditioning in 4 rooms; evening hors d'oeuvres.*
Rates: *$70–$175, suites $100–$175; full breakfast. AE, D, DC, MC, V.*
Restrictions: *No pets.*

Garden Street Inn

Nostalgia is the theme at this Stick-style Italianate inn just a block from Mission San Luis Obispo and only a few steps from the town's Old California-style downtown. Innkeepers Dan and Kathy Smith retained the 1887 structure's high ceilings, skylighted grand staircase, 8-foot-tall wooden doors, stained glass, and squared bay windows. The thematic decor draws from the Smiths' family histories as well as that of the community. The Field of Dreams Room is dedicated to Kathy's sportswriter father and contains baseball memorabilia; Walden, sporting family wood carvings and New Zealand art, honors Dan's dad, who loved the outdoors; and the Ah Louis Room, containing an antique Oriental curio cabinet, celebrates an early Chinese labor leader who organized Central Coast railroad workers.

The couple are a good source of information about local history, beaches, restaurants, and the Thursday-night farmers' market that takes place nearby.

Address: *1212 Garden St., San Luis Obispo, CA 93401, tel. 805/545–9802.*
Accommodations: *9 double rooms with bath, 4 suites.*
Amenities: *Afternoon refreshments; air-conditioning, radio with tape deck in rooms, fireplace in 5 rooms, whirlpool tub in 6 rooms.*
Rates: *$90–$120, suites $140–$166; full breakfast. AE, MC, V.*
Restrictions: *Smoking outside only, no pets; 2-night minimum on holiday and special-event weekends.*

Harbour Carriage House

An 1896 Victorian cottage on busy Montecito Street, not far from the beach, this B&B was skillfully transformed in 1985 from a musty private home to an inn that combines beach brightness with English- and French-country touches. Beams were whitewashed, skylights and French doors installed, wicker chairs added, and botanical prints hung. Though tiny, the sitting room is inviting. In the more imposing solarium, where windows reach up to a mile-high ceiling, manager Kim Pegrem serves a tasty full breakfast—egg casseroles, fruit sundaes, homemade breads.

Many of the rooms have a sort of a Martha Stewart–meets–Ralph Lauren look—for example, Flowering Peach, done in pale peach and white with a comfy, green-stripe overstuffed chair. Though the huge Lily of the Valley room has an old claw-foot tub in the bathroom, most baths are more modern, with country-pine vanities.

Address: *420 W. Montecito St., Santa Barbara, CA 93101, tel. 805/962–8477 or 800/594–4633.*
Accommodations: *9 rooms with bath.*
Amenities: *Fireplace in 6 rooms, fans in 8 rooms, air-conditioning in 1 room, in-room phones available; evening wine and hors d'oeuvres.*
Rates: *$85–$185; full breakfast. AE, MC, V.*
Restrictions: *Smoking outside only, no pets; 2-night minimum on weekends.*

Inn at Summer Hill

The best-known landmark in Summerland, a small seaside town just south of Santa Barbara, had long been the Big Yellow House restaurant, but the 1989 opening of the Inn on Summer Hill changed the status quo. Built as a showcase for the talents of interior designer Mabel Schults, the newly constructed Craftsman-style inn consists of two long, narrow buildings with rooms on the first and second floors, each with a motel-style private entrance.

All rooms have private balconies and ocean views and are lavishly decorated—practically overflowing with furniture, much of it rattan with floral fabrics. White pine is used in the ceilings, wainscoting, paneling, and most of the furniture. Guest rooms on the second level have pine-paneled vaulted ceilings, feel larger, and seem to get less highway noise.

Address: *2520 Lillie Ave., Box 376, Summerland, CA 93067, tel. 805/969–9998 or 800/845–5566, fax 805/969–9998.*
Accommodations: *15 rooms with bath, 1 suite.*
Amenities: *Afternoon and evening refreshments; air-conditioning, TV with VCR, 2 phones, fireplace, refrigerator, robes, hair dryer, and ironing board in rooms, irons available; spa.*
Rates: *$155–$185, suites $210–$250; full breakfast. AE, MC, V.*
Restrictions: *Smoking outside only, no pets; 2-night minimum on weekends and holidays.*

J. Patrick House

This inn is set on a pine-shaded acre above East Village Cambria, in an area known as Lodge Hill, and is convenient to shops, galleries, and restaurants, though it's some distance from the beach. The inn consists of two buildings connected by a garden and a trellised arbor. The front building is a contemporary log cabin, where innkeeper Molly Lynch greets guests, tends to the living room fireplace, and cooks up the unusual breads served at breakfast.

There is one bright, spacious guest room upstairs, and the remaining rooms and a separate guest sitting room are in the cedar-sided two-story building out back. Each of the rooms is named for a county in Ireland: Cork, Clare, Galway, Dublin.

Furnishings are simple and eclectic. Beds are of wicker, willow, or painted wood, and guest rooms are adorned with floral wallpapers and spreads. Flowers abound, and woodland bouquets are tucked into every corner throughout the inn—in rooms, on tables in hallways, on windowsills. Each room has a window seat with a garden view.

Address: *2990 Burton Dr., Cambria, CA 93428, tel. 805/927-3812.*
Accommodations: *8 rooms with bath.*
Amenities: *Fireplace or wood-burning stove in rooms; afternoon refreshments, guest refrigerator.*
Rates: *$100–$120; Continental breakfast. MC, V.*
Restrictions: *No smoking, no pets.*

La Mer

La Mer offers a bit of European ambience in a distinctly southern California seaside setting. Presided over by German-born Gisela Baida, the inn is visible from afar on its perch high up on a hillside and is decorated with a collection of European flags. The inn has five rooms, each decorated in a theme of a different European country. The French Room is powder blue, with an antique carved walnut bed and a ceiling-tall ficus tree. The Norwegian Room has a nautical theme, with a ship's bed, wood paneling, and brass fixtures in the bathroom. The bright and airy rooms are surrounded by balconies and porches.

Gisela serves a sumptuous Bavarian-style breakfast in the parlor, with its view of the ocean; the buffet fea-tures cheeses and Black Forest ham in addition to fruit, pastries, and beverages. She promotes the inn as a romantic midweek getaway by offering attractive packages that include dinners, visits to nearby Wheeler Hot Springs, and therapeutic massages.

Address: *411 Poli St., Ventura, CA 93001, tel. 805/643-3600.*
Accommodations: *5 rooms with bath.*
Amenities: *Old-fashioned radio in rooms, fireplace in 1 room; afternoon refreshments, beach towels; antique carriage rides, picnic baskets extra.*
Rates: *$105–$155; full breakfast. MC, V.*
Restrictions: *Smoking outside only, no pets.*

Montecito Inn

L ike the San Ysidro Ranch, this small hotel is located in swank Montecito and has a show-biz history, having been built by Charlie Chaplin and Fatty Arbuckle in 1928. But it's more urban than country, situated on the edge of one of Montecito's two main shopping streets (great for strolling) and backing up to the freeway (which can be heard from the rear-facing rooms). An admirable small hotel, it combines the friendliness of an inn with the amenities of a hotel.

The red-tile roof, courtyard entrance, and gorgeous tile lobby are resolutely Spanish, but the smallish rooms are French-country, all done in Pierre Deux fabrics; an ongoing renovation has given 18 of the rooms a lovely new lavender-and-blue color scheme. Off the lobby is the Montecito Cafe, a terrific, bargain-priced California-cuisine restaurant (under separate ownership) with tile floors and a beautiful old fountain.

Address: *1295 Coast Village Rd., Montecito, CA 93108, tel. 805/969–7854 or 800/843–2017.*
Accommodations: *48 double rooms with bath, 5 suites.*
Amenities: *Cable TV, phone, ceiling fans in rooms; some nonsmoking rooms, limited room service; air-conditioning in public rooms; pool, spa, fitness center, bicycles.*
Rates: *$105–$175, suites $150–$245; Continental breakfast. AE, D, DC, MC, V.*
Restrictions: *No pets; 2-night minimum on weekends.*

Olallieberry Inn

W here time stands still" is the motto of this 1873 Greek Revival house, but that's not entirely accurate—a just-completed remodeling gave the inn much-appreciated improvements, from new bathrooms to a spiffy new kitchen, in which owner Peter Irsfield intends to spend time once he flees his Los Angeles law practice. Peter plans to live here full-time by 1994; his wife, CarolAnn, is already in residence, running the place with friendly efficiency. (Once Peter trades the law books for the cookbooks, the Irsfields will offer dinner to weekend guests.)

At the edge of Cambria's cutesy downtown, the Olallieberry is decorated in a style that suits its era. The front parlor's crystal chandelier and Victorian sofa are rather formal for funky Cambria; the white-wicker, fireplace-warmed "gathering" room is more casual. The Cambria room has a wall fireplace, high ceilings, and Queen Anne furniture; bathers will love the huge tub in the cozy, low-ceilinged Olallieberry room. The grassy backyard, which leads to a thicket of trees and a creek, boasts a porch swing.

Address: *2476 Main St., Cambria, CA 93428, tel. 805/927–3222.*
Accommodations: *3 rooms with attached baths, 3 with detached baths.*
Amenities: *Fireplace in 2 rooms; evening wine and hors d'oeuvres.*
Rates: *$85–$115; full breakfast. MC, V.*
Restrictions: *Smoking outside only, no pets.*

The Olive House

I n 1987, Lois Gregg and her then-husband sold their Hearthside Inn in Bar Harbor, Maine, and bought this 1904 shingled Craftsman-pattern house in the bougainvillea-draped foothills near the mission. Lois is a hands-on innkeeper, and her warm, relaxed style (she's typically attired in shorts and running shoes) perfectly suits laid-back Santa Barbara.

Lois recently spruced the place up some, adding thick forest-green wall-to-wall carpeting and Victorianish floral wallpapers that are more delicate than fussy. The turn-of-the-century details—dark-wood beams, paneling, and headboards—throughout are offset by such lightening touches as miniblinds and simple white curtains. The best room is the Master Bedroom, a large corner room with ocean breezes, a claw-foot tub, and a bit of a view. A buffet breakfast—fruit, pastries, eggs, cereals—is served in the dining room, furnished with American antiques. Extras include a studio grand piano in the living room and a sunny little patio in the side yard.

Address: *1604 Olive St., Santa Barbara, CA 93101, tel. 805/962-4902 or 800/786-6422.*
Accommodations: *5 rooms with bath.*
Amenities: *Evening wine and hors d'oeuvres.*
Rates: *$85-$125; full breakfast. MC, V.*
Restrictions: *Smoking outside only, no pets; 2-night minimum on weekends.*

Pickford House

T he small town of Cambria dates back to the 19th century, but this residential subdivision is a product of the early 1980s. Perhaps in order to compensate for its newness, Pickford House is a riot of American antiques and reproductions: Headboards are carved and heavy, tubs are claw-footed, carpets are floral; fussy lace doilies are scattered about. Off the ordinary lobby an extraordinary parlor is replete with a brass-railed 175-year-old bar and loads of antiques.

It might be rather out-of-place and forced, but the Pickford House offers a lot of comfort for the price, along with views and easy access to Hearst Castle (its rooms are named for the celebrities who visited the publishing magnate there). And owner Anna Larsen makes a mean plate of *aebleskive* (Danish pancakes) for breakfast. Perhaps the best Victorian-style room, large and bright, is named for Mary Pickford. If you're not a fan of the period, try the spacious, king-bedded Fairbanks room, with subdued art-deco furniture, a fireplace, and a lovely view of the hills.

Address: *2555 MacLeod Way, Cambria, CA 93428, tel. 805/927-8619.*
Accommodations: *8 rooms with bath.*
Amenities: *Cable TV in rooms, fireplace in 3 rooms; evening wine and hors d'oeuvres.*
Rates: *$85-$120; full breakfast. MC, V.*
Restrictions: *Smoking in lobby only, no pets.*

Rose Victorian Inn

Roses and romance are the dual themes at the Rose Victorian Inn, a striking 1885 Stick-style house that has become a hideaway for many Hollywood celebrities. On the outskirts of Arroyo Grande, a small farming community about 100 miles north of Santa Barbara, the inn offers seclusion, comfortable rooms, a popular restaurant, and the warm family feeling created by innkeeper Diana Cox. The building is surrounded by lush gardens containing a 30-foot rose arbor and a gazebo. The five rooms in the main house make up the original inn and are simply furnished, decorated in earthtones. The rooms in the carriage house are sunnier and more contemporary in decor, featuring big, bright floral-bouquet prints on the walls and furnishings.

Breakfast features ample servings of eggs Benedict and mimosas. A popular wedding site, this inn is not only a good place for hiding out but also for exploring, since it's near Pismo Beach, where there's good clamming, and close to Oceano, known for its massive white sand dunes.

Address: *789 Valley Rd., Arroyo Grande, CA 93420, tel. 805/481–5566.*
Accommodations: *7 rooms with bath, 4 rooms share 2 baths.*
Amenities: *Restaurant, afternoon refreshments.*
Rates: *$130–$175 MAP. MC, V.*
Restrictions: *Smoking outside and in restaurant only, no pets; 2-night minimum on weekends. Inn closed Mon.–Wed.*

Simpson House Inn

The very Victorian Simpson House Inn seems a bit out of place in Spanish-style Santa Barbara. This 1870s Folk Victorian house is deliberately British in character because Scotsman Robert Simpson built it to remind him of his homeland. Now presided over by innkeeper Gillean Wilson, a native of England, the house is set amid an acre of English gardens. Guests especially enjoy the wraparound verandas furnished with white wicker, which is adorned with blue linens and cushions.

The rooms are surprisingly large, bright, and appealing; two have big private decks reached through lace-curtain-covered French doors. The color scheme throughout the inn is bright and bold, particularly the elec-

tric blue in the sitting rooms and the deep, dark mauve walls in the dining room. Antiques abound: tapestry settees and chaise longues, Victorian armchairs, brass or iron beds, a collection of china teacups.

Address: *121 E. Arrellaga, St., Santa Barbara, CA 93101, tel. 805/963–7067 or 800/676–1280.*
Accommodations: *6 rooms with bath.*
Amenities: *Air-conditioning in 1 room; robes, afternoon refreshments, bicycles, beach chairs, towels, croquet.*
Rates: *$95–$155; full breakfast. AE, MC, V.*
Restrictions: *Smoking outside only, no pets; 2-night minimum on weekends, 3-night minimum on holidays.*

Tiffany Inn

Prim, pretty Victorians may seem anomalous in Spanish-mad Santa Barbara, but this neighborhood just west of State Street's shops and cafés is positively thick with them. This tan-and-green Stick-style model from 1898 is particularly well restored, with its hipped roof, shingled second and third floors, large front porch, jutting bays, and covered rear patio furnished with high-quality green wicker. The only fly in the ointment is the street traffic outside.

Owners Carol and Larry MacDonald respected the interior's Victoriana without being slaves to it—puffy floral curtain valances, white walls, and solid pastel bedspreads add a welcome touch of English cheerfulness. Up a steep staircase on the third floor is the marvelous Penthouse Suite, a rambling, nook-filled hideaway complete with fireplace, ceiling fan, love seats, view-rich deck, and a second bedroom with twin bed and whirlpool tub.

Address: *1323 De la Vina St., Santa Barbara, CA 93101, tel. 805/963-2283.*
Accommodations: *3 rooms with bath, 2 rooms share a bath, 2 suites.*
Amenities: *Fireplace in 5 rooms, refrigerator in suites; evening wine and hors d'oeuvres.*
Rates: *$75–$175; full breakfast. AE, DC, MC, V.*
Restrictions: *Smoking outside only, no pets; 2-night minimum on weekends.*

The Upham

A Victorian Italianate building topped with a cupola, wrapped with porches, and cheered by rose gardens, the Upham was built in 1871 by a Boston banker turned hotelier. Over the years additions have been made, including several cottages behind the main building. One of the cottages holds the extravagant Master Suite, complete with fireplace, wet bar, and large private yard. The rest of the quarters are humbler but comfortable in a masculine sort of way: wall-to-wall carpeting, white shutters, ginger-jar lamps, reproduction four-poster Colonial beds, wing chairs.

The public areas are equally eclectic. One large, comfortable sitting area looks like an English drawing room, and the grassy courtyard is dotted with Adirondack chairs. Perhaps most charming of all is the veranda seating at Louie's, the admirable California-cuisine restaurant.

Address: *1404 De la Vina St., Santa Barbara, CA 93101, tel. 805/962-0058 or 800/727-0876.*
Accommodations: *46 double rooms with bath, 3 suites.*
Amenities: *Cable TV and phone in rooms, fireplace in 7 rooms and 1 suite; restaurant, conference and banquet rooms; evening wine and cheese.*
Rates: *$95–$165, Master Suite $295; Continental breakfast. AE, D, DC, MC, V.*
Restrictions: *Smoking outside only, no pets; 2-night minimum on weekends.*

Villa Rosa

An antidote to Santa Barbara's many Victorian B&Bs, this small inn pays proud tribute to the city's Spanish architectural heritage, with its tile roof, archways, wrought-iron balconies, rough-hewn beams, and saltillo-tile courtyard. A low-key, sophisticated place, Villa Rosa is a short walk from the beach and from Stearns Wharf.

In the lobby areas and guest rooms, colors are muted and earthy, upholstered chairs and sofas are straight-lined and contemporary, and wood furniture is southwestern in style. The accommodations all pretty much look alike. Some lower-floor rooms have shutter-clad French doors opening to the courtyard and small pool, but they can be rather dark; upper-floor rooms are more cheerful. On the down side, the breakfast is pretty unimpressive and service can be amateurish; on the plus side, the inn is cool, quiet, and very comfortable. It's a good place for those who prefer chic monochromaticism to color and antiques.

Address: *15 Chapala St., Santa Barbara, CA 93101, tel. 805/966–0851 or 800/727–0876.*
Accommodations: *18 rooms with bath.*
Amenities: *Phone in rooms, fireplace in 4 rooms; afternoon wine and cheese, evening port and sherry; pool and spa.*
Rates: *$80–$190; Continental breakfast. AE, MC, V.*
Restrictions: *No pets; 2-night minimum on weekends.*

Monterey Bay

Monterey Bay
Including Santa Cruz and Carmel

A semicircle about 90 miles across, Monterey Bay arcs into the California coast at a point about two hours' drive south of the San Francisco Bay Area. Santa Cruz sits at the northern end of the curve, and the Monterey Peninsula, containing Monterey, Pacific Grove, and Carmel, occupies the southern portion. In between, Highway 1 cruises along the coastline, passing windswept beaches piled high with sand dunes. Along the route are fields of artichoke plants, the towns of Watsonville and Castroville, and Fort Ord, the army base where millions of GIs got their basic training.

A beneficent climate, stunning scenery, and the sweep of history have combined to bring visitors to this area for hundreds of years. Although evidence suggests that Native Americans lived here 10,000 years ago, the first written records date from 1542, when Portuguese explorer Juan Rodríguez Cabrillo sighted the beaches and pine forests where Carmel now lies. The Spanish later settled here, building missions in Carmel and Santa Cruz, and eventually naming Monterey the capital of Alta California. Monterey remained the center of government for California until 1850, when Sacramento became the state capital upon California's admission to the Union.

During the late 1800s, the cool summers attracted a seasonal colony of Methodists who came to Pacific Grove on retreat; they later built the Victorian homes for which the town is now famous. At about the same time, wealthy easterners discovered Monterey's splendid scenery and mansions sprang up along Pacific Grove and Pebble Beach.

The Monterey Bay area has attracted artists and writers for more than a century. The best known on the long list of names include novelists Robert Louis Stevenson, Mary Austin, and John Steinbeck; poet Robinson Jeffers; and photographers Edward Weston and Ansel Adams. Carmel's heritage as an art colony lives on in dozens of art galleries scattered throughout the town.

As Monterey was becoming a mecca for artists and the wealthy, Santa Cruz was developing as a working community with logging, fishing, tanning, and farming being the major industries. The arrival of the railroad brought visitors from San Francisco and the hot inland valleys to the seaside pleasures of Santa Cruz and Capitola, and the establishment of the University of California at Santa Cruz added yet another dimension to the town's character.

Monterey Bay is one of the loveliest spots on the West Coast. With its combination of rugged natural beauty and sophisticated local culture, this remarkably diverse area offers fine restaurants, bed-and-breakfast inns, tourism attractions (both natural and man-made) that reflect and respect its history and heritage, a lively arts community, and varied shopping.

Places to Go, Sights to See

Big Sur. A 26-mile drive south of Carmel via Highway 1 yields breathtaking views at every turn: The rugged Santa Lucia Mountains rise sharply on one side of the highway, and the Pacific pounds against the shore on the other. Big Sur's intractable landscape was home to author Henry Miller and many famous artists.

Cannery Row (765 Wave St., Monterey, tel. 408/649–6690) is a restored area of shops, restaurants, and galleries where the 16 sardine canneries immortalized in John Steinbeck's novel *Cannery Row* once stood.

Carmel Mission (3080 Rio Rd., Carmel, tel. 408/624–3600). With beautifully landscaped gardens, this is one of the loveliest of the 21 California missions. It is the burial place of Father Junipero Serra, founder of nine of the missions.

Monterey Bay Aquarium (886 Cannery Row, Monterey, tel. 408/648–4888). The centerpiece of Cannery Row, this sealife museum houses more than 6,500 marine creatures. Exhibits include a 28-foot-tall kelp forest, a shark display, and examples of the undersea life of Monterey Bay.

Monterey State Historic Park (525 Polk St., Monterey, tel. 408/649–7118). This is a collection of adobe structures and other historic buildings from the Spanish and Mexican eras, when Monterey was the capital of California.

Point Lobos State Reserve (Hwy. 1, Carmel, tel. 408/624–4909) is an outdoor museum of unmatched beauty. Nearly 10 miles of trails weave along the shoreline, and there are 750 acres of underwater reserve, a portion of which is open to scuba and skin divers with permits. The many tidal pools contain starfish, anemones, and other examples of marine life; sea lions, otters, and harbor seals are in residence most of the time.

Seventeen Mile Drive. Running along the outer rim of the Monterey Peninsula, this scenic drive offers some of the most photographed ocean vistas in the world. The route passes through the famous Pebble Beach and Cypress Point golf courses, Lone Cypress, Restless Sea, and numerous magnificent estates. Entrance gates are at Lighthouse Avenue in Pacific Grove, and off Highway 1 and North San Antonio Avenue in Carmel.

Tor House (26304 Ocean View Ave., tel. 408/624–1813) is the unique house and tower built by poet Robinson Jeffers during the early 1900s from stones gathered on Carmel beach. Docent-led tours cover the early history of Carmel as an artists' colony.

Restaurants

Central 159 (tel. 408/372–2235), in Pacific Grove, is known for its eclectic menu featuring the lighter side of new American cuisine. Also in Pacific Grove, **El Cocodrilo** (tel. 408/655–3311) features spicy Central American and Caribbean cuisines. **Fresh Cream** (tel. 408/375–9798), in Monterey, is acclaimed for its classic French cuisine, as well as for its outstanding service. In Santa Cruz, **Gilbert's on the Wharf** (tel. 408/423–5200) offers casual seafood dining with an ocean view. **Shadowbrook Restaurant** (tel. 408/475–1511), in Capitola, serves Continental cuisine. Locally popular for its atmosphere, it is reached by cable car. In Aptos, the Bayview Hotel's **Veranda Restaurant** (tel. 408/685–1881) offers inventive California cuisine in a Victorian setting.

Tourist Information

Monterey Peninsula Chamber of Commerce and Visitors & Convention Bureau (380 Alvarado St., Box 1770, Monterey, CA 93942–1770, tel. 408/648–5354, fax 408/649–3502); **Santa Cruz County Conference and Visitors Council** (701 Front St., Santa Cruz, CA 95060, tel. 408/425–1234 or 800/833–3494).

Reservation Services

California Bed and Breakfast Innkeepers (2715 Porter St., Soquel, CA 95073, tel. 800/284–INNS) has a voice-mail reservation system.

Apple Lane Inn

Diana and Doug Groom acquired Apple Lane Inn in a romantic moment. They were celebrating their wedding anniversary at the inn where they were married a couple of years earlier, when they learned that the property might be for sale if the right buyers could be found. "The right buyers were sitting there in the parlor," Diana laughs. Before long, the high school teacher and flight instructor—plus kids and animals—had moved into the inn and put their own stamp on it.

This four-story, gray-and-blue farmhouse, built in the 1870s, is perched on a 3-acre ocean-view hillside, once part of a Spanish land grant. It's surrounded by a Victorian cutting garden, rows of vegetables, and old apple orchards. Alongside the lane, a large red barn contains a horse corral and a chicken house where hens lay tomorrow's breakfast.

Of the guest rooms, Blossom in the back of the house is the most interestingly furnished. A huge, 150-year-old reproduction of a 14th-century bed once owned by Diana's Aunt Mildred is flanked by a pair of Eastlake chairs and stands on a 400-year-old Persian carpet next to an amazing buffet with 22 beveled mirrors. Uncle Chester's Room, also on the second floor, contains a 40-inch-high, 400-year-old four-poster bed that Diana's uncle found in Spain during World War I. Two bedrooms and

a bathroom share an unfinished attic on the third floor, unusual because it has exposed rafters and shingles. The Orchard room offers the inn's best view of meadows, gazebo, and distant Monterey.

Common rooms are comfortably Victorian. A long double parlor contains a dining table set up for breakfast at one end and a sitting room-library at the other. A player piano and stacks of games and books are available for guest use, and the wine cellar is set up with a table for card games.

Food is an essential part of the experience at this inn. Diana loves to cook, and breakfast is likely to feature ham-and-cheese soufflé, eggs Christy, or morning Monte Cristo accompanied by fruit, coffee cake, cereal, and beverages. Home-baked desserts are offered after dinner in the upstairs sitting room.

Address: *6265 Soquel Dr., Aptos, CA 95003, tel. 408/475-6868.*
Accommodations: *3 double rooms with bath, 2 double rooms share a bath.*
Amenities: *TV room, guest phone, fireplace in parlor, afternoon and evening refreshments, picnic baskets available.*
Rates: *$70–$125; full breakfast. D, MC, V.*
Restrictions: *Smoking outside only, no pets.*

Babbling Brook Inn

P resided over by the vivacious Helen King, this inn offers a combination of romantic setting, California history, and a convenient location for business travelers. In the heart of Santa Cruz, the inn's wooded grounds and gardens make it appear to be worlds away from the city.

The inn consists of four cedar-shingle-sided buildings set on different levels of the hillside property. Portions of the main house's stone foundation date from 1796, when the mission fathers built a gristmill for grinding corn. In 1981, when it became a bed-and-breakfast inn, three cottages were added.

The rooms are decorated in French-country style: soft colors, floral-print curtains, and iron beds covered with floral spreads. Some guest rooms are just big enough for a bed and a chair; others have a spacious sitting area. The most charming guest rooms are in the main house: The romantic Honeymoon Suite hideaway offers couples seclusion as well as a view from a private deck that overlooks the waterfall. The expansive Garden Room has a wood-burning stove, a great garden view, and complete privacy. The rooms in the outbuildings get more street and parking-lot noise, but they also have decks facing the garden. The Babbling Brook's gardens are often the setting for weddings, with the big wrought-iron white gazebo as the centerpiece, the brook meandering through the property, and flowers adorning every inch of hillside.

Helen King, a onetime organizer of international tours, is acutely aware of business travelers' needs; she accommodates them by offering an early breakfast, late check-in, and copies of the *Wall Street Journal.* And in the afternoon, Helen hosts a congenial wine-hour gathering in front of the fire in the comfortable living room.

The buffet-style breakfast of frittatas, fresh fruits, and croissants with jam is set out in the living room, although guests can go either into the adjacent dining room or outside to enjoy their meal in the shade of the redwood trees.

Address: *1025 Laurel St., Santa Cruz, CA 95060, tel. 408/427-2437 or 800/866-1131, fax 408/427-2457.*
Accommodations: *12 double rooms with bath.*
Amenities: *Cable TV and phone in rooms, fireplace in 10 rooms, whirlpool tub in 2 rooms; picnic baskets available, afternoon refreshments.*
Rates: *$85–$135; full breakfast. AE, D, MC, V.*
Restrictions: *Smoking outside only, no pets; 2-night minimum on weekends.*

Green Gables Inn

The Green Gables Inn, a striking landmark along the oceanfront of Pacific Grove, dates from 1888, when Los Angeles businessman William Lacy built the two-story, half-timbered and gabled Queen Anne for his lady friend, Emma Murdoch.

Lacy was also an amateur architect, and he probably designed this elegant house in which nearly every room has a three-sided bay window that takes in the ocean view just across the street. Framed entirely of redwood, it has solid maple floors, countless angles, slopes and nooks, exposed ceiling beams, intricate moldings, woodwork and arches, and even stained-glass windows framing the fireplace and set into pocket doors dividing rooms in what's now the Lacy Suite. The windows, fixtures, and woodwork all date from the original construction.

Roger and Sally Post bought the house as a family home for their four daughters. The Posts began renting out rooms to summer visitors, and in 1983 the Green Gables became a full-time inn (and the cornerstone of the Four Sisters collection of seven large inns in California, operated by the Roger Post family).

Guest rooms in the carriage house, perched on a hill out back, are larger than those in the main house and have more privacy as well as views of the ocean. They also offer more

modern amenities, but the rooms in the main house, with their intricately detailed molding and woodwork, have more charm. The Lacy Suite on the main floor, doubtless a converted parlor and library, has a fireplace, built-in bookshelves, and a claw-foot tub in the bathroom. Upstairs in the Gable Room, a window seat under leaded-glass windows overlooks the ocean. The Balcony Room is like a sleeping porch, and the Chapel Room actually resembles a church, with a vaulted ceiling and a pewlike window seat stretching across the front of the room.

The food, always fresh, is served in a family-style setting. The ample buffet breakfast includes frittatas, a fruit plate, an assortment of breads and scones, and apple pancakes. Afternoon refreshments include wine and hors d'oeuvres. The young staff is gracious and can offer assistance with dinner reservations and sightseeing information.

Address: *104 5th St., Pacific Grove, CA 93950, tel. 408/375–2095.*
Accommodations: *6 double rooms with bath, 4 double rooms share 2 baths, 1 suite.*
Amenities: *Fireplace in carriage-house rooms; afternoon refreshments, picnic baskets available, bicycles, some parking spaces.*
Rates: *$100–$160; full breakfast. AE, MC, V.*
Restrictions: *No smoking in main house, no pets.*

Inn at Depot Hill

nnkeeper Suzie Lankes and her partner, Dan Floyd, have created one of the most beautiful bed-and-breakfasts in California—perhaps anywhere. And they provide guests with exquisite pampering to complement the splendid surroundings.

Once a historic railroad station in the beachside village of Capitola, the Inn at Depot Hill is now a vision of turn-of-the-century European-style luxury. Most rooms have a Continental theme: Dutch Delft, for example, a two-room corner suite, includes a big blue-and-white sitting room, a bedroom with a huge featherbed draped in Battenberg lace and real linen, a private patio filled with tulips and irises, and a gray-marble bathroom with double shower. Romantic Paris, a study in black and white, has walls upholstered in French toile, windows curtained in lace, and a bath done in black marble. Portofino captures a sunny Italian mood, with a vine-and-leaf-decorated bed and a private Mediterranean garden planted with orange and lemon trees. Departing from the European motif, the Railroad Baron's room honors local history. This masculine accommodation, resembling a posh railroad car, has deep red brocade upholstery, a red-and-gold sitting room, rich woods with gold leaf, a circular lit dome over the bed—and an eagle presiding over all.

This is first and foremost a romantic inn. While Suzie and her staff encourage guests to mingle, most prefer to retreat to the privacy of their rooms. Thus guests are likely to have private use of the inn's gardens, the parlor-library with piano tucked into one corner, and even the dining room, where an unusual glass-topped table can fit 10.

The food here is ample and well prepared. A late-afternoon hors d'oeuvre buffet features a canape tray, meatballs, and chips and dip. A dessert buffet and sherry welcome guests returning from dinner. For breakfast there are breads, fruit, cereal, and an egg entrée. Service is elegant, with silver, linens, and china displaying the inn's logo.

Address: *250 Monterey Ave., Box 1394, Capitola by the Sea, CA 95010, tel. 408/462–3376, fax 408/458–0989.*
Accommodations: *4 double rooms with bath, 4 suites.*
Amenities: *TV with VCR, stereo, phone with modem, hair dryer, robes, steamer, coffee maker, fireplace in rooms, private landscaped patio and hot tub in 5 rooms; afternoon and evening refreshments.*
Rates: *$155–$250; full breakfast. AE, MC, V.*
Restrictions: *Smoking outside only, no pets; 2-night minimum on weekends.*

The Jabberwock

"Things are not always as they seem," observes Alice in *Through the Looking Glass.* That's certainly the case at this delightful inn, perched on a quiet residential street in the hills above Monterey Bay and just a short walk from Cannery Row and the Aquarium. Take breakfast, for example, where you're likely to sit down to a repast of Sharkleberry Flumptios or Brundt Blumbleberry. Or have a look at the clocks, all of which run backward. Guest rooms have names from the pen of Lewis Carroll. If you need to make a call, you'll find the phone in the Burbling Room.

This fantasy is the creation of Jim and Barbara Allen, who left jobs in Los Angeles—he was a firefighter, she worked in the hotel industry—in 1982 to open an inn in "a better climate." The 1911 building they bought had seen better days, but the Allens tackled the needed restoration with the humor that now pervades the inn.

In short order, they had the place fixed up, with rooms as comfortable as they are engaging. Momerath, for example, has a superking-size bed with an elaborately carved mahogany headboard as its centerpiece; the private bathroom has a claw-foot tub. Borogrove is a huge corner room with an expansive ocean view and a telescope for scanning the horizon, a Victorian settee, and a fireplace. The best view can be had from the third-floor tower, where two rooms share a bath and a small sitting area. The Mimsey room is tiny, but it has wall-to-wall windows and the oldest piece of furniture in the house, a wood-frame bed bought in 1886 for $6.45.

One of the most pleasant spots is the huge wraparound sun porch, from which guests can watch otters and sea lions frolicking in the bay.

Guests usually drift into the comfortable living room after dinner to discuss their dining adventures and sample the milk and cookies guarded by Vorpal Bear, who warns, "Before bedtime . . . not dinner. Vorpal Bear attacks if you cheat."

Jim and Barbara keep up to date on the local restaurants. Fresh Cream, for example, is described as "where Jim takes Barbara when he's in trouble."

Address: *598 Laine St., Monterey, CA 93940, tel. 408/372-4777.*
Accommodations: *3 double rooms with bath, 4 double rooms share 2 baths.*
Amenities: *Afternoon refreshments, off-street parking.*
Rates: *$100–$175; full breakfast. No credit cards.*
Restrictions: *Smoking outside only, no pets; 2-night minimum on weekends, 3-night minimum on holidays.*

Mangels House

Once the country home of California sugar barons Claus Mangels and his brother-in-law Claus Spreckles, Mangels House is set on 4 acres of lawn and orchard. The big, white square Italianate structure with deep verandas is close to the entrance of the Forest of Nisene Marks State Park and surrounded by nearly 10,000 acres of second-growth redwoods.

The Mangels family built the house in 1886 as a retreat from San Francisco; each summer the family—with children, governess, and servants—would move to the then logged-out forest for a three-month stay. At the time of its construction, the house boasted some of the most modern conveniences, including fully plumbed marble-topped vanities, still in use in the bedrooms today. Vintage gaslight fixtures in the ceilings have recently been converted to electricity.

English-born innkeeper Jackie Fisher is the force behind the inn's genteel ambience. She came to the business naturally, after raising children, living abroad with radiologist husband Ron, and serving as hostess on many occasions. "I love meeting new people," she explains as she pours late-afternoon tea for guests in the inn's 40-foot-long sitting room. Usually conversation turns to shared experiences and personal adventures, such as the time the family lived in Zaire.

Indeed, the inn reflects the family's life. One African-themed bedroom displays artifacts collected in Kenya and Zaire, including a collection of carved animals, banana-leaf art, dolls, and medicine men. By contrast, Timothy's Room features a pair of beautiful, locally thrown vases and a unique carved wooden headboard that Jackie herself designed.

Guests gather each morning in the dining room for a hearty English breakfast, which Jackie serves family-style. It starts with Jackie's homemade crumpets, "a vehicle for getting melted butter to your mouth." Accompaniments include fruit compote, spicy cheese-egg puff, oatmeal scones, and dessert—plenty to keep one going on a long morning hike through the forest.

Address: *570 Aptos Creek Rd., Box 302, Aptos, CA 95001, tel. 408/688-7982.*
Accommodations: *6 double rooms with bath.*
Amenities: *Guest phone, fireplace in sitting room and 1 guest room; English garden, games including table tennis and darts, afternoon refreshments.*
Rates: *$98–$125; full breakfast. MC, V.*
Restrictions: *Smoking in sitting room only, no pets; 2-night minimum on weekends.*

Martine Inn

Elegance and grace are the keys to the Martine Inn, a nearly 100-year-old mansion perched on a hillside above the tiny cove of the Monterey Bay that frames Pacific Grove. Originally a Queen Anne with turrets and towers, the home was owned until World War II by Laura and James Parke (of Parke Davis Pharmaceutical Co.), who remodeled it in Mediterranean style, with a stucco exterior and windows framed by arches. Don Martine's family acquired the house in 1972; by 1984 he and wife Marion had opened it as an inn.

Don and Marion have assembled one of the most extensive antiques collections to be found in any California bed-and-breakfast inn, mostly American pieces dating from 1840 through 1890: an Eastlake suite used by publisher C.K. McClatchy; a mahogany suite exhibited at the 1893 Chicago World's Fair; Academy Award costume designer Edith Head's bedroom suite; and an 1860 Chippendale Revival four-poster bed.

Guest rooms are located on the ground and second floors of the main house, with stunning views of the water through arched front windows upstairs in the Parke, Victorian, and Maries rooms. Other rooms are in what was once the carriage house off the courtyard.

The inn has many common areas. The parlor, which occupies the glassed-in front of the house's main floor, lures guests to savor the stunning ocean view. A small library contains a personal collection of books and magazines, and two small solarium sitting rooms adjoin guest rooms on the ground and second floor. A games room contains an 1870 oak slate pool table, a 1917 nickelodeon, and a slot machine from the 1930s.

Breakfast may be the best time of the day at the Martine. In the dining room, Marion sets up a buffet table from which guests can select eggs poached in cream sauce, cereal, muffins, and fruit. Guests eat at large lace-clad tables set with Marion's best Sheffield silver and look out at a sweeping sea vista that competes with the food and decor for their attention.

Address: *255 Ocean View Blvd., Pacific Grove, CA 93950, tel. 408/373–3388, fax 408/373–3896.*
Accommodations: *19 double rooms with bath.*
Amenities: *Phone, refrigerator, and robes in rooms, fireplace in 7 rooms; afternoon refreshments, conference facilities, picnic meals available, garden, outdoor whirlpool tub, antique sauna.*
Rates: *$95–$225; full breakfast. MC, V.*
Restrictions: *Smoking in fireplace rooms only, no pets; 2-night minimum on weekends, 3-night minimum on holidays.*

Old Monterey Inn

Ann and Gene Swett have elevated the business of innkeeping to a high art, offering
their guests quietly elegant accommodations in a historic home—and
the type of pampering that antici-
pates every need. Just a few blocks
from downtown Monterey, a woodsy,
flower-lined driveway leads to the
English Tudor–style home built in
1929 by Carmel Martin, then the
mayor of Monterey.

When Gene Swett was transferred to
Monterey from the Bay Area in
1968, the family needed a house that
was big enough for eight. Although
the Martin house was run-down, the
Swetts purchased it, renovated it,
and created what would become one
of the loveliest inns in California.

Outside, Gene made an oasis of year-
round color. The house was Ann's
domain. She began haunting flea
markets as well as garage and yard
sales. The quest continues, and the
themes and color schemes of guest
rooms are always subject to change.
Thus the room once known as Madri-
gal is now Serengeti, evoking
a turn-of-the-century African safari,
with mosquito netting over the bed,
rattan chairs, pith helmets, antique
leather hatboxes, and a brass-ele-
phant bird-cage stand. In the Library
Room, floor-to-ceiling bookshelves
contain volumes of nostalgic children's literature. The Garden Room
feels almost like a tree house set in
the upper branches of the massive
oak just outside the window.

Guests have the option of having
breakfast in bed. But unless you're
honeymooning, don't take it. Breakfast is served in front of the fireplace in the formal dining room, at
a table set for 14 with exquisite Oriental china. Guests dine on fruit,
breads, quiche, or stratta served
course by course. Gene is the con-
summate host, mingling and getting
to know each and every guest to determine food preferences before
sending everyone off to dinner. He
can recommend a half dozen romantic picnic spots and can advise
guests on which galleries and shops
they should visit.

The Swetts offer guests a chance to
get away from it all. "You come to
our inn to talk to each other . . . to
get your life back together," explains Gene.

Address: *500 Martin St., Monterey,
CA 93940, tel. 408/375-8284.*
Accommodations: *8 double rooms
with bath, 1 suite, 1 cottage suite.*
Amenities: *Fireplace in 8 rooms,
whirlpool bath in 1 room, robes; afternoon and evening refreshments,
picnic baskets available.*
Rates: *$160–$220; full breakfast. No
credit cards.*
Restrictions: *Smoking in garden
only, no pets; 2-night minimum on
weekends, 3-night minimum on holidays. Closed Christmas Day.*

Stonepine

To enter this fabulous 330-acre Carmel Valley estate, originally the weekend home of the Crocker banking family, you'll pass through two electronically controlled gates, drive by the Equestrian Center with its adjacent paddock, survey acres of oak-covered hillsides, and eventually pull into the parking area where a Phantom V Rolls-Royce waits to whisk guests to the far corners of the property.

The Mediterranean-style château, built in the 1920s, was designed for lavish entertaining. The elegantly appointed public rooms have graceful stone arches, Roman columns, and gracious gardens shaded by rare Italian stonepines. Antiques abound: a hand-carved limestone fireplace from Italy in the grand living room; 18th-century French tapestries in the living room, the foyer, and the spiral staircase; a carved French writing desk in the Cartier bedroom; 19th-century burnished-oak paneling in the library and dining room.

Guest rooms in the château are elegantly but simply furnished with overstuffed chairs and canopy beds. Bathrooms are dramatic, offering sweeping garden views, sunken marble Jacuzzis, and expansive marble countertops with double sinks. Tattinger, the original master bedroom done in black and white, offers a sitting room–office, separate his and hers bathrooms, and a hidden tower room. Four bedrooms in the

Paddock House are done in casual country plaids with horsey themes.

Following an evening champagne reception, guests are escorted to dinner in the château dining room, where tables are set with Baccarat crystal, Limoges china, and sterling silverware. A typical six-course menu offers choices such as roasted Chateaubriand and sautéed salmon dill–beurre blanc accompanied by soup, salad, dessert, Stilton and port.

Service here, as one might expect, is attentive and discreet.

Address: *150 E. Carmel Valley Rd., Carmel Valley, CA 93924, tel. 408/659–2245, fax 408/659–5160.*
Accommodations: *8 rooms with bath, 4 suites, 1 two-bedroom cottage.*
Amenities: *TV with VCR, fireplace, Jacuzzi, phone, robes in rooms; video and book library, restaurant, room service, honor bar, picnic baskets, gardens, tennis, pool, croquet, archery, health club, hiking and riding trails, equestrian center.*
Rates: *$195–$575; Continental breakfast. Dinner $50 per person; service charge added to bill. AE, MC, V.*
Restrictions: *No pets; 2-night minimum on weekends and holidays.*

Bayview Hotel

This striking mansard-roofed hotel looks a bit out of place on a busy corner in historic Aptos Village. A three-story building dominating the single-story shops surrounding it, the Bayview (which has no view) dates back to the 1870s, when, as the Anchor House, it provided luxury accommodations in this tiny lumber town. Some remnants of the era remain: guest rooms with 10-foot-tall ceilings adorned with ornate plaster rosettes, massive hand-painted wood furnishings imported from Spain, and brass lighting fixtures.

Two stories of the three-story building are in use. The first floor contains a popular local restaurant, the Veranda (where breakfast is served), and a small Victorian parlor for inn guests. Bedrooms on the second floor are generally spacious with simple Victorian furnishings, carved wooden beds, straight-back chairs, and Battenberg lace.

Address: *8041 Soquel Dr., Aptos, CA 95003, tel. 408/688-8654.*
Accommodations: *8 double rooms with bath; 2 rooms can combine for family suite.*
Amenities: *TVs available, guest phone, fireplace in parlor, gardens, restaurant.*
Rates: *$90-$125; full breakfast. AE, MC, V.*
Restrictions: *No smoking, no pets; 2-night minimum on weekends.*

Blue Spruce Inn

This pair of Victorian farmhouses, tucked behind a white-picket fence on a busy city street, offers comfortable, no-nonsense bed-and-breakfast accommodations—plus a few surprises. There are outdoor fountains in secret corners; interconnecting decks adorned by colorful rose gardens; birdbaths; an enormous, green-tiled shower lit by a full-length, stained-glass mural; skylights above the beds; a full-body shower described as a "human car wash"; handmade Amish quilts in Irish chain and broken star patterns; work of local artists on the walls; window seats; and a cozy common area filled with books and magazines.

Innkeeper Pat O'Brien, a former teacher, presides with Irish charm, offering a ready smile and laugh for all who cross her threshold.

Address: *2815 S. Main St., Soquel, CA 95073, tel. 408/464-1137.*
Accommodations: *6 double rooms with bath.*
Amenities: *Fireplace in 5 rooms, whirlpool tub in 2 rooms, phone in 4 rooms, TV with VCR in 1 room; private decks, gardens with outdoor hot tub, afternoon refreshments, picnic baskets available.*
Rates: *$80-$125; full breakfast. AE, MC, V.*
Restrictions: *Smoking outside only, no pets; 2-night minimum on weekends.*

Cliff Crest Bed and Breakfast Inn

Innkeeping may seem an unlikely retirement career choice for an aerospace engineer and a recipe tester for Carnation foods, but it's the one Bruce and Sharon Taylor made when they moved from Los Angeles to this seaside town in 1986, purchasing Cliff Crest.

A smallish, modest Queen Anne, Cliff Crest was the home of William and Jenny Jeter. William was a mayor of Santa Cruz, lieutenant governor of California from 1895 to 1899, and founder of a local bank. Historic photographs on the walls illustrate the active life the Jeters led.

Like the Jeters, the Taylors enjoy visiting with guests in the parlor or in the sunny solarium. The guest rooms on the first and second floors contain antiques from the Taylors' personal collection: an Eastlake bedroom suite, an original Morris chair, an antique walnut dresser.

Sharon's penchant for experimenting with recipes continues, and results in such unusual breakfast entrées as chili egg puff, one of her most popular creations.

Address: *407 Cliff St., Santa Cruz, CA 95060, tel. 408/427-2609.*
Accommodations: *5 double rooms with bath.*
Amenities: *Robes; fireplace in 1 room; evening refreshments.*
Rates: *$80–$135; full breakfast. AE, MC, V.*
Restrictions: *Smoking outside only, no pets; 2-night minimum on weekends.*

Country Rose Inn

Innkeeper Rose Hernandez has created a remote retreat out of this big, white Dutch colonial farmhouse, just a few miles south of bustling Silicon Valley. It's set back on a country lane and surrounded by fields, ancient oaks, and flowering magnolias.

Many of the furnishings and decor come from Rose's family: her mother's wedding dress hanging in an antique armoire; a marriage trunk; a *metate y mano* stone Rose's mother used for grinding corn during the early days of her marriage; a baby grand piano in the music room. The Rambling Rose suite offers a lavish, romantic cathedral-ceiling hideaway comprising a bedroom and separate sitting room with Franklin stove, and a huge bathroom featuring a double Jacuzzi, oversize steam shower, and an enormous double-sink vanity.

Common areas include a large dining room–bar, where Rose serves breakfast, a cozy antiques-filled sitting room, and a music room.

Address: *455 Fitzgerald Ave. No. E, San Martin, CA 95046, tel. 408/842-0441.*
Accommodations: *4 double rooms with bath, 1 suite.*
Amenities: *Air-conditioning, fireplace, Jacuzzi in 1 room; gardens; afternoon refreshments, picnic baskets available.*
Rates: *$79–$169; full breakfast. MC, V.*
Restrictions: *No smoking, no pets; 2-night minimum on weekends.*

Gatehouse Inn

This Italianate Victorian house has a somewhat literary history. John Steinbeck, whose grandparents lived across the street, used to visit with owner Alice Langford to discuss poetry and King Arthur. The house dates from 1884 and is one of the oldest in Pacific Grove.

The original decor has either been retained or re-created: lincrusta on walls, Bradbury & Bradbury silkscreen wallpapers and antique white wicker furnishings, lending a bright and airy ambience in both the main house and the sympathetic addition. About half of the rooms are faithfully decorated in the Victorian style; the others are done up in fantasy themes: One is like a sultan's tent, with Persian carpet, brass headboard with inlaid mother-of-pearl, and a chair made from a camel saddle. Some rooms have claw-foot tubs set in their corners or alcoves.

Kristi and Doug Aslin, a charming couple, preside over the inn.

Address: *225 Central Ave., Pacific Grove, CA 93950, tel. 408/649–1881 or 800/753–1881.*
Accommodations: *8 double rooms with bath.*
Amenities: *Fireplace in 4 rooms, radio and tape player, phone in rooms; guest kitchen, afternoon refreshments.*
Rates: *$95–$170; full breakfast. AE, MC, V.*
Restrictions: *Smoking outside only; 2-night minimum on weekends.*

Gosby House

The Gosby House is a gabled and turreted landmark dating from 1887, when J. E. Gosby built one of the first boardinghouses in town. The addition of the turret tower, a bay window with stained glass, white spindled gingerbread adorning the front porch, and the shingled exterior transformed the homely building—ugly duckling-style—into a graceful Queen Anne Victorian.

Guest rooms vary in size, and all are decorated with late Victorian antiques and period reproductions. The inn has an informal, country air about it, and at breakfast guests feel comfortable choosing among the buffet offerings of cinnamon rolls, quiche, muffins, scones, omelets, and Mexican eggs, and taking them out to the garden; in the afternoon, they can enjoy a glass of wine in the parlor. The young innkeepers are knowledgeable and can offer tourism or restaurant suggestions.

Address: *643 Lighthouse Ave., Pacific Grove, CA 93950, tel. 408/375–1287.*
Accommodations: *20 double rooms with bath, 2 double rooms share bath.*
Amenities: *Phone in rooms, kitchen in 2 rooms, fireplace in 12 rooms; afternoon refreshments; picnic baskets and wine available; bicycles.*
Rates: *$85–$130; full breakfast. AE, MC, V.*
Restrictions: *Smoking in rooms with outside entrance only; no pets.*

Happy Landing Inn

This 1920s inn is a collection of pastel-colored Hansel and Gretel cottages set in a sea of flowers. Flagstone paths wind through the gardens, which include a beckoning lily pond and a lattice gazebo. Stone benches and lawn statuary abound.

Designed by Hugh Comstock, the architect responsible for much of Carmel, the two master suites and five bedrooms share the gardens, the great room, and the kitchen. The rooms have cathedral ceilings, lace curtains, brass beds, and an eclectic assortment of antiques. Each room has its own garden entrance, and a Continental breakfast will be served to the rooms when "you raise the shade to let us know you're ready," according to owner Dick Stewart.

Coffee and tea are served by a great stone fireplace. The inn is within easy walking distance of the beach, shops, and art galleries of Carmel.

Address: *Monte Verde St. between 5th and 6th Aves., Box 2619, Carmel, CA 93921, tel. 408/624-7917.*
Accommodations: *5 double rooms with bath, 2 suites.*
Amenities: *Cable TV in rooms, fireplace in suites and 1 room; afternoon refreshments.*
Rates: *$90–$145; Continental breakfast. MC, V.*
Restrictions: *Smoking outside only, no pets; 2-night minimum on weekends.*

Sandpiper Inn

Longtime innkeepers Graeme and Irene Mackenzie, originally from Scotland, are true to the spirit of hospitality conveyed by the Gaelic motto hanging in the Sandpiper Inn's spacious, bay-view living room: "Ceud Mile Failte: A hundred thousand welcomes."

The prairie-style inn, located near scenic Carmel Point and built in the 1920s, features bands of horizontal casement windows, a stucco finish, and a long, flat roofline. It offers a selection of spacious rooms, many with sweeping ocean views, on the first and second floors of the main house and in two garden cottages. There are open-beam ceilings, skylights, fireplaces, reproduction and antique furnishings, canopy beds, and local art on the walls.

Lovely gardens, with sitting areas tucked in all corners, are filled with pink, white, and red rhododendrons, camellias, azaleas, and geraniums.

Address: *2408 Bayview Ave., Carmel, CA 93923, tel. 408/624-6423.*
Accommodations: *16 double rooms with bath.*
Amenities: *TV in 1 room, fireplace in 3 rooms; fireplace in living room, guest phone, gardens, afternoon refreshments; French and German spoken.*
Rates: *$90–$165; expanded Continental breakfast. AE, MC, V.*
Restrictions: *Smoking outside only; 2-night minimum on weekends.*

Sea View Inn

A few blocks from the madding crowd that sometimes overwhelms Carmel, the Sea View typifies what longtime visitors to Carmel come for: peaceful seclusion amid stunning natural beauty. Diane Hydorn and husband Marshall, a former airline pilot and now a writer and artist (whose paintings grace many of the inn's rooms), have been the hosts here since 1975.

Inside the Craftsman cottage there's lots of dark woodwork in open-beam ceilings, paneled walls, milled moldings, hardwood floors topped with Oriental and braided rugs, overstuffed chairs, sofas in subdued colors, and brick fireplaces that keep the living room and games room warm on cool days (in other words, most of the time). Books, magazines, and games abound, and classical music plays softly in the background.

Breakfast, which consists of quiche, home-baked breads, fruits and cheeses, is served by candlelight.

Address: *Camino Real between 11th and 12th Aves., Box 4138, Carmel, CA 93921, tel. 408/624-8778.*
Accommodations: *6 double rooms with bath, 2 double rooms share bath.*
Amenities: *Afternoon refreshments, rental bicycles.*
Rates: *$80–$110; Continental breakfast. MC, V.*
Restrictions: *Smoking outside only, no pets; 2-night minimum on weekends, 3-night minimum on holidays.*

Seven Gables Inn

T his inn is actually a collection of four yellow, gabled clapboard buildings that share a corner lot and a breathtaking view of the ocean. The main house was built in 1886, one of the first of the many showy Victorian homes in Pacific Grove; the three outbuildings were put up during the 1910s and 1940s.

The Flatley family (who opened the Green Gables Inn during the 1950s) has filled the buildings with a collection of European antiques from various periods, marble statues, and bric-a-brac. Gold-leaf mirrors, picture frames, a Tiffany window, crystal chandeliers, inlaid wood furnishings, beveled-glass armoires, and Oriental rugs and marble statues create a formal European atmosphere. Susan Flatley, who manages the inn day to day, grew up in this house and is quite knowledgeable about the area; she happily provides advice and insight on visiting nearby Cannery Row, the Aquarium, and various Monterey historic sites.

Address: *555 Ocean View Blvd., Pacific Grove, CA 93950, tel. 408/372-4341.*
Accommodations: *14 double rooms with bath.*
Amenities: *Afternoon tea, picnic baskets, refrigerators.*
Rates: *$95–$185; full breakfast. MC, V.*
Restrictions: *Smoking in garden only; 2-night minimum on weekends, 3-night minimum on holidays.*

Stonehouse Inn

This handcrafted stone cottage dates back to 1906, when San Francisco socialite Nana Foster hosted Bay Area artists and writers at her weekend retreat. Rooms named for those notables—Jack London, Sinclair Lewis, Lola Montez—are smallish, some tucked in gables, others with ocean views lined up across the front; furnishings include brass and canopy beds, hand-carved armoires, and skylights.

The common areas, with distinctive Craftsman architectural touches, are particularly inviting. The centerpiece of the board-and-batten living room is a great stone fireplace flanked by shelves of books, a Victorian sofa, and a pair of wing chairs. An indoor garden–sun room is furnished with a rattan sofa and an antique wicker perambulator. Innkeeper Barbara Cooke serves homemade breads, Stonehouse granola, quiche, and egg dishes buffet-style in the sunny breakfast room, which opens to the cottage's backyard.

Address: *8th Ave. below Monte Verde St., Box 2517, Carmel, CA 93921, tel. 408/624-4569.*
Accommodations: *6 double rooms with 3 shared baths.*
Amenities: *Fireplace in living room, guest phone, gardens, afternoon refreshments.*
Rates: *$90–$125; expanded Continental breakfast. MC, V.*
Restrictions: *Smoking outside only, no pets; 2-night minimum on weekends.*

San Francisco

San Francisco
From North Beach to the Castro District

Sailboats gliding past Alcatraz Island, the hand-tooled finial of a restored Victorian, the clang of a cable-car bell, the aroma of Italian roast coffee, the spices of Szechuan cooking, the old '60s holdover and the new '90s individualist—San Francisco dazzles, provokes, and never disappoints. A jewel on the tip of a peninsula, the city is surrounded by water—the Pacific to the west of the Golden Gate Bridge, San Francisco Bay to the east. Victorian "painted ladies" cling to hills so steep they rival any roller coaster. Although driving can be nerve-racking and walking challenging, panoramic views reward at every turn.

Many visitors begin their tour of San Francisco at the vibrant waterfront. On a sunny weekend day, tourists and residents alike throng the unique shops, T-shirt stands, historic and hokey museums, and bay-view restaurants. Pier 39, a two-story wooden boardwalk of boutiques, eateries, and an old-fashioned carousel, juts into the ocean. Just up the street are the Cannery and Ghirardelli Square, a former chocolate factory, with more fun shops and restaurants. Along the way, you'll be enticed by the catch of the day cooked and sold at sidewalk stalls along Fisherman's Wharf. This is the northern terminus of the cable car, the nation's only moving National Historic Landmark.

The cable car climbs and dips over the city's hills to North Beach, the Italian neighborhood. Open-air cafés, pastry shops, delis, coffee-roasting companies, bakeries, and pizza parlors ensure that visitors never go hungry as they explore the Italian import shops and the Romanesque-Gothic cathedral of Saints Peter and Paul. Many of these businesses have been run for generations by the same Italian families that started them. On the adjacent

Telegraph Hill, residents have some of the best views of San Francisco as well as the most difficult ascent to their aeries.

The next stop is Chinatown, alive and exotic with crowds of Chinese and more recently arrived Southeast Asians scrutinizing the abundant vegetable stands and snapping up bargains on embroidered linens, jade, and ceramics in the import shops along Grant Avenue. Roast ducks hang in restaurant windows, Chinese characters cover marquees, and teahouses offer cups of steaming ginseng, reputed to induce good health. Nearby is Union Square, the heart of downtown and the city's premier shopping district. Within a few blocks are I. Magnin, Neiman-Marcus, F.A.O. Schwarz, Gump's, Shreve Co., a spate of world-famous retailers, and many smaller, exclusive boutiques. Chances are that many of the shoppers who frequent these pricey establishments live in Pacific Heights, where many-splendored mansions and town houses dominate some of San Francisco's most expensive real estate.

Continuing on the west side of the city, you'll find the stunning Golden Gate Park, home to world-class museums and delightful gardens. Although the park stretches from Stanyan Street to the sea, several highlights are clustered in one section. The M. H. de Young Memorial Museum, known for its American works, and the renowned Asian Art Museum share the same building. Next door is the serene four-acre Japanese Tea Garden, with its winding paths, a 200-year-old Buddha, a bonsai forest, and the always busy Tea House, where fortune cookies were invented. Across the street, the Strybing Arboretum is a microcosm of the plant kingdom, divided into such theme plantings as the New World Cloud Forest and the Scent Garden. The California Academy of Science and its magnificent aquarium are across the concourse.

Due north is an other urban oasis, the 1,500-acre Presidio, an area of rolling hills, majestic woods, and attractive

*redbrick army barracks. Just outside its eastern boundary
is the rosy and rococo Palace of Fine Arts, which houses
the Exploratorium, an innovative science museum.
Crowning the Presidio is the Golden Gate Bridge.*

*Since its bawdy, boomtown birth in the wake of the 1848
gold rush, San Francisco has pulsed with ethnic diversity,
free enterprise, a thirst for the good life, and a love for the
natural beauty of the West. Take a stroll away from the
tourist spots and you'll discover this spirit still very much
alive. Although occasional earthquakes may rattle the city
temporarily, San Francisco remains unsinkable.*

Places to Go, Sights to See

Alcatraz Island. Al Capone, Machine Gun Kelly, and Robert Stroud, the
"Birdman of Alcatraz," were inmates at this former maximum-security
federal penitentiary. You can walk through the prison and grounds on
a self-guided tour. Seating on the ferries of the Red and White Fleet (tel.
415/546–2882), which leave from Pier 41, is in great demand and should be
reserved in advance.

Asian Art Museum (Golden Gate Park, tel. 415/668–8921). With an estimated
12,000 works spanning 6,000 years, this is the largest museum outside Asia
that is devoted to Asian art. Highlights include the Magnin Jade Room and
the Leventritt collection of blue-and-white porcelain. The adjoining *M. H. de
Young Memorial Museum* (tel. 415/750–3600) is especially strong in
American art, including works by Sargent, Whistler, Cassatt, and Remington.

Cable Car Museum (Washington and Mason Sts., tel. 415/474–1887) displays
the brawny inner workings of the cable-car system, scale models, and
memorabilia.

California Academy of Sciences (Golden Gate Park, tel. 415/750–7145). One
of the five top museums of natural history in the country, the Academy
encompasses the first-rate *Morrison Planetarium*, featuring star and laser
shows; the *Steinhart Aquarium*, with its 100,000-gallon Fish Roundabout,
which is home to 14,000 creatures; and such exhibits as an "earthquake
floor," which enables visitors to ride a simulated California quake.

Coit Tower (atop Telegraph Hill, tel. 415/274–0203). An elevator to the top of
this art-deco monument, decorated with murals dedicated to the workers of
California, offers panoramic views of the city and the bay.

Exploratorium (Bay and Lyon Sts., tel. 415/561–0360). This science museum
at the end of the marina, packed with more than 600 hands-on exhibits, gives

children a chance to run off excess energy. You can create a giant soap bubble, freeze your shadow, or play computerized musical instruments. Be sure to include the pitch-black, crawl-through Tactile Dome in your visit.

Golden Gate Bridge. For the best views of this 54-year-old symbol of San Francisco, see it from Lincoln Boulevard, which forms the western boundary of the Presidio, or drive across the bridge to the parking lot on the Marin side.

Golden Gate Park. The best way to see this 1,000-acre park is by car. Highlights include the *Conservatory* (tel. 415/666–7077), an elaborate Victorian crystal palace that was designed after one in London's Kew Gardens, and the *Japanese Tea Garden* (tel. 415/752–1171), a 4-acre village of small ponds, streams, and flowering shrubs created for the 1894 Mid-Winter Exposition. Visitors especially enjoy paddle-boating on Stow Lake, the expansive picnic grounds, and the first-class museums located in the eastern section of the park (*see* above).

Hyde Street Pier (just west of the Cannery, tel. 415/556–6435). Climb aboard and explore a 19th-century three-masted schooner, paddle-wheel ferry, steam tug, and other historic ships that have been restored to look as though they just reached port.

Lombard Street (between Hyde and Leavenworth Sts.). Cars line up to zigzag down this "crookedest street in the world," where pedestrians negotiate stairs instead of sidewalks.

Mission Dolores (16th and Dolores Sts., tel. 415/621–8203). The sixth of 21 missions founded in California by the Franciscans and the oldest building in the city, this structure, dating from 1776, retains the appearance of a small-scale outpost, dwarfed by the towers of the adjacent basilica.

Tourist Information

San Francisco Convention and Visitors Bureau (lower level of Hallidie Plaza at Powell and Market Sts., tel. 415/391–2000).

Reservation Services

Bed & Breakfast Innkeepers of Northern California (Box 7150, Chico, CA 95927, tel. 800/284–4667); **Bed & Breakfast International** (Box 282910, San Francisco, CA 94128–2910, tel. 415/696–1690, fax 415/696–1699); **Bed & Breakfast San Francisco** (Box 349, San Francisco, CA 94101, tel. 415/931–3083 or 800/452–8249, fax 415/921–2273); **Lodging San Francisco** (421 North Point, San Francisco, CA 94133, tel. 415/292–4500 or 800/356–7567, fax 415/771–8309).

Archbishops Mansion

The Archbishops Mansion is an elegant European manor reborn in San Francisco. The Second Empire–style residence, built in 1904 for Archbishop Patrick Riordan, faces Alamo Square and its "postcard row" of restored Victorians. Designers Jonathan Shannon and Jeffrey Ross have restored the home to that era of opulence. Ornate Belle Epoque furnishings and reproductions fill the rooms, such as the crystal chandelier that hung in Scarlett O'Hara's beloved Tara in *Gone with the Wind*. Everything about the mansion—the scale, the ornamentation, the Napoleon III antiques—is extravagant.

A three-story redwood staircase rises majestically from the coffered foyer. Above, sunlight filters through a 16-foot-wide, oval leaded-glass dome, which miraculously survived the 1906 earthquake. While you sip your complimentary evening wine in the front parlor, dominated by a massive redwood fireplace with fluted Corinthian columns, you'll be serenaded from the hall by a 1904 ebony Bechstein piano once owned by Noel Coward.

Inspired by the Opera House six blocks away, guest rooms are unabashedly romantic. The gold-hued Don Giovanni Suite conveys a Renaissance formality and, not surprisingly, has a huge bed. The zebrawood canopy four-poster bed found in a castle in southern France was masterly carved during the Napoleonic period.

The Carmen Suite's outstanding feature is its bathroom: A claw-foot tub sits in front of a fireplace with, naturally, a tubside champagne stand. A second fireplace warms the Carmen's bedroom, where the 1885 settee has its original horsehair covering. Billowing draperies, canopied beds, and ceramic-tile fireplaces are routine here.

A breakfast of bakery muffins, scones, and tea or coffee is brought to your room in a picnic basket, or you can join the other guests in a formal dining room.

Address: *1000 Fulton St., San Francisco, CA 94117, tel. 415/563–7872 or 800/543–5820, fax 415/885–3193.*
Accommodations: *10 double rooms with bath, 5 suites.*
Amenities: *Phone and cable TV in rooms, fireplace and robes in many rooms, whirlpool tubs in 2 suites; evening refreshments, elevator, laundry service; room service for wine, beer, and snacks; conference facilities, off-street parking.*
Rates: *$115–$185, suites $195–$285; Continental breakfast. AE, MC, V.*
Restrictions: *No smoking in common areas, no pets; 2-night minimum on weekends.*

Chateau Tivoli

stay in this ornate fin de siè-
cle château in the historic
Alamo Square district may
forever alter your decorating sensibilities. Built in 1892, this historic
painted lady wears no fewer than 22
colors, from raisin brown to turquoise, with ornamentation picked
out in 23-karat gold leaf.

The château's past is even more colorful than its exterior. Designed by
19th-century American architect William Armitage, the house once belonged to lumber baron Daniel
Jackson and later to Ernest Krelling,
owner of the Tivoli Opera House.
Over the past few decades, when the
Alamo Square district saw some
rough times, the building was everything from a halfway house to
a famed ashram. Current owners
Rodney Karr and Willard Gersbach
purchased the château from new-age
guru Jack Painter in 1985.

Rodney and Willard have carried the
flamboyant appearance of the exteri-
or inside, tightly packing every
room, hallway, and wall with antique
furnishings and art (some from the
estates of Cornelius Vanderbilt and
Charles de Gaulle), housewares,
knickknacks, and a somewhat haunting taxidermy collection. Competing
for attention are the cornices and
carved oak paneling of the entrance
hall, double parlor, and staircase.

The riotous, museumlike quality of
the château's busy public areas is
carried over into the guest rooms.
A sultan and his elephant could both
stay comfortably in the glorious
Mark Twain suite; its Renaissance
Revival–style parlor alone is 500
square feet. Romantics will relish
the Luisa Tettrazine suite's marble
bath with double shower head, huge
French Renaissance canopy bed, and
frescoed ceilings. Five additional bedrooms are equally spacious. From
the bowed windows and Aesthetic
Movement furniture in the Joaquin
Miller room to the intimate tower
dining nook and French wash walls
of the Jack London room, there's
something at the Chateau Tivoli for
anyone open to the owners' flair for
dramatic decorating.

A Continental breakfast of scones,
cereals, juices, and fresh fruit is
served at a grand dining room table
that seats more than a dozen.

Address: *1057 Steiner St., San
Francisco, CA 94115, tel. 415/776–
5462 or 800/228–1647, fax 415/776–
0505.*
Accommodations: *1 double room
with bath, 4 double rooms share 2
baths, 1 suite, 1 double suite.*
Amenities: *Phone in rooms; complimentary wine, fireplace in 1 room
and 1 suite.*
Rates: *$80–$125; suites $160–$200.
Continental breakfast weekdays,
full breakfast weekends. AE, MC,
V.*

Hotel Triton

The newest acquisition of the Kimko Hotel and Restaurant Management Company, which oversees a rash of small hotels in San Francisco, the Triton is by far the zaniest. Guests enter via a whimsical lobby of shimmering silk-taffeta furniture, star-studded carpeting, and inverted gilt pillars, stylized spoofs of Roman columns.

The result of a $10 million makeover of the old Beverly Plaza Hotel, a former haven of Japanese businessmen, today's Triton caters to fashion, entertainment, music, and film-industry folks, who seem to like the iridescent pink-and-gold-painted rooms, harlequin diamonds on the walls, and *s*-curved dervish chairs with tassels. Indeed, it's right in the downtown gallery district, several blocks from Union Square, just steps from the Chinatown gates, and an uphill hike to the coffeehouses and celebrated nightlife of North Beach. The South of Market area, home to the Showplace Design Center and other smart fashion-design outlets, is a five-minute drive away.

A team of local artists coordinated the Triton look, with original art in every room and an assortment of curly-necked lamps and oddball light fixtures. Geometric patterns dominate—diamond-shaped, gilt-painted end tables and beige checkerboard-painted walls. These themes and unexpected color combinations, such as big navy silk pillows with magenta buttons, give the rooms an avant-garde appeal.

Such playfulness makes you forgive the rooms' diminutive dimensions. For enough space to stretch out, try the junior suites. The roomy master suite, number 221, includes a whirlpool bath tucked in a mirror-lined sideroom with its own TV. Comfort has not suffered for the sake of trendiness. Asymmetrical wooden armoires offer plenty of closet space, and beds covered with duvets are extremely comfortable.

A restaurant serving Mediterranean cuisine and a coffeehouse-newsstand are attached to the hotel. Among the Triton's more quirky services are rollerblade rentals.

Address: *342 Grant Ave., San Francisco, CA 94108, tel. 415/394–0500 or 800/433–6611, fax 415/394–0555.* **Accommodations:** *133 double rooms with bath, 7 junior suites.* **Amenities:** *Phone, TV, and minibar in rooms, CD stereo and VCR in suites, whirlpool bath in 1 suite; fireplace in lobby, complimentary coffee, tea and evening wine in lobby, conference facilities, complimentary limousine service to South of Market design community, room service 6 AM–9 PM, valet-laundry service, business-secretarial services, valet parking.* **Rates:** *$125, suites $165–$195. AE, MC, V.* **Restrictions:** *No pets.*

Inn at the Opera

Half-hidden behind the Opera House, Symphony Hall, and Museum of Modern Art near the Civic Center, this impeccable inn with its lavish floral arrangements and elegant furnishings manages to be a paradigm of superb taste without being stuffy. In 1986, owner-manager Tom Noonan turned a neglected seven-story hotel into a resplendent hideaway for performing artists and their fans: Mikhail Baryshnikov, Luciano Pavarotti, Herbie Hancock, and Dizzy Gillespie are among the notables who have stayed here. Noonan is a congenial host, overseeing every detail and maintaining the inn's reputation for fine service and hospitality.

The plush little lobby, all pale green with Oriental porcelain and damask chairs, resembles the foyer of a European inn. Excellent California-Mediterranean cuisine is served in the adjoining Act IV restaurant, against the swank backdrop of wood paneling, tapestry-covered walls, leather chairs, and a green marble fireplace; a formally dressed pianist plays old standards on a glossy black grand. The inn offers a package including show, dinner, dessert and champagne, and overnight accommodations.

The hotel's 48 rooms are discreetly romantic, glowing with pastel colors and Old World finesse, from the half-canopy beds and fluffy pillows to the handsome antique armoires

and gorgeously framed color reproductions of delicately etched flowers and birds. Subtle grace notes abound, such as a basket of red apples and armoire drawers lined with sheet music. Under filmy curtains and drawn-back drapes, window shades gently let in the morning light through a lacy diamond-shaped cutout near the bottom. Larger suites have two bedrooms, each linked to its own bath, and a central sitting room with a well-stocked minibar and microwave. Guests can have breakfast brought to their rooms with a morning newspaper or head for Act IV's buffet breakfast.

Address: *333 Fulton St., San Francisco, CA 94102, tel. 415/863–8400 or 800/325–2708, 800/423–9610 (in CA), fax 415/861–0821.*
Accommodations: *30 double rooms, 18 suites.*
Amenities: *Phone, minibar, robes, cable TV in rooms, microwave in suites; irons and ironing boards, hair dryers available, fireplace in restaurant/bar, morning newspapers, complimentary pressing, overnight shoeshine, 24-hour room service, complimentary limousine service to financial district, business-secretarial service, laundry service, packing service, staff physician, valet parking.*
Rates: *$110–$155, suites $175–$205; Continental breakfast. AE, MC, V.*
Restrictions: *Most pets not permitted.*

The Mansions Hotel

If inns were awarded prizes for showmanship, the Mansions Hotel would win top honors. First, there's the decapitated head of the resident ghost who reads minds. And where else can you see the innkeeper, clad in sequined dinner jacket, play the saw? They're just part of the live "magic extravaganzas" held every weekend at the Mansions.

The inspiration behind this zaniness is the aforementioned innkeeper, Bob Pritikin. The author of *Christ Was an Adman*, Pritikin isn't afraid of innovation in his hotel, two adjacent Queen Anne Victorians a short walk from the chic boutiques and eateries of Pacific Heights. The cabaret, free to overnight guests, also draws diners from the highly praised restaurant.

The Mansions Hotel is as visually flamboyant as its entertainment, although the west wing (a hotel bought two years ago) has a simpler, country-inn look. In the public areas no surface has been left unembellished. Objets, wall murals, curios (a selection of ugly ties, for example), and sculptures, many by Beniamino Bufano, are everywhere. The porcine theme in the breakfast dining room is tough to miss, surrounded as you are by an old wooden carousel pig and wall painting depicting a swine-filled picnic in progress.

All of the west-wing rooms have murals that depict the famous San

Francisco personage for whom the room is named. The authentic and Victorian reproduction decor might include a rolltop desk, four-poster canopy bed, and Tiffany-style lamp. The west-wing rooms have Laura Ashley flower-print wallpaper and matching bedding, with a preponderance of pine furniture. Particularly lavish is the Louis IV room, where such guests as Barbara Streisand, Robert Stack, and Michael York have enjoyed the immense gold-leaf half-tester bed and wardrobe and private redwood deck.

A full breakfast of fresh fruit, cereal, eggs cooked to order, crumpets, bangers, potatoes, and juice can be delivered to your room. There you'll find a replica of a Victorian silk rose to take home—and a little chocolate version of the Mansions, which, chances are, will never leave the premises.

Address: *2220 Sacramento St., San Francisco, CA 94115, tel. 415/929–9444, fax 415/567–9391.*
Accommodations: *22 double rooms with bath, 3 suites.*
Amenities: *Restaurant, evening entertainment, phone in rooms, TV on request, fireplace in some rooms, whirlpool tub in 1 room; complimentary newspaper, coffee, and sherry, limited room service, laundry service, billiard table.*
Rates: *$89–$325, suites $250–$350, full breakfast. AE, D, DC, MC, V.*
Restrictions: *None.*

The Queen Anne

This majestic, four-story Victorian ranks among the loveliest of San Francisco's classic painted ladies. Its rose and green gables and distinctive corner turret rise proudly above a neighborhood of vivid Victorians in lower Pacific Heights; walking tours of this colorful district can be arranged at the hotel. Japantown with its restaurants and the Fillmore shopping area are just around the corner.

The building's roots as a luxurious boarding school for girls, constructed by silver mogul and senator James G. Fair in 1890, still show in its rich cedar and oak paneling and the lofty staircase winding four flights up past stained-glass windows to an antique skylight. A sprawling lobby full of Victoriana—from brocade chairs to crimson walls—encompasses most of the ground floor. Guests can curl up with coffee or sherry before a crackling fire or partake of the breakfast buffet here each morning (many prefer to take a tray back to their room). This spacious public area, which fans into adjoining conference chambers, makes the hotel ideal for weddings and business meetings.

All 49 rooms and suites are different, blending contemporary comforts with historic accents. The plush carpeting, modern bedspreads, and hair dryers in the baths are offset by old-fashioned details like brass-necked

lamps, English antiques, and lacy curtains. Fireplaces warm many quarters; one enormous room has two brick hearths at either end. The accommodations, large for a small hotel, range from a two-bedroom, split-level town house with a private deck to a snug top-story room with slanted ceilings and a framed picture of George Washington.

Address: *1590 Sutter St., San Francisco, CA 94109, tel. 415/441-2828 or 800/227-3970, fax 415/775-5212.*
Accommodations: *49 rooms with bath. 1 town house.*
Amenities: *Phone and TV in rooms, fireplace and wet bar in many rooms, minifridge in suites; fireplace in parlor, irons and ironing boards available, conference and reception facilities, evening room service, laundry service, morning newspaper, afternoon tea and sherry, complimentary morning limousine downtown, passes to nearby health club, off-street parking, concierge-secretarial service.*
Rates: *$99–$150, suites $175–$275; Continental breakfast. AE, MC, V.*
Restrictions: *No smoking in lobby, no pets.*

The Sherman House

The words "crème de la crème" best describe this French-Italianate white mansion in Pacific Heights. More showcase than home-sweet-home, the Sherman House exudes old money, from the silken-striped Empire chairs of the second-floor gallery-salon and the sweeping staircase to the Old World splendor of the music hall.

Built in 1876 by music lover–instrument maker Leander Sherman, the house once attracted patrons and world-class musicians such as Enrico Caruso and pianist Jan Paderewski, who performed in the magnificent music hall; string quartet and piano concerts still make the chandeliers quiver today. Iranian economist Manouchehr Mobedshahi and his art historian wife, Vesta, saved this urban palace from demolition when they bought and restored it in 1980. Designer William Gaylord added antiques and objets d'art from estates and auctions, largely in French Second Empire style. A solarium with diamond-shaped windowpanes and a connecting chamber lit by a flickering fire make up the petite (and expensive) in-house restaurant, which serves California cuisine.

Great care went into the guest rooms, one more sumptuous than the next. Marble fireplaces with gas jets, bowls of heady potpourri, and featherbeds enclosed in heavy drapery are common denominators. The dark, wood-beamed, and wainscoted look of the Biedermeier and Paderewski suites contrasts sharply with the airy feel of the Leander Sherman Suite; its enormous rooftop terrace could hold a party of 100. Behind the main house, half an acre of garden—a princely estate in land-pinched San Francisco—encircles a carriage house containing the hotel's largest, priciest quarters, the Garden Suite. Decorated in a rattan motif, with a house-in-the-country aura and its own gazebo and private garden, this set of rooms is popular for wedding parties.

Address: *2160 Green St., San Francisco, CA 94123, tel. 415/563–3600 or 800/424–5777, fax 415/563–1882.*
Accommodations: *7 double rooms with bath, 7 suites.*
Amenities: *Phone and cable TV with stereo in rooms, fireplace, bath, robes, whirlpool bath, hair dryer in many rooms; fireplace in main salon and restaurant; garden, restaurant, music room with live concerts, conference facilities, personal valet service, massage service, private chauffeur available, laundry service, 24-hour room service, business-secretarial services, valet parking.*
Rates: *$235–$375, suites $550–$750. AE, MC, V.*
Restrictions: *No smoking in public areas, no pets.*

Victorian Inn
on the Park

Overlooking the so-called pan-handle of Golden Gate Park, this Queen Anne Victorian is a riot of gables, finials, and cornices. The most unusual feature is the open belvedere in a cupola, one of only two existing in the city; it's a private retreat for guests in the Belvedere Suite.

Renowned San Francisco architect William Curlett designed the mansion in 1897 for a prominent lawyer. In 1980, attorneys Lisa and William Benau, looking for a way to raise their children while working at a job they love, transformed the house into one of San Francisco's first bed-and-breakfasts.

If you've ever wanted to experience the more luxurious aspects of life in the Gay '90s, this is the place to do it. Step across the threshold to a grand entrance of rubbed mahogany paneling and oak parquet floors; they look even more burnished when a fire is lit in the immense brick fireplace framed by a sculpted wood mantel. The parlor is rather formal, with a graceful Rococo Revival fainting couch in floral brocade and a velvet settee. Wine is served here in the evening by the white-tile and painted-wood hearth, which almost touches the ceiling. Light filters through period fringed and embroidered lampshades.

Guest rooms, decorated with Rococo Revival and Eastlake antiques and

peppered with modern reproductions, are most noteworthy for their wall treatments. The wallpapers, combining different floral motifs in rich blues, purples, greens, and gold, are reproductions of William Morris designs, meticulously hand-silkscreened by Bradbury & Bradbury, a local firm.

Piles of pillows, marble bathroom counters, Victorian-era prints and photos, and a decanter of sherry in every room are some of the inn's special touches. The rooms on the street level are quiet and removed but a bit dark, and noise from the busy street can be heard in the upper-story rooms. These, however, are small complaints that never overshadow the friendly ambience and elegant presentation at the Victorian Inn on the Park.

Address: *301 Lyon St., San Francisco, CA 94117, tel. 415/931–1830, fax 415/931–1830.*
Accommodations: *12 double rooms with bath, 1 suite, 1 double suite with 2 baths.*
Amenities: *Phone and clock radio in rooms, some rooms with fireplace; TV available, meeting facilities.*
Rates: *$88–$144, suites $144–$280; Continental breakfast. AE, D, DC, MC, V.*
Restrictions: *No smoking in breakfast room, no pets; 2-night minimum on weekends, 3-night minimum on holiday weekends.*

White Swan Inn

Fireplaces in every room, romantic furnishings, delicious food, top-notch amenities, and a location just two blocks from Union Square make the White Swan Inn one of the premier bed-and-breakfasts in San Francisco. This circa-1908 building has the look of a London town house, and the decoration is studiously English. Walk into the library, and you'll think you've been admitted to an exclusive gentleman's club, with tufted wing chairs; rich, dark wood; sparkling brass fixtures and hardware; hunting scenes on the pillows; and a red tartan couch.

The guest rooms, predominantly green and burgundy with touches of yellow and rose, have a more informal look than the public rooms. All are similarly furnished with reproduction Edwardian pieces in cherry and other dark woods. Four-poster beds, wingback or barrel chairs, TVs enclosed in an armoire or a cabinet, wooden shutters, and Laura Ashley–style floral wallpaper are standard. A bedside switch allows you to control the gas fireplaces.

The hotel is one of the Four Sisters Inns, owned and operated by the Post family, and each evening and morning, a family member greets guests in the common rooms. At the White Swan, it's usually Kim, one of the four Post sisters for whom their family business was named. Their trademark teddy bears cuddle in the reception area, peeking through banisters and perched on the mantel over the perpetually lit fire. A plush bear also adorns each guest room.

The Four Sisters properties are known for their food, so you're urged to find an excuse to be back at the White Swan in the afternoon. You'll be rewarded by such complimentary snacks as lemon cake, vegetables with curry dip, stuffed grape leaves and specialty cheeses, accompanied by wine, sherry, and other drinks. Typical breakfast fare includes Mexican quiche, soda-bread toast, Swiss oatmeal, fresh fruit, granola, and doughnuts. Everything is homemade. Guests have made so many requests for the recipes that the family has released its own cookbook.

Address: *845 Bush St., San Francisco, CA 94108, tel. 415/775–1755, fax 415/775–5717.*
Accommodations: *26 double rooms with bath, 1 suite.*
Amenities: *TV, wet bar, refrigerator, hair dryer, robes, phone in rooms; afternoon refreshments, laundry service, wine-only room service, complimentary newspaper and shoe-shine service; valet parking available, conference and catering facilities.*
Rates: *$145–$160, suites $250; full breakfast. AE, DC, MC, V.*
Restrictions: *No smoking in common areas, no pets.*

The Alamo Square Inn

his inn spans three buildings encircling a flower-filled patio overlooking a small garden. The most attractive of the three is the 1895 Neo-Classical Revival Baum House, with delicate reliefwork in the form of wreaths and ribbons.

In the guest rooms, innkeepers Wayne Morris Corn and Klaus Ernst May have opted for reproduction and contemporary furnishings. One upstairs suite features an ultramodern black-laminate bedroom set and a sunken whirlpool bath. Another bright attic suite with dormers has white wicker furniture and opens onto a rooftop sun deck. Several rooms overlook Alamo Square.

The second building is an 1896 Tudor Revival, but the rooms are darker, with small windows. The third house features a modern garden apartment with full kitchen.

Address: *719 Scott St., San Francisco, CA 94117, tel. 415/922-2055 or 800/345-9888, fax 415/931-1304.*
Accommodations: *9 double rooms with bath, 3 suites, 1 housekeeping suite.*
Amenities: *Phone in rooms, Jacuzzi in 1 suite, TV in 4 rooms, fireplace in 4 rooms; refreshments, conference room, off-street parking.*
Rates: *$85–$135; suites $175; full breakfast. AE, DC, MC, V.*
Restrictions: *Smoking outdoors only, no pets; 2-night minimum on weekends, 3-night minimum on some holidays.*

Albion House Inn

ucked away several blocks from the Civic Center, the serene and cozy Albion is within walking distance of many restaurants and the city's opera, ballet, and modern art museum. Formerly a flophouse where 1960s rock stars crashed, this prequake Victorian was restored and fitted out with bird-print wallpaper and Turkish kilim rugs. An enormous and inviting lobby–living room has teak beams, a grand piano, a marble fireplace, and a dining table where a generous breakfast steams every morning.

The rooms, though small, are cheerful and homey, decorated with an English-country flair. The rather inappropriately named Janis Joplin suite—a favorite of honeymooners— has sweet floral fabrics and a half-canopy bed and thronelike wicker chair. Other rooms complement the peach, green, and ivory color scheme with a warm mix of antiques and rattan, brightened here and there by floral arrangements.

Address: *135 Gough St., San Francisco, CA 94102, tel. 415/621-0896.*
Accommodations: *9 double rooms with private bath.*
Amenities: *Phone in rooms; fireplace in living room, TV available, complimentary brandy, afternoon tea, restaurant.*
Rates: *$55–$85; full breakfast. MC, V.*

The Bed and Breakfast Inn

This 1885 Italianate Victorian row house is nestled in a quiet mew just off Union Street. The Bed and Breakfast Inn, which also includes an adjacent house, may be the closest you'll come to staying in a native's home. Although owners Bob and Marily Kavanaugh don't reside here, most of the furniture and cherished antiques have descended through the two families.

Guest rooms are cozy, with traditional pieces (some of them love seats), the family china on display, and impressionistic landscape paintings by Marily. Fresh flowers perfume each room. One spacious suite, decorated with comfortable contemporary furnishings, boasts a living room, dining area, full kitchen, and a balcony overlooking the deck. A spiral staircase climbs to a sleeping loft. Most rooms that have private bathrooms also have phones and TVs. Pension rooms that share a bath are simple but affordable.

Address: *4 Charlton Ct., San Francisco, CA 94123, tel. 415/921–9784.*
Accommodations: *3 double rooms with bath, 4 double rooms share 3 baths, 2 suites, 1 housekeeping suite.*
Amenities: *Phone in 6 rooms, TV in 5 rooms, complimentary coffee, sherry in rooms with baths; sherry in parlor.*
Rates: *$70–$140, suites $215; Continental breakfast. No credit cards.*
Restrictions: *No smoking except on deck, no pets.*

Golden Gate Hotel

The family-run Golden Gate Hotel is ideal for budget-conscious visitors. With rooms as low as $55 for a shared bath (and a sink in each guest room), this circa-1913 Edwardian is just two blocks from Union Square. Hosts John and Renata Kenaston provide complimentary afternoon tea and cookies, served in the hotel's cozy parlor, which is simply decorated with ivory-sponged walls, gray-blue carpeting, a contemporary, "deconstructivist" fireplace, and Rococo Revival love seat and coffee table. Coffee lovers can look forward to what is billed as "the city's strongest coffee."

Guests reach their rooms by riding the town house's original birdcage elevator. The rooms are small, clean, and reasonably quiet given the hotel's downtown location. Each is cheerfully furnished, with white or blue wicker chairs, wicker headboards, and 19th-century mahogany wardrobes. Laura Ashley floral-print wallpaper with matching curtains and comforters are featured in all rooms with private baths (some of these have antique claw-foot tubs).

Address: *775 Bush St., San Francisco, CA 94108, tel. 415/392–3702 or 800/835–1118.*
Accommodations: *14 double rooms with bath, 9 double rooms share 3 baths.*
Amenities: *TV in rooms, phone in 10 rooms; afternoon refreshments.*
Rates: *$55–$89; Continental breakfast. AE, DC, MC, V.*

Hotel Griffon

With its clean, contemporary design and proximity to San Francisco's financial district, the Hotel Griffon attracts mostly corporate clients, but its setting on the historic Embarcadero, its glittering views of the bay, and its restaurant also make it a romantic getaway on weekends.

Occupying a five-story 1906 building, transformed—at a cost of $10 million—from a run-down sailor's inn several years ago, the hotel now has a spare European look. Rooms and suites are quietly elegant, most done in ivory and beige with exposed-brick walls, rich cherry and mahogany furniture, tapestried window seats, and, in the bathrooms, marble vanities and sinks. Bayside rooms, only slightly more expensive, offer beautiful vistas of the Bay Bridge; protected from traffic noises by two sets of double-paned windows, these get snapped up quickly.

Address: *155 Steuart St., San Francisco, CA 94105, tel. 415/495–2100, fax 415/495–3522.*
Accommodations: *53 double rooms with bath, 9 suites.*
Amenities: *Phone with modem, cable TV, minibar in rooms, terrace in penthouse suites; VCR available, complimentary newspaper, boardroom, laundry, use of nearby fitness center, room service 11:30–2:30 PM and 5:30–10 PM, off-street parking.*
Rates: *$120–$140, suites $140–$190; Continental buffet breakfast. AE, MC, V.*
Restrictions: *No pets.*

Inn at Union Square

A half block west of Union Square, the Inn at Union Square is a friendly, more personal alternative to the area's skyscraping hotels. Interior designer Nan Rosenblatt has endowed the guest rooms and parlors with the rich, inviting ambience of a gracious country home.

At the end of each of five floors is a cozy sitting area warmed by a wood-burning fireplace. High tea, complete with a generous selection of cucumber sandwiches, cakes, and cookies, is served here.

Guest rooms feature furniture in Chippendale and Federal styles, heavy draperies, and floral-print canopies and half-canopies. Don't expect a view in this crowded part of town, where buildings are squeezed next to one another.

Address: *440 Post St., San Francisco, CA 94102, tel. 415/397–3510 or 800/288–4346, fax 415/989–0529.*
Accommodations: *23 double rooms with bath, 7 suites.*
Amenities: *Phone and TV in rooms, fireplace in 2 rooms, wet bar in 2 rooms, whirlpool bath, sauna, and refrigerator in 1 suite; refreshments, complimentary newspaper and shoe-shine service, laundry service, room service, honor bar, catered dinner in room available, valet parking.*
Rates: *$120–$180, suites $145–$300; Continental breakfast. AE, DC, MC, V.*
Restrictions: *No smoking.*

Inn San Francisco

The Inn San Francisco, in Mission Hill, is quintessential northern California: a beautifully restored 1870s Italianate Victorian with a hot tub out back. Featherbeds, 19th-century British and American furnishings throughout, a delightful garden and cottage, and a rooftop patio complete the picture.

The spacious double parlor is elegantly decorated in true Victorian fashion with forest-green walls, rubbed redwood trim, velvet side chairs, a tapestried fainting couch, and Oriental rugs. One popular guest room opens onto a private, sheltered deck with its own traditional redwood hot tub. Another room has a double whirlpool bath beneath a stained-glass skylight. Manager Jane Bertorelli adds her own special touches: fresh flowers and truffles by San Francisco's best-known chocolatier in every room.

Address: *943 S. Van Ness Ave., San Francisco, CA 94110, tel. 415/641–0188 or 800/359–0913, fax 415/641–1701.*
Accommodations: *17 double rooms with bath, 5 double rooms share 2 baths.*
Amenities: *Phone, TV, refrigerator and clock radio in rooms, hot tub on deck of 1 room, whirlpool tub in 5 rooms, fireplace in 4 rooms; complimentary tea, coffee, and sherry, hot tub in garden, limited off-street parking.*
Rates: *$75–$175; Continental breakfast. AE, D, DC, MC, V.*
Restrictions: *No smoking in parlor, no pets in public areas.*

Jackson Court

This charming, old 1900 brownstone in the heart of Pacific Heights houses an exemplary San Francisco bed-and-breakfast: tasteful, personal, and serene. From the walk-in courtyard, doors open into a cordial sitting room where scarlet silk tulips catch the glow of a blazing fire. Floors are parquet and ceilings wood-beamed.

Each room has its own personality and color scheme. Some are done in old-fashioned ivory, others in lush burgundy; some have marble basins in the rooms, and all have antique writing desks. Off the main parlor, the spacious Executive Suite is sophisticated in a masculine way with its brass bed and coatrack; a door connects to the hotel's wood-paneled conference room. The Garden Court Suite looks out on a private garden. Upstairs, the library wins raves for its sunny grandeur and gracious hearth. Breakfast is served in the small, bright upstairs kitchen, where guests can stash perishables in the fridge or cook their own meals.

Address: *2198 Jackson St., San Francisco, CA 94115, tel. 415/929–7670.*
Accommodations: *10 double rooms with bath.*
Amenities: *Phone and TV in rooms, fireplace in many rooms; fireplace in lobby, afternoon sherry, off-street parking.*
Rates: *$95–$140; Continental breakfast. AE, MC, V.*
Restrictions: *No smoking in public areas, no pets.*

The Monte Cristo

Originally a bordello, the Monte Cristo occupies a deep burgundy Italianate building with white awnings and window boxes. It dates back to 1875 and was refurbished in 1980. At the edge of Presidio Heights, this now modest, low-key guest house is within a few blocks of chic shopping on Sacramento Street and about 10 minutes from downtown San Francisco.

Though it lacks the drama and personality of many other small inns, the Monte Cristo offers good value in a peaceful environment. The Chinese wedding room features a unique carved Cantonese bed, as well as a deep tiled tub, tasseled lamp, and other Oriental accoutrements. A grandiose four-poster bed dominates the secluded upstairs Georgian room. The other rooms are simpler and more Victorian, with sunny bay windows, crocheted bedspreads, and antiques. Breakfast is served downstairs in a pretty, flowery parlor at tables for two, and complimentary wine is offered in the tiny sitting room.

Address: *600 Presidio Ave., San Francisco, CA 94115, tel. 415/931–1875.*
Accommodations: *11 double rooms with bath, 3 double rooms share 1 bath, 1 deluxe suite.*
Amenities: *Phone in some rooms, TV in some rooms, minifridge in deluxe suite; TV rentals, pay phone.*
Rates: *$63–$98, suites $108; Continental breakfast. AE, MC, V.*
Restrictions: *No pets.*

Petite Auberge

Just two blocks from Union Square, this circa-1915 Baroque Revival inn is a romantic retreat with a small garden patio in the heart of downtown. Owned and operated by the Four Sisters Inns (*see* the White Swan Inn, above), the Petite Auberge features dainty floral wallpaper, French-country oak armoires and matching headboards carved in flower and vine reliefs, and fireplaces framed with hand-painted floral tiles. Other French touches include glazed terra-cotta tiles in the lobby and Pierre Deux fabrics in some of the rooms.

The lace-curtained guest rooms, predominantly peach, French-country blue, and rose, have thoughtful features, such as reading lights above each side of the bed, a selection of old books, fresh apples, hair dryers, and a wine list. Color TVs are tucked away in armoires. Some rooms have bay windows with sitting areas; others have charming tables with hand-painted flowers.

Address: *863 Bush St., San Francisco, CA 94108, tel. 415/928–6000, fax 415/775–5717.*
Accommodations: *26 double rooms with bath.*
Amenities: *Phone in rooms, fireplace in many rooms, whirlpool tub in 1 room; laundry service, afternoon refreshments, wine-only room service, catered dinner in room available, valet parking.*
Rates: *$105–$155, suites $215; full breakfast. AE, MC, V.*
Restrictions: *No smoking in common areas, no pets.*

Savoy Hotel

San Francisco is blessed with nearly as many small, European-style hotels as Paris, and this newcomer is one of the very best for the money. Named for the Savoy region of France and housed in one of the many late-Victorian, postearthquake buildings surrounding Union Square, the hotel is exceptionally comfortable given its modest scale and price. Featherbeds, down pillows and cotton Matelasse bedspreads help ensure a good night's sleep; etchings, polished Provençal-style furniture, and Toile de Jouy fabrics with bucolic country scenes set the French-country tone. The suites, with their modest vestibules, black-granite bathrooms, and sitting rooms with Louis-Philippe sleeper sofas, are worth the few extra dollars.

Off the tiny lobby, Brasserie Savoy, which would fit in well on Paris's Left Bank, is a superb spot for a glass of Sancerre and a seafood dinner.

Address: *580 Geary St., San Francisco, CA 94102, tel. 415/441-2700 or 800/227-4223.*
Accommodations: *70 rooms with bath, 13 suites.*
Amenities: *Phone, cable TV, hair dryer, minibar, robes in rooms; restaurant, concierge, conference center, no-smoking floors.*
Rates: *$89–$109, suites $139–$159; Continental breakfast. AE, D, DC, MC, V.*
Restrictions: *No pets.*

Spencer House

A short walk from Golden Gate Park and the hippie haven of Haight-Ashbury, this classic 1887 Queen Anne Victorian once was residence of a San Francisco milliner and gold-mine speculator.

Innkeepers Barbara and Jack Chambers purchased the Spencer House as their home in 1984 and spent two years painstakingly restoring it before opening it as an inn in 1986. The French château influence can be seen in the elegant silk wall coverings, Louis XVI antiques, and half-canopy beds suitable for royalty. Rooms are also outfitted with claw-foot tubs, old-fashioned light fixtures, and linens trimmed with antique lace. Many of the original features of the house can be enjoyed, including faceted stained-glass windows, and combination gas-and-electric brass chandeliers. Guests are greeted as if they were long-lost friends, and many of them are. The Spencer House doesn't have a listed telephone number; instead, Barbara and Jack rely on word of mouth and repeat business.

Address: *1080 Haight St., San Francisco, CA 94117, tel. 415/626-9205, fax 415/626-9208.*
Accommodations: *6 double rooms with bath.*
Amenities: *Fireplace in parlor, off-street parking.*
Rates: *$95–$155; Continental breakfast. No credit cards.*
Restrictions: *Smoking in kitchen only; 2-night minimum on weekends, 3-night minimum on holiday weekends.*

Union Street Inn

Window-shopping in San Francisco's most fashionable shopping district, one would never guess that it possesses a garden carriage house, the favorite retreat of Diane Keaton and other celebrities when they visit the city. Of course, guests needn't stay in the cottage to have a view of Union Street Inn's beautiful backyard English-style garden.

The parlor of this 1901 Edwardian features a brick and redwood gas fireplace and padded salmon-colored velvet walls with wainscoting; French doors open onto a gardenside redwood deck. Certainly the cottage accommodations are the most sybaritic: In the center of the 300-square-foot room is an indulgent double whirlpool tub glowing beneath a skylight and hemmed by greenery. The Holly Room has a 19th-century brass bed, wedding-ring quilt, and an English walnut dresser with three hinged, beveled mirrors. The Wild Rose Room features a white wicker bed, striped chaise and ottoman, and classic modern posters.

Address: *2229 Union St., San Francisco, CA 94123, tel. 415/346-0424.*
Accommodations: *6 double rooms with bath.*
Amenities: *Phone and robe in rooms, TV on request, whirlpool in 2 rooms; evening refreshments, limited off-street parking.*
Rates: *$125–$175, carriage house $225; Continental breakfast. AE, MC, V.*
Restriction: *Smoking in garden only, no pets.*

Washington Square Inn

One of San Francisco's prettiest small, modern hotels, this inn overlooks verdant Washington Square and the cathedral of Saints Peter and Paul in North Beach.

Co-owner and interior designer Nan Rosenblatt has captured the ambience of a gracious country home with dramatic floral draperies, half-testers, bedspreads, sofas, and bay-window seats. There isn't a bad view to be had: Some rooms look over Washington Square while others face an inner patio filled with potted plants and flowers.

In the afternoon, complimentary high tea with cucumber sandwiches is served by the fireplace in the downstairs parlor, followed by evening wine and hors d'oeuvres. Breakfast is served in your room or at the dining table in the parlor, from which you can watch the Chinese residents performing their morning *t'ai chi* exercises in the square.

Address: *1660 Stockton St., San Francisco, CA 94133, tel. 415/981-4220 or 800/388-0220.*
Accommodations: *10 double rooms with bath, 5 double rooms share 2 baths.*
Amenities: *Phone in rooms, complimentary paper and shoe-shine service, afternoon refreshments, laundry service, room service for beer, wine, and soft drinks; valet parking available.*
Rates: *$85–$180; Continental breakfast. AE, DC, MC, V.*
Restrictions: *No smoking, no pets.*

Bay Area

Bay Area
Marin, East Bay, and the Peninsula

Like a twilight fog, the Bay Area beyond San Francisco's city limits defies set boundaries. The peninsula, the East Bay, and Marin are names used knowingly by locals and terms dictated somewhat by geography, but they tell only part of the story. These three areas, all within a 30-mile radius of downtown San Francisco, encompass forested coastal mountains, high-tech industrial centers, majestic shorelines, enclaves of academia, quiet seaside villages, sunny inland suburbs, and one-of-a-kind nature preserves.

The peninsula stretches south from San Francisco, through Silicon Valley and down to San Jose, and is the only part of the Bay Area that's reachable from the city without crossing a bridge. Along the Pacific coastline here, the air is often moist with fog in the morning and late afternoon but bright with sunshine during midday. Commercial florists and backyard gardeners make much of this mild climate. In South San Francisco you can take a greenhouse tour at Rod McClellan's, the world's largest hybridizer of orchids, and around Half Moon Bay you'll find one of the most prolific flower-growing regions in the world. Here, too, you can shop in boutiques or head to the beach for a picnic or horseback ride on the sand. Swimmers, however, will find the Pacific waters goose-bumpingly cold at any time of the year. To the southeast is Filoli, whose magnificent estate and gardens were used as the setting for the TV series Dynasty.

San Jose is inland, just below the southern curve of San Francisco Bay. High-tech industry has pumped new life into this city, and a museum called the Tech Museum of Information offers a fun, hands-on peek into computers, including a simulated "clean room," where silicon chips are made. From San Jose north along the bay toward San Francisco there's a string of high-tech–oriented towns, including Mountain View, where you can take tours of wind tunnels and prototypical aircraft at the Ames Research Center, and Palo Alto, home to Hewlett-Packard, Apple, and the elegant Spanish Revival–style campus of Stanford University.

The East Bay is just that: the area east of San Francisco Bay beginning at Oakland and Berkeley. The University of California at Berkeley holds a long-standing rivalry with Stanford in both football and academics. Berkeley's reputation as a hotbed of radical thinking has always spilled off campus, and during the past decade the city has become known for spawning a generation of innovative young chefs of the "California cuisine" school, their inspiration being Alice Waters and her Chez Panisse restaurant.

Oakland boasts such attractions as the Oakland Museum, a microcosm of the Golden State's cultural heritage, art, and natural history. The parks and gardens around Lake Merrit, pleasant hillside and bayside neighborhoods, shopping at Jack London Square along the revitalized waterfront, and generally warmer–than–San Francisco weather offer as much to the visitor as to the commuting resident.

North of the Golden Gate Bridge is Marin, with its redwood forests, well-preserved coastline, and golden-brown hills, interspersed with clusters of suburban towns. Artsy, upscale Sausalito, just across the bridge, is a favorite getaway for both locals and tourists. Whimsical shops and art galleries line the main street, and restaurants cantilevered over the water offer panoramic views of San Francisco Bay and the skyline. Curving mountain roads lead west to the tallest living things on earth—redwood trees—in Muir Woods. Nearby is Muir Beach, a secluded cove along the Pacific, and Stinson Beach, one of the most popular—and crowded—strips of shore in northern California. Point Reyes National Seashore is an expansive

*coastal preserve encompassing rolling hills, long, nearly
deserted sandy beaches, a lighthouse built in 1870, a re-
created Miwok Indian village, an interpretive walk along
the San Andreas Fault, and a free-roaming herd of tule
elk. Many consider Point Reyes to be northern California
at its best.*

Places to Go, Sights to See

Filoli (Canada Rd., Woodside, tel. 415/364–2880). This 654-acre estate is one
of California's best-loved gardens and is open by tour only. Advance
reservations are required.

Muir Woods National Monument (off Hwy. 1, 17 miles northwest of San
Francisco, tel. 415/388–2595). This awe-inspiring grove of coastal redwoods,
the tallest living things on earth, has some specimens that are 250 feet high,
with diameters of more than 12 feet.

Oakland Museum (10th and Oak Sts., Oakland, tel. 510/238–3401). The
museum is devoted to California's natural history, man-made heritage, and
art.

Point Reyes National Seashore (off Hwy. 1, Point Reyes, tel. 415/663–1092).
Encompassing 74,000 acres of rolling hills, forests, pastureland, estuaries,
and beaches, the preserve has a visitor center, re-created Miwok Indian
village, the Morgan Horse Ranch (where horses are bred and trained for the
National Park Service), and Earthquake Trail, which traces the San Andreas
Fault.

Rod McClellan's Acres of Orchids (1450 El Camino Real, South San
Francisco, tel. 415/871–5655). Orchid cultivation is explored in daily tours
through this 35-acre complex of greenhouses.

Winchester Mystery House (525 S. Winchester Blvd., San Jose, tel. 408/247–
2101). The eccentric heiress to the Winchester Arms fortune designed this
mansion to baffle evil spirits with 160 rooms, 2,000 doors, 10,000 windows,
blind closets, secret passageways, and 40 staircases.

Beaches

You can stop at virtually any spot along Highway 1 within an hour's drive
north or south of San Francisco for some spectacular coastline scenery. The
beaches tend to be fairly narrow strips of sand, backed either by craggy
bluffs or rolling hills. The water is often much too cold for swimming;

sunbathing is catch-as-catch-can and usually possible only very early in the afternoon.

Point Reyes, Muir Beach, and **Stinson Beach,** to the north, are well-kempt and popular; to the south, the beaches along **Half Moon Bay** skirt quaint seaside villages.

Restaurants

In Marin County, the small town of Inverness is a good place to stop for lunch on the way out to the seashore, or dinner on the way back. At **Manka's** (tel. 415/669–1034), California cuisine is served up in a dining room warmed by a huge fireplace. Restaurants and cafés line Sausalito's main street, and seafood, plain or fancy, is the specialty in most. **The Spinnaker** (tel. 415/332–1500) offers fresh seafood and homemade pasta dishes in a spectacular setting near the yacht club. Devotees of California cuisine pay homage at Berkeley's landmark **Cafe at Chez Panisse** (tel. 510/548–5049) for fresh and innovative light lunches and dinners from a daily changing menu of grilled dishes, pastas, pizza, and salads. Near the magnificent Filoli estate in Woodside, the **Village Pub** (tel. 415/851–1294) features California fare, including a variety of main-course salads, pastas, and seafood. Even if San Jose were not the fast-food franchise capital of California (no mean feat), the **Lion and Compass** (tel. 408/745–1260) would be popular for its good and extensive menu, ranging from pork chops and prime rib to such lighter fare as ahi tuna and generous salads.

Tourist Information

Half Moon Bay Coastside Chamber of Commerce (225 S. Cabrillo Hwy., Box 188, Half Moon Bay, CA 94019, tel. 415/726–5202); **San Jose Convention and Visitors Bureau** (333 W. San Carlos St., Suite 1000, San Jose, CA 95110, tel. 408/295–9600); **Sausalito Chamber of Commerce** (333 Caledonia St., Sausalito, CA 94965, tel. 415/332–0505); **West Marin Chamber of Commerce** (Box 1045, Point Reyes Station, CA 94956, tel. 415/663–9232).

Reservation Services

The California Association of Bed and Breakfast Inns (2175 Porter St., Soquel, CA 95073, tel. 800/284–4667); **Bed & Breakfast International** (Box 282910, San Francisco, CA 94128–2910, tel. 415/696–1690, fax 415/696–1699); **Bed & Breakfast San Francisco** (Box 420009, San Francisco, CA 94142, tel. 415/931–3083 or 800/452–8249); **Inns of Point Reyes** (Box 145, Inverness, CA 94937, tel. 415/663–1420).

Captain Dillingham's Inn

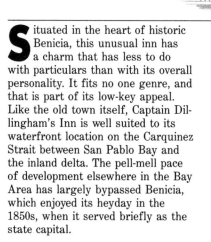

Situated in the heart of historic Benicia, this unusual inn has a charm that has less to do with particulars than with its overall personality. It fits no one genre, and that is part of its low-key appeal. Like the old town itself, Captain Dillingham's Inn is well suited to its waterfront location on the Carquinez Strait between San Pablo Bay and the inland delta. The pell-mell pace of development elsewhere in the Bay Area has largely bypassed Benicia, which enjoyed its heyday in the 1850s, when it served briefly as the state capital.

The main house was built in the 1850s as a residence for Captain William Wallace Dillingham, who sailed from Massachusetts around Cape Horn and out to Hawaii before settling here. He married a local widow, and they made a home in this clapboard Cape Cod–inspired residence behind a storybook white-picket fence. Given the inn's salty heritage, it would be easy to imagine that its eclectic assortment of furnishings was collected by the old captain as he sailed the seven seas. How else to explain the presence of, say, a headboard from Brittany or a bridal chest from Yugoslavia or navigational charts from the 1800s? The truth is a bit more prosaic. Roger Steck, who bought the place in 1985, more or less cannibalized his antiques store for the treasures that give the inn much of its character.

As a result, no room is like any other. The one common trait of the accommodations is that they are all spacious. In the original structure, the Captain's Quarters boasts a working fireplace fashioned from black onyx and can be coupled with an adjacent room to form a suite in space once occupied by a parlor. The four rooms in the newer Pepper Wing (built in 1984, the year before the present owners took over) all have cathedral ceilings. The second-floor accommodations share a deck sheltered by trees; the lower two have brick patios fronting a garden carefully planted for successive blooms, from the bright marigolds of summer to the more subdued chrysanthemums of autumn. The cozy reception parlor is walled with bookshelves with enough titles for a long weekend of reading, either in your own quarters or in the garden. A 12-foot-long antique French pine table makes the morning meal memorable.

Address: *145 E. D St., Benicia, CA 94510, tel. 707/746-7164.*
Accommodations: *10 double rooms with bath, 1 suite.*
Amenities: *Phone, TV, minifridge in rooms, 9 rooms with spa tub, 1 room with fireplace; garden, off-street parking, walking distance to shops, restaurants, and marina.*
Rates: *Rooms $70–$110, suites $160; full breakfast. AE, DC, MC, V.*
Restrictions: *No pets.*

Casa del Mar

This pale stucco Mediterranean-style villa perches at the top of a landscaped knoll a scant block from the Pacific Ocean. The original structure on this site was built in 1906 as the Buckeye Lodge, named after a tree common to the area. A two-story cabin, it was favored by hikers who would frequently ferry from San Francisco across the Golden Gate (before the bridge was built) and then traipse across the wild slopes of Mt. Tamalpais. The trailhead near the inn is as popular now as it was then, but today most visitors arrive by car.

The place was purchased in 1987 by Rick Klein, a local lawyer and sometime builder Klein bought it as a private home but found that making it an inn was the only way he could support his passion for restoring the gardens, which cascade down to sea level, a riot of flowering bulbs, citrus trees, and other vegetation common to the Mediterranean. Klein has also added a vegetable garden and, in the shaded corner that backs up to the mountain slope, a dell of trillium, ferns, and other shade-loving plants. Indeed, Klein has become so enamored of his greenery that he offers occasional tours, charging a nominal fee that he hopes will help bankroll maintenance and expansion of the grounds.

Inside, the crisp decor is also a refreshing antidote to those hot and sticky summer days when the fog fails to roll in at sunset. The entry level has an open-space floor plan, with a breakfast room at one end flanked on two sides by large windows and warmed by sunlight or heat from a dark blue, tile wood-burning stove. Here guests are served the morning meal. The Mexican paver floor extends to the parlor area, which has its own built-in fireplace. Everywhere are selections from Klein's extensive collection of local artwork, bright paintings (many seascapes), and amusing animal sculptures. The rather small upstairs accommodations are made to seem larger by the use of pale painted walls, lots of windows, and simple furnishings. The rooms derive their names from the charming motifs (shell, passionflower, etc.) painted on the tilework within each shower stall. Two rooms face the ocean; two, the forest behind.

Address: *37 Belvedere Ave., Box 238, Stinson Beach, CA 94970, tel. 415/868-2124.*
Accommodations: *Four double rooms with bath.*
Amenities: *Fireplace in public rooms.*
Rates: *$100–$225 ($6 less for singles); full breakfast. MC, V.*
Restrictions: *No smoking, no pets; 2-night minimum on weekends, 3-night minimum on holiday weekends.*

Casa Madrona Hotel

The Casa Madrona was a decaying 1885 Victorian mansion that was on the verge of tumbling from its steep hillside perch above the Sausalito Marina until John Mays renovated and reopened it as a hotel during the late 1970s. The New Casa, a multilevel addition, is stepped down to the street below like an Italian hill town.

The New Casa's guest rooms all share a magnificent view of the marina across the street, Belvedere and Angel islands, and the forested hills of Tiburon beyond. Many rooms have private balconies. Each room of the New Casa has a distinct personality. The Renoir Room, hung with prints of the artist's work, has a window seat, large deck, fireplace, and, in the bathroom, a claw-foot tub surrounded by an impressionistic mural of a flower garden. In the Artist's Loft, an easel and watercolor paints set beneath a skylight await your talents.

Guest rooms in the original Victorian building are decorated in period style, with high ceilings, Victorian-era American furniture, and four-poster or brass beds. Rooms facing east or south have views. There are also three private cottages done up as rustic mountain cabins.

Casa Madrona is more small hotel than homey bed-and-breakfast, and except for a large outdoor deck of the New Casa, the Victorian's parlor and balcony are the inn's only common areas. In the evening, wine, cheese, and fruit are served in the parlor, and guests can relax in the antique settees or in the balcony's wicker chairs while taking the night air.

A buffet-style breakfast is served in the award-winning Casa Madrona Restaurant, which is attached to the original building. In warm weather the glass walls and ceiling of this terrace dining room slide open to enhance the already panoramic view, which on a clear day can include the San Francisco skyline. The contemporary American cuisine makes much of the area's ethnic influences, and specialties include rack of lamb with roasted garlic glaze and minted *gremoulata* ice, and dry-aged New York steak with caramelized onion flan. The hotel's bakery, where the restaurant's excellent desserts are prepared daily, is on an upper level.

Address: *801 Bridgeway, Sausalito, CA 94965, tel. 415/332–0502 or 800/288–0502, fax 415/332–2537.*
Accommodations: *34 rooms.*
Amenities: *Phone in rooms, TV in 23 rooms, fireplace in 18 rooms, minibar in 17 rooms; room service during restaurant hours, conference facilities, outdoor hot tub.*
Rates: *$105–$225; Continental breakfast. AE, MC, V.*
Restrictions: *No smoking in restaurant; 2-day minimum on weekends.*

Claremont Resort and Spa

The statuesque Victorian gables and towers of the Claremont dwarf the surrounding homes in the Oakland hills. In 1915, when the Claremont was built, city dwellers used to make the trek out to the country by ferry and take the train back. Thanks to the freeway and the Bay Bridge, the hotel is now within a half hour's drive of San Francisco, but the 22-acre resort feels secluded in its woodsy residential neighborhood, and despite its massive scale, it has the individuality and charm of a small hotel. Through a recent $30 million facelift, the Claremont has again become one of the Bay Area's loveliest getaways.

Its gardens and public areas are a gallery for the intriguing collection of northwestern art of owner Harold Schnitzer and his wife, Arlene. The plush pink dining room and terrace café present equally aesthetic views of the bay and hills. In keeping with the resort's health theme, the two restaurants serve calorie-conscious "crossover cuisine" in spa portions along with standard fare.

Largely acclaimed as the Bay Area's premier urban spa, the Claremont attracts a steady following of locals in addition to its overnight visitors. Its posh new facilities include two pools, a workout center, and an aerobics gym, and you can opt for every sort of relaxation and beauty treatment you might think of, such as high-tech underwater massage.

The rooms, all large and individually designed, have earned the Claremont the nickname "the largest B&B on the West Coast." The top honeymoon suite comes with floor-to-ceiling windows, a sunken living room, and whirlpool bath. Another suite has a pale yellow color scheme, a wraparound window seat, and a telescope. Some of the junior suites have canopy beds, overstuffed sofas and chairs, and huge walk-in closets. It's worth springing for the slightly more expensive rooms with bayside rather than hillside views.

Address: *Ashby and Domingo Aves., Oakland, CA 94623, tel. 510/843–3000 or 800/551–7266, fax 510/848–6208.*
Accommodations: *239 double rooms with bath, 23 junior suites, 6 suites.*
Amenities: *Phone, cable TV, hair dryer, robes, iron and ironing board in rooms, minifridge in some suites or on request, whirlpool bath in 1 suite; fitness center, 10 tennis courts, 2 pools, 2 spas, saunas, steam rooms, beauty salon, jogging course; 28 meeting rooms, business-secretarial services, restaurant, café, deli, bar-lounge, 24-hour room service, laundry service, complimentary shuttle to downtown Oakland and BART stations, off-street parking.*
Rates: *$169–$209, suites $295–$720. AE, MC, V.*
Restrictions: *No pets.*

The Mill Rose Inn

et amid a lush flower garden, the Mill Rose Inn is one of the most indulgent, romantic hostelries in northern California. The word *pampered* takes on new meaning here—guests are provided virtually everything they need for a carefree stay. Most of the guest rooms have Eastlake and Arts and Crafts antique furnishings, brass beds, down comforters, billowing draperies, and fireplaces framed with hand-painted tiles. All come equipped with a stereo, TV with VCR, refrigerator stocked with beverages, fruit and nut basket, candies, coffee maker with herb teas and cocoa, sherry and brandy, hair dryer, and more. Sinfully rich desserts are always available in the parlor, and you'll wake to a generous champagne breakfast.

The Mill Rose Inn is 30 miles south of San Francisco, in the oceanside hamlet of Half Moon Bay. Innkeepers Eve and Terry Baldwin both hold degrees in horticulture and take full advantage of the gentle climate. The front garden is an explosion of color, with more than 200 varieties of roses, lilies, sweet peas, daisies, Iceland poppies, irises, delphiniums, lobelias, and foxgloves, all framed by the inn's crisp white exterior. Tourists and local residents stop by just to photograph the spectacular floral displays. Located in the town's historic district, the inn is five blocks from Half Moon Bay and a short drive to Pacific coast beaches.

In contrast to the building's spare exterior, virtually no corner of the guest rooms has gone undecorated. Each is done in rich, deep tones with floral-patterned wall coverings, burgundy carpeting, custom-made brass chandeliers and wall sconces, and watercolor paintings. All have private entrances opening to a balcony that faces the back courtyard, with its hanging potted flowers, brick patio, and whirlpool spa secluded in an old-fashioned gazebo.

In the breakfast room, bouquets on each table and a fire in the hearth, with its hand-painted tiles reading "Welcome All to Hearth and Hall," set the stage for evening desserts and sumptuous breakfasts. Courses might include an orange-banana frappé, fresh fruit, raspberry, crème fraiche soufflé, crisp bacon, enormous croissants, local champagne, and Mexican hot chocolate made with cinnamon and almonds.

Address: *615 Mill St., Half Moon Bay, CA 94019, tel. 415/726-9794.*
Accommodations: *4 rooms with bath, 2 suites.*
Amenities: *Phone, TV with VCR, stereo, clothes steamers in rooms, fireplace in 5 rooms; afternoon wine and snacks, conference facility.*
Rates: *$175–$275; full breakfast. AE, D, MC, V.*
Restrictions: *No smoking, no pets; 2-day minimum on weekends.*

The Pelican Inn

Upon first seeing the Pelican Inn, you may think you've taken a wrong turn and somehow stumbled into the English countryside. Just off Highway 1 in Marin County, the Pelican Inn is fronted by a formal English garden and set in an expanse of lush lawn. This whitewashed Tudor with black timbers is a replica of a 16th-century British inn—the realized dream of Englishman Charles Felix, who built it in 1977.

Now run by Englishman Barry Stock, the hostelry is a favorite stopping place for San Franciscans out to celebrate a special occasion and for tourists visiting the nearby Muir Woods. Muir Beach is just a short walk from the inn.

Guests are especially drawn to the Pelican's pub. Amiable bartenders, a dart board, an assortment of beers, stouts, and ales, and an inviting selection of ports, sherries, and British dishes create a convivial setting. The aptly named Snug is a parlor set aside for registered guests only. English-country antiques, old books, prints and curiosities that Stock has brought back from his homeland, as well as a comfortable sitting area by the woodburning fireplace, make this an ideal sanctuary.

The inn's restaurant is right out of Merry Olde England, with heavy wooden tables, and a dark, time-worn atmosphere, enhanced by fox-hunt prints and an immense walk-in hearth with large cast-iron fittings. During dinner and breakfast, the room is lit only by the fireplace, the tall red tapers on each table, and cut-tin lanterns on the walls. Tasty, moderately priced meals include beef Wellington, prime rib, and chicken dishes. Breakfast, served here or in your room, is hearty fare, with eggs cooked to order, breakfast meats, and toasted breads. Lunch specialties include bangers and mash and fish-and-chips. In the backyard beer garden, sunlight filters through a greenery-entwined trellis, and a brick fireplace keeps things cozy.

Planked doors with latches open to the guest rooms, some of which are decorated with antiques from different periods. Each room has leaded, multipane windows, Oriental scatter rugs, English prints, heavy velvet draperies, hanging tapestries, and half-tester beds. Even the bathrooms are special, with Victorian-style hardware and hand-painted tiles in the shower.

Address: *Star Rte. (Hwy. 1), Muir Beach, CA 94965, tel. 415/383-6000.*
Accommodations: *7 rooms with bath.*
Amenities: *Restaurant on premises.*
Rates: *$135–$150; full breakfast. MC, V.*
Restrictions: *No pets; closed Christmas Eve and Christmas Day.*

Blackthorne Inn

The Blackthorne Inn is an adult-size fantasy tree house. A four-story spiral staircase winds its way to the guest rooms, and secluded balconies nest in the treetops. The adventurous can slide down a fireman's pole from one of the inn's decks to the driveway.

Handcrafted in 1978 by owner Bill Wigert, the imaginative structure is highlighted by a 3,500-square-foot deck with stairways to higher decks. A single, 180-foot Douglas fir was milled to create the planks in the living room's vaulted ceiling. Boulders in the room's fireplace were gathered from eight counties. The solarium was made with timbers from San Francisco wharves; the outer walls are salvaged doors from a railway station. The inn is crowned with a glass-sheathed octagonal tower called the Eagles Nest. Guests there pay a price for the drama: They must traverse an outdoor walkway to reach the private bath. They are, however, near the inn's hot tub. Guest rooms are uncluttered, with redwood trim, and floral-print comforters.

Address: *266 Vallejo Ave., Box 712, Inverness Park, CA 94937, tel. 415/663-8621.*
Accommodations: *3 rooms with bath, 2 rooms share a bath.*
Amenities: *Afternoon dessert and tea, outdoor hot tubs.*
Rates: *$105–$175; full breakfast. MC, V.*
Restrictions: *Smoking on decks only, no pets; 2-day minimum on weekends, closed Christmas Day.*

Cowper Inn

The Cowper Inn encompasses two homes, their front porches connected by a wide, painted Plexiglas deck. One is an 1893 Queen Anne Victorian, and the other is an 1897 Craftsman house. Many guests choose the Cowper for its location, a five-minute walk from downtown Palo Alto and ¼ mile from the train to San Francisco.

Innkeeper Peggy Woodworth has created a home away from home for frequent visitors to nearby Stanford University and Silicon Valley; they appreciate the quiet neighborhood and unfussy atmosphere inside. The largest common room is in the Craftsman house: an open living room that's arranged so guests can either join each other in conversation or settle into a secluded corner.

A long dining table is set near a row of windows overlooking the elaborately restored Queen Anne Victorian across the street.

The guest rooms in both houses are furnished simply, decorated in warm, light tones, and have wicker chairs, unobtrusive floral wallpaper, and Amish quilts on the beds.

Address: *705 Cowper St., Palo Alto, CA 94301, tel. 415/327-4475, fax 415/329-1703.*
Accommodations: *12 rooms with bath, 2 rooms share a bath.*
Amenities: *Phones and TV in rooms, kitchenettes in 3 rooms, conference facility.*
Rates: *$55–$98; Continental breakfast. AE, MC, V.*
Restrictions: *No smoking, no pets.*

Gramma's Inn

A ten-minute walk from Berkeley's university campus, this inn is a complex of five buildings. The two oldest, the 1903 Shingle-style Fay House, and the Main House, an 1899 half-timber, sit at a corner, and a garden area connects them with the other buildings.

The inn is a blend of well-worn comfort and more upscale luxury. The common rooms, in the Main House, have a lived-in feel. The parlor's pink-and-white checkered wing chairs and floral-print overstuffed sofas face the fireplace. The breakfast room resembles a greenhouse and opens to the patio, with umbrella-covered tables and the garden beyond. A full breakfast of omelets and fresh-baked breads is served here.

The newer buildings are somewhat quieter. Rooms in the Garden House are sunlit, with modern bleached-wood furnishings, tile fireplaces, brass beds, and private entrances. The Carriage House rooms all have fireplaces but lack the character of the older buildings. The Cottage House offers larger rooms, all with fireplaces, desks, and sitting areas.

Address: *2740 Telegraph Ave., Berkeley, CA 94705, tel. 510/549–2145, fax 510/549–1085.*
Accommodations: *38 rooms with bath.*
Amenities: *Phones and TV in rooms, fireplace in 20 rooms; off-street parking.*
Rates: *$85–$175; full breakfast. DC, MC, V.*
Restrictions: *No smoking, no pets.*

The Hensley House

This 1884 Queen Anne Victorian, with its steeply pitched roof and witch's hat tower, is a short walk to the light rail for the five-minute ride to downtown San Jose.

A stately grandfather clock graces the entryway, and in the parlor, velvet brocade high-back chairs, a rosewood settee, and red velvet side chairs surround an ivory-hued grand piano. The room leads out to a sunny backyard deck. The full breakfast includes such entrées as eggs Florentine and waffles and is sometimes served in the library, dominated by an 11-foot-high walnut vestment cabinet from a Jesuit monastery, and a 500-year-old stained-glass window.

Deep, cool color schemes and Victorian antique and reproduction wardrobes highlight the guest rooms. The largest room is in the tower and features a corner gas fireplace, whirlpool tub, half-canopy bed, and a bay-window sitting area.

Address: *456 N. 3rd St., San Jose, CA 95112, tel. 408/298–3537, fax 408/298–4676.*
Accommodations: *5 rooms with bath.*
Amenities: *Phone, TV with VCR, clock radio, hair dryer, robes in rooms; fireplace, spa, refrigerator in 1 room; air-conditioning, conference facility, off-street parking.*
Rates: *$75–$125; full breakfast. AE, D, DC, MC, V.*
Restrictions: *Smoking outside only.*

Mountain Home Inn

Early in the century, hikers and railroad passengers had their choice of lodgings on Mt. Tamalpais. The only recommended inn on the mountain now is this architectural wonder, built in 1912 by a Swiss couple who must have pined for their Alpine homeland. Ed and Susan Cunningham bought the property after a fire in the mid–1980s and transformed it into a slightly rustic inn.

Four slim redwood trunks shoot up through the airy, high-ceilinged lobby, which shares the top floor with a lounge and a deck cantilevered 1,000 feet above San Francisco Bay, visible in the distance. The floors below are oddly angled to encompass a number of small accommodations and two larger, deluxe rooms. Despite handmade hickory furniture and lovely views, the rooms don't look as fresh as they did in the early days. Still, they are comfortable, decorated in combinations of pastels. Most romantic is number 6, a spacious, secluded room with a fireplace.

Address: *810 Panoramic Hwy., Mill Valley, CA 94941, tel. 415/381–9000, fax 415/381–3615.*
Accommodations: *10 double rooms with bath.*
Amenities: *Phone in rooms, TV available on request; fireplace and Jacuzzi tub in 4 rooms, private terraces in 2 rooms; off-street parking; restaurant and lounge.*
Rates: *$121–$178; full breakfast. MC, V.*
Restrictions: *No pets.*

Old Thyme Inn

This understated Queen Anne house's rosy hues and white-picket fence set a tone of comfort and good cheer. Innkeepers Anne and Simon Lowings lovingly restored the house and enjoy sharing it with their guests.

Anne's pride and joy is her herb garden, where more than 80 varieties of herb sweeten the air, some imported from the couple's native England. Fresh herbs garnish the inn's breakfast specialties, and guests are invited to take cuttings home with them.

The Garden Suite features a four-poster bed and whirlpool tub beneath skylights. The Thyme Room has a whirlpool, fireplace, and a half-canopy bed. Even with its up-to-the-minute luxuries, the inn retains a genuine air of old-fashioned friendliness and hospitality.

A full breakfast of home-baked breads, fruit, yogurt, granola, a hot item such as English crumpets, and a dessert of, say, hot cherry flan is served family-style.

Address: *779 Main St., Half Moon Bay, CA 94019, tel. 415/726–1616.*
Accommodations: *6 rooms with bath, 1 suite.*
Amenities: *Phone available, refreshments; fireplace, whirlpool tub in 2 rooms; TV with VCR, fireplace, whirlpool tub, refrigerator in suite; health club next door.*
Rates: *$90–$135, suites $210; full breakfast. AE, D, MC, V.*
Restrictions: *Smoking in garden only.*

Pillar Point Inn

One of few California inns with an ocean view, Pillar Point sits on a tiny harbor, separated from the sea by a breakwater visible through the bobbing masts of fishing boats. Built in 1986 to resemble the homes on Cape Cod, it was bought in 1989 by a management group.

The gray-blue, two-story inn has immaculate rooms decorated in shades of blue with white accents. Linens are Laura Ashley style, but the seminautical decor stops just short of being precious. Café curtains flanking the window seats leave plenty of room for sunlight to flood the rooms. Aside from the white metal-and-brass bedframes, all the furniture is oak reproduction. Blue and white tiles surround the fire-places. Close to restaurants, shops, and the marina, the inn gets a good deal of foot traffic on weekends.

A cozy parlor, separated from the breakfast room by a glass-enclosed fireplace, is stocked with cookies, port and sherry. Upstairs, a small deck is available for sunning and barbecuing.

Address: *380 Capistrano Rd., Princeton-by-the-Sea, CA 94018, tel. 415/728-7377.*
Accommodations: *11 double rooms with private bath.*
Amenities: *Phone, TV, minifridge, fireplace in rooms; deck, off-street parking.*
Rates: *$150; full breakfast. AE, MC, V.*
Restrictions: *No smoking, no pets.*

Roundstone Farm

Owner Inger Fisher describes Roundstone Farm as "my hillside haven." Nestled among the hills near Point Reyes National Seashore, this farmhouse was constructed in 1987. From the rambling shed-style building, you'll see pastoral scenes of Inger's horses grazing by the pond, meadows stretching to wooded hillsides, and a glimmer of Tomales Bay.

A 16-foot-high skylighted and beamed cathedral ceiling and tall windows keep the living room bright. The wood stove, country-casual furniture, and stone floors confirm that you've gotten away from it all. The decor throughout the inn is low-key, in keeping with—perhaps creating—the relaxed atmosphere. Guest rooms are uncluttered, with floral-print curtains and bedspreads, a Windsor side chair or two, and white wood headboards fashioned after garden gates, all harmonizing with antique armoires from England and Denmark. Breakfast is served family-style in the dining room, whose sliding glass doors lead to a patio and garden.

Address: *9940 Sir Francis Drake Blvd., Box 217, Olema, CA 94950, tel. 415/663-1020.*
Accommodations: *5 rooms with bath.*
Amenities: *Fireplace in 4 rooms.*
Rates: *$115–$125; full breakfast. AE, MC, V.*
Restrictions: *Smoking on deck only, no pets; 2-night minimum on weekends, closed first 2 weeks of Dec.*

Ten Inverness Way

Veteran innkeeper and columnist Mary Davies has created a coastal country-style bed-and-breakfast in Inverness, on Tomales Bay. The weathered 1904 Shingle-style house is convenient to the Point Reyes National Seashore and close to the fine Czechoslovakian or French restaurants in town.

The inn's living room is warmed by a large stone fireplace, and the walls are lined with bookshelves. Windows look out onto the trees and gardens.

The atmosphere is country-cottage casual, and the decor takes its cues from the stone fireplace, redwood interior, and Oriental rugs. Hand-sewn quilts enhance the guest rooms. There's nothing fancy or fussy here,

but then again, people come to get *away* from fancy and fussy.

Breakfasts feature banana-buttermilk buckwheat pancakes and chicken-apple sausage.

Address: *10 Inverness Way, Box 63, Inverness, CA 94937, tel. 415/669-1648.*
Accommodations: *4 rooms with bath, 1 suite.*
Amenities: *Hot tub, complimentary beverages.*
Rates: *$110–$160; full breakfast. MC, V.*
Restrictions: *Smoking in garden only; 2-day minimum on weekends, 3-day minimum on holidays.*

Wine Country

Wine Country
Napa and Sonoma Counties

*Less than an hour north of the cosmopolitan streets of San
Francisco lies the gateway to California's wine country, the
premium grape-growing region in the United States. Well-
traveled highways gradually give way to country roads that
meander through lush valleys, along hillsides dotted with
orchards, and past thousands of acres of vineyards whose
color and character change dramatically with the season.*

*The counties of Napa and Sonoma, which garner the lion's
share of wine-tasting awards, are separated by the majestic
Mayacamas Mountains. To the north of them, Mendocino
County is best known for its rugged coastline and for the
quaint New England–style town of Mendocino. More
recently, however, the area has been gaining a reputation
for the grapes that are grown inland, particularly in the
scenic Anderson Valley, which may one day become as
famous as its Napa and Sonoma cousins.*

*The 21-mile-long Napa Valley, which stretches from the top
of San Francisco Bay to the unassuming town of Calistoga,
boasts more than 200 wineries. But it is dwarfed by its
neighbor to the west. Sonoma's 1,600 square miles consist of
rolling hills, scenic valleys, and five distinct wine-growing
regions, including one that straddles the dynamic Russian
River as it wends its way west to meet the waters of the
Pacific Ocean.*

*It has been said that Napa is reminiscent of parts of the
French countryside while Sonoma resembles Italy,
especially Tuscany. The analogies with Europe are
particularly apt, given the local emphasis on fine wines
and extraordinary cuisine. Moreover, many of the region's
earliest wineries were established during the 1800s by
immigrants from France and Italy as well as from
Germany and Hungary. Gradually orchards of apples,*

pears, walnuts, and plums were replanted with grapes, though Sonoma is still famous for its apples and other produce. Sonoma's numerous ranches and farms produce everything from beef and poultry to strawberries and melons, and it's all available at the hundreds of produce stands scattered along the county's 1,450 miles of roadsides.

The wine country's abundant open space is endangered, however, by encroaching development. The county seat itself has mushroomed, making it difficult to travel easily between the Sonoma Valley and the Russian River area.

Despite recent urban growth, particularly in the vicinity of Santa Rosa, the wine country is still largely rural—fertile ground for dozens of small inns that attract a constant stream of visitors year-round. In Napa, summer weekends find cars snaking along Highway 29, the main north–south thoroughfare. An increasingly popular option is the Silverado Trail, a two-lane road that parallels the highway on the eastern side of the valley.

Sonoma bears myriad reminders of the county's mission heritage; in Napa, the hot springs and mud baths bear testimony to the valley's volcanic history. Napa has a reputation for elitism, whereas Sonoma remains close to its agricultural heritage. Combined, the two areas constitute one of California's prime attractions.

The Anderson Valley is the strongest lure of the lesser-known Mendocino wine country, encompassing the area around Ukiah along the four- to six-lane Highway 101. Located some 100 miles north of San Francisco, the 25-mile-long valley lies on either side of Highway 128, which zigzags through rocky outcroppings as it leads west into more-open countryside. Still known for its apples, the region has increasingly been settled by urban escapees of all stripes, as well as by winemakers appreciative of the soil and climate of this hidden valley. The towns are tiny, ranging from Boonville (population 715) to the handful of

*buildings which compose Navarro, but innkeepers are
gradually discovering the charms of the Anderson Valley
and playing host to a growing number of visitors.*

Places to Go, Sights to See

Horseback Riding (tel. 707/996–8566). The *Sonoma Cattle Company* offers
guided one- and two-hour excursions at Jack London State Historic Park and
Sugarloaf Ridge State Park. Picnic and full-moon rides are also available.

Hot-Air Ballooning. *Sonoma Thunder* (4914 Snark Ave., Santa Rosa, tel.
707/538–7359 or 800/759–5638, fax 707/538–3782) operates hot-air balloons
above the vineyards and west along the Russian River, allowing visitors to
view the coastline.

Jack London State Historic Park (2400 London Ranch Rd., Glen Ellen, tel.
707/938–5216). Memorabilia from the life of the prolific author-sailor-farmer
are displayed in a museum home. The remains of Wolf House, London's
dream home that burned down mysteriously in 1913, can be seen through
a grove of redwood trees.

Luther Burbank Memorial Gardens (Santa Rosa and Sonoma Aves., Santa
Rosa, tel. 707/576–5115). The renowned horticulturist Luther Burbank chose
this area for his extensive plant-breeding experiments. He is remembered in
this well-maintained National Historic Landmark home, carriage house, and
greenhouse, all of which can be seen on docent-guided tours.

Mud Baths. Nineteenth-century settlers discovered the health benefits of the
natural mineral waters and volcanic ash of Mt. St. Helena. Establishments on
Lincoln Avenue in Calistoga tout health regimens ranging from immersion in
mud baths to soaking in hot baths to full massage treatments.

The Petrified Forest (4 mi. west of Hwy. 128, between Calistoga and Santa
Rosa, tel. 707/942–6667). Ancient trees, some more than 100 feet tall, were
covered by volcanic ash 6 million years ago when nearby Mt. St. Helena
erupted. Also visible are petrified seashells, clams, and other remains of
marine life.

Russian River (between Hwy. 101 and the Pacific Ocean along the Russian
River Rd., tel. 800/253–8800). Secluded beaches, angling spots, and boats,
canoes, and inner tubes for rent can all be found along the shady banks of
this popular resort area.

Sonoma State Historic Park (Sonoma, tel. 707/938–1578). Facing the plaza
in the center of the old city is *Mission San Francisco Solano* (1st St. and
Spain St. E), the site where the original flag of California was first flown in
1846. Barracks, an old hotel, and other historic structures, including *La Casa
Grande* (General Mariano Vallejo's former home), are part of this complex.

Sugarloaf Ridge State Park (Hwy. 12, just outside Kenwood, tel. 707/833–5712). Some 25 miles of trails lead through grassy meadows and groves of redwood and laurel trees within this 2,500-acre park, where bird-watching, picnicking, camping, and horseback riding are popular.

Wineries

Choosing which of the 400 or so wineries to visit will be difficult, and the range of opportunities makes it tempting to make multiple stops. The wineries along the more frequented arteries of the Napa Valley tend to charge nominal fees for tasting, but in Sonoma County, where there is less tourist traffic, fees are rare. In Sonoma, you are more likely to run into a wine grower willing to engage in convivial conversation than you are along the main drag of the Napa Valley, where the waiter serving yards of bar has time to do little more than keep track of the rows of glasses.

One of California's first premier wineries, **Buena Vista Winery** (18000 Old Winery Rd., Sonoma, tel. 707/938–1266) was built in 1857 by Hungarian Count Agoston Harazthy, who enclosed his limestone caves within large stone buildings that still house barrels of wine. The Napa Valley cousin of France's Moët et Chandon label, **Domaine Chandon** (California Dr., Yountville, tel. 707/944–2280) offers a close-up of how sparkling wines are produced and bottled. **Hakusan Sake Gardens** (1 Executive Way, Napa, tel. 707/258–6160) is a refreshing change from winery tours; you can taste both warm and cold sake in the Japanese garden. **Husch Vineyards** (4400 Hwy. 128, Philo, tel. 707/895–3216) is the classic Anderson Valley winery, a place so unpretentious it could be mistaken for a toolshed, but one should never underestimate its Pinot Noir and Chardonnay. No tour of the Napa Valley would be complete without a visit to **Robert Mondavi** (7801 St. Helena Hwy., Oakville, tel. 707/963–9611), the winery owned by one of the most famous and admired winemakers in the United States. **Roederer Estates** (4501 Hwy. 128, Philo, tel. 707/895–2288), a French sparkling-wine maker, is one of very few wineries where visitors feel comfortable smoking—no doubt the French influence. Set atop a hill at the northern end of the Napa Valley, **Sterling Vineyards** (1111 Dunaweal La., Calistoga, tel. 707/942–5151) features an aerial tramway. In 1990 Vicki and Sam Sebastiani opened the Tuscan-style **Viansa Winery** (Hwy. 12, Schellville, tel. 707/945–4747) overlooking the Sonoma Valley.

Restaurants

The Diner (tel. 707/944–2626) in Yountville is a homey American-Mexican diner specializing in hearty, simply prepared dishes that range from waffles or *huevos rancheros* at breakfast to seafood tostadas at dinner. North of Yountville is **Mustards Grill** (tel. 707/944–2424), an unpretentious roadside restaurant serving such fresh, flavorful fare as roast rabbit, grilled fish, and a long list of noteworthy appetizers. In the El Dorado Hotel in Sonoma, **Ristorante Piatti** (tel. 707/996–2351), like its namesake in the Napa Valley, is known for its homemade pastas, calzones, and pizzas prepared in a wood-burning oven; grilled meats are another specialty. In St. Helena, **Tra Vigne** (tel. 707/963–4444) has high ceilings, gilded moldings, and hearty Italian fare. **Big 3** (tel. 707/938–9000) in Boyes Hot Springs is a casual restaurant at the Sonoma Mission Inn & Spa known for fresh local produce, poultry, and seafood. The breakfast and Sunday-brunch menus feature spa dishes as well as eggs, waffles, and Sonoma sausages. **Floodgate Store and Grille** (tel. 707/895–3000) in Philo specializes in freshly prepared foods, including hearty sandwiches and innovative salads.

Tourist Information

Healdsburg Chamber of Commerce (217 Healdsburg Ave., tel. 707/433–6935 or 800/648–9922 in CA); **Napa Valley Visitors Bureau** (4260 Silverado Trail, Yountville, CA 94599, tel. 707/258–1957); **Sonoma County Visitors and Convention Bureau** (10 4th St., Santa Rosa, CA 95401, tel. 707/575–1191); **Sonoma Valley Visitors Bureau** (435 E. 1st St., Sonoma, CA 95476, tel. 707/996–1090). For information on Mendocino, contact the **Ukiah Chamber of Commerce** (495E E. Perkins St., Ukiah, CA 95482, tel. 707/462–4705).

Reservation Services

Bed & Breakfast Inns of Sonoma County (Box 51, Geyserville, CA 95476, tel. 707/433–4667).

Auberge du Soleil

Partially obscured by groves of gray-green olive trees, the "inn of the sun" is nestled into a hillside on the eastern edge of the Napa Valley. Claude Rouas, the French-born restaurateur who made San Francisco's L'Etoile the virtual headquarters of the society set, opened a restaurant on this site in 1981. "The restaurant took off immediately," recalls Rouas. "But I had always dreamed of opening an inn in the style of the country inns in.Provence, like La Colombe d'Or. I wanted something with that Provence feeling but also something that would be fitting in the Napa Valley."

The guest accommodations also had to suit the existing restaurant, a stunning structure with light-colored walls and an extended balcony entwined with grapevines. To this end, Rouas went back to the original design team—architect Sandy Walker and designer Michael Taylor. Together they built nine *maisons* (each named for a French region) on the 33-acre site below the restaurant; two others were added in 1987. The result is a low-rise blend of southwestern French and adobe-style architecture.

Each room has its own entrance and a trellis-covered veranda facing the valley. The rooms have a fresh, streamlined look with smooth, hand-glazed terra-cotta tiles on the floors and framing the fireplaces. The walls are a soothing pale stucco, and tall double doors, covered with white wooden shutters, open onto the balcony. High ceilings and air-conditioning fight the summer heat; on winter nights, however, guests may want to pull the soft leather chairs close to the fireplace for warmth.

The Auberge du Soleil is eminently suited to honeymooners, who can remain sequestered, thanks to room service. But the inn also has ample public spaces where groups can gather. The restaurant, whose reputation suffered after the departure of the original chef, is now one of the valley's most popular. Although Rouas is often on the premises, the day-to-day business of management is left to George A. Goeggel, another European, who came to the inn from the Rosewood Hotel Group.

Address: *180 Rutherford Hill Rd., Rutherford, CA 94573, tel. 707/963–1211, fax 707/963-8764.*
Accommodations: *27 rooms with bath, 21 suites.*
Amenities: *Air-conditioning; fireplace and refrigerator in rooms, whirlpool baths in 12 rooms; outdoor pool and whirlpool bath, tennis courts, tennis pro, massage room, restaurant, beauty salon, 24-hour room service, conference facilities.*
Rates: *$295–$345, suites $445–$495; Continental breakfast. AE, D, MC, V.*

The Boonville Hotel

It's hard to miss the Boonville Hotel if you drive through the quiet Anderson Valley on Route 128. The white, two-story 19th-century hotel is right on the road, its entrance only a few yards and the width of the porch from the center divider. At first glance, it would seem more appropriate to arrive on horseback and simply tether your mount to the porch railing.

The property became famous in northern California in the early 1980s, when it was operated as a restaurant that gained a fanatical following of those devoted to fresh-from-the-garden cuisine. Fame turned to notoriety, however, when the former owners disappeared amid rumors of financial scandal. John Schmitt and his wife, Jeanne Eliades, took possession in 1988. Like its predecessor, the hotel's restaurant uses fresh herbs from the garden, but the menu is less elaborate and more in keeping with that of the restaurant Schmitt owned before taking over the Boonville Hotel.

After remodeling downstairs and gutting the upper floor, Schmitt and Eliades decided to redecorate the century-old hotel with handcrafted pieces from local artisans. An abundance of bare wood and contemporary Craftsman-style furnishings makes this one of the most distinctive hotel interiors anywhere in the wine country.

All the accommodations have wood-slatted window coverings, custom tilework in the baths, and pale beige Berber-weave carpeting. Many have four-paneled doors topped with transoms that flood the rooms with natural light. The suites are especially impressive, with their vaulted ceilings and white cotton curtains suspended from simple rods. Number 1 has a bed and an armoire made of ash, a wet bar, and a sofa, chair and ottoman covered in mint-green fabric. French doors open onto the street-front porch shared with the adjacent suite, which is done in shades of mustard yellow and gray. Among the myriad details deserving of notice are the verdigris lamps and the highly idiosyncratic assortment of vases (including simple pitchers and small buckets) with fresh flower arrangements. All the guest accommodations are on the second floor, opening onto a central hallway. Despite the location, the rooms are quiet; there is very little traffic here except on Saturday morning or Sunday afternoon.

Address: *Hwy. 128 and Lambert Lane, Box 326, Boonville, CA 95415, tel. 707/895-2210.*
Accommodations: *6 double rooms with bath, 2 suites.*
Amenities: *Restaurant, off-street parking, proximity to brew pub and nearby wineries.*
Rates: *$70–$125, suites $145; Continental breakfast. MC, V.*
Restrictions: *No smoking, no pets.*

Camellia Inn

This graceful jewel is the real thing. Few California inns match the perfect appearance of this lovingly maintained Italianate Victorian set amid a garden of camellias on one side and, on the other, a tiny tiled pond in a shaded patio. Inside, it is replete with 12-foot ceilings, Oriental rugs, and a plethora of four-poster, queen-size canopy beds best entered via upholstered stepstool. The pale apricot-and-white ground-floor double parlor has twin marble fireplaces. High ceilings keep the rooms cool even during Healdsburg's warm summers, and a pool out back provides a good respite from the heat on superhot days.

The inn was built in 1869 by Ransome Powell, a tailor from Tennessee, and then appropriated as an infirmary by J.W. Seawell in 1892. Luther Burbank, a family friend of the Seawells, is responsible for many of the 50-odd varieties of camellia here. Remodeled in 1981, the inn was opened the following year by Ray and Del Lewand. Ray, who used to be in the insurance industry, oversees the property and, in his spare time, makes a limited supply of award-winning wines. Both he and Del, formerly the owner of a sportswear business, share guest-tending duties, except in the few months they spend at their Puerto Vallarta inn, when daughter Lucy (an antiques dealer) takes over.

Of the nine double rooms (most of them named for varieties of camellia), three are upstairs in the main house, two in the rear, two in a separate building that once housed the dining room, and two in the former water tower, which was remodeled in 1989. Accessible via private entrance, Firelight has a carved oak mantel atop a gas-log fireplace and a Queen Anne–style bay window. Royalty, with a private entrance of its own, is equally impressive: It has a massive bed originally from a Scottish castle and three arched windows. Tiffany is done in Bradbury & Bradbury hand-silkscreened wallpaper, with a stained-glass window in the bath. Upstairs in the main house are Moonglow, Memento (which can be opened into a suite), and Demitasse, which features a double antique iron bedstead and an antique dresser inherited from Del's Michigan grandmother. In contrast to the other rooms, which are ornate, the latter two—Tower East and Tower West—are a refreshing vision of white-washed pine, with willow furnishings.

Address: *211 North St., Healdsburg, CA 95448, tel. 707/433–8182.*
Accommodations: *9 double rooms with bath, 1 suite.*
Amenities: *Pool, off-street parking, close to shops and restaurants.*
Rates: *$70–$115; full breakfast. D, MC.*
Restrictions: *No smoking, no pets; 2-night minimum on weekends.*

Highland Ranch

The approach to the Highland Ranch is enough to make the nearby town of Philo look like an urban metropolis, but after 4 miles of narrow twists and turns, one arrives on a knoll overlooking a broad clearing. To one side, the 100-year-old ranch house is hidden in the shade of old oaks; to the left of the road, a handful of cabins look like little more than bunkhouses. Only slowly does the newcomer notice the strategically located ponds, the tennis court and small pool, the barn and riding ring in the back, and four hammocks strung beneath ancient redwood trees.

Highland Ranch didn't look this good in 1988, when George Gaines and his family took possession of what had become a rather run-down retreat. It took a mammoth effort to bury the electrical wires and perform the other feats of illusion that have resulted in a smooth-running operation. After a globe-trotting career as an international businessman, West Virginia–born Gaines came to California so that his wife, Mary Moore, could complete her studies to become an Episcopal priest. Depending on one's inclinations toward sociability, a sojourn here may be centered in the farmhouse, where guests gather in a well-worn living room lined with books, games, and memorabilia of the family's residences abroad, or in the privacy of one of the 11 cabins. These are homespun affairs, with good reading chairs and plenty of

windows through which to watch deer and jack rabbits bound across the landscape.

This is not a turn-down-service, basket-of-amenities type of place but one where travelers can get some exercise and fresh air, good food, and a sense of peace so pervasive it might unnerve a big-city dweller. After breakfast, guests may take a short or an all-day horseback ride or hike, go clay-pigeon shooting or fishing; at the end of the day, they may enjoy the sunset on their small private decks. Given the natural beauty of the setting, few visitors care that the walls of their cabin are fir plywood, the floors are Douglas-fir plank with only sparse carpeting, or that decoration consists of family collections of china or framed paintings—or even an old nonfunctioning camel horn that Gaines used to toot whenever he closed a particularly good deal.

Address: *Philo, CA 95466, tel. 707/895-3600, fax 707/895-3702.*
Accommodations: *11 cabins with bath.*
Amenities: *Fireplace, deck, phone in rooms; pool, tennis court (racquets and balls provided), fishing, hiking, clay-pigeon shooting, cribs available.*
Rates: *$150 per person, including all meals, beverages, and activities. No credit cards.*
Restrictions: *No pets; 2-night minimum.*

Kenwood Inn

Terry and Roseann Grimm deserve an award for transforming a ramshackle antiques shop into a romantic Italian-style retreat facing the vineyards that lie on the hillsides across Highway 12. The two-lane road, in fact, is the biggest drawback to the Kenwood Inn, although there is little traffic noise after dark. This inn is separated from the road by a large flagstone patio, a swimming pool, and extensive grounds landscaped with dozens of rose bushes, as well as persimmon, fig, apple, and—most appropriately—olive trees.

The inn's most seductive features lie in the lavish attention to detail, from the down mattresses covered with Egyptian-cotton sheets to the aromatic sprigs of fresh-from-the-garden herbs used to garnish breakfast dishes. Although there is no regular food service beyond the morning meal, guests are welcome to make special requests, whether it's a late-afternoon platter of fruits and cheeses or a specially catered dinner for private parties. Advance notice for the latter is, of course, required.

Room Three, decorated in leafy green and lush burgundy, has a queen-size bed and a separate living room with paisley wallpaper and moss-color draperies. It also has a private patio and garden entrance and is separated from the other two ground-floor accommodations by a large living room furnished simply with glass-and-wrought-iron console tables along the walls, antique ebony straight-back chairs imported from Mozambique, and two overstuffed sofas, upholstered in Italian prints, flanking the fireplace. Room Six, located upstairs, claims the most privacy and the best view. A four-poster king-size bed is canopied in fabrics of mango, burgundy, and black.

Innkeeper Laurance van Valkenburg, who once worked for a large chain hotel in the Bay Area, clearly relishes the opportunity to meet guests on a more intimate basis. He prides himself on embellishing the guest rooms with flowers picked from the gardens. Breakfast may consist of a plate of fresh fruits, a slice of rock-shrimp quiche, and a poached egg served on a square of polenta and drizzled with pesto. Other specialties del villa include blintzes and crepes.

Address: *10400 Sonoma Hwy., Kenwood, CA 95442, tel. 707/833-1293.*
Accommodations: *2 rooms with bath, 2 suites.*
Amenities: *Fireplaces, feather mattresses, down comforters and pillows; pool, off-street parking.*
Rates: *$125–$225; full breakfast. MC, V.*
Restrictions: *No smoking, no pets; 2-night minimum on weekends.*

Larkmead

Set back in regal seclusion off a country lane, this 1919 inn could pass for a winemaker's residence. In fact, it was built as a farmhouse on the property that once encompassed the adjacent Hanns Kornell Sparkling Wines estate. In the 1880s, the winery was owned by Lillie Hitchcock Coit, the pioneer San Franciscan whose bequest to the city led to the erection of an observation tower on Telegraph Hill now known as Coit Tower. The property eventually came into the hands of the Italian-Swiss Salmina family, and the house was constructed by one of the Salmina sons for his bride. It was bought in 1978 by an East Bay couple, Gene and Joan Garbarino—he a dentist and she a former grade-school teacher—who transformed the place into a residential-style inn.

Larkmead has both Victorian and Palladian elements, the latter evident in such details as the second-floor window arranged directly above the entryway. One enters through an octagonal, wisteria-covered loggia flanked by two wings; the living quarters were established on the second floor, typical of structures built by Italian-Swiss families who wanted to enjoy afternoon breezes while gazing out over their surrounding vineyards.

The house is wonderfully quiet; even on busy summer weekends, traffic moves slowly on Larkmead Lane.

Sheltered by magnolia, cypress, and sycamore trees, the inn has lawns for strolling outdoors, and Persian carpets and favorite family paintings in the living room. Joan, who tends to her guests on weekends (a manager takes over during the slower, midweek days), is a fastidious hostess who holds nothing back, not even the Imari china or the Grand Baroque silver used for breakfast in the formal dining room. In fact, the entire inn is somewhat stiff, in the manner of a favorite great-aunt's home, where the bedroom furnishings match almost too well. Four rooms, all named for Napa Valley varietals, have their idiosyncracies, however: Chenin Blanc is swathed in green-and-white floral fabric, right down to the wonderful chaise longue; Chablis has an enclosed porch; Chardonnay is evocative of the art-deco rage; and Beaujolais looks out over the loggia to the vineyards.

Address: *1102 Larkmead La., Calistoga, CA 94515, tel. 707/942-5360.*
Accommodations: *Four double rooms with bath.*
Amenities: *Air-conditioning, fireplace in living room, afternoon wine and cheese, off-street parking.*
Rates: *$110–$145; Continental breakfast. No credit cards.*
Restrictions: *No pets, but exceptions may be made for small dogs.*

Madrona Manor

Afraction of its former size, this estate dates from 1881, when San Franciscan John Paxton commissioned a mansion to be built on 240 acres on the outskirts of Healdsburg. To the Eastlake-style architecture he added gingerbread flourishes, steeply pitched dormers, gables, a mansard roof, and a wraparound porch. He filled it with massive furniture; many pieces, including a rosewood square grand piano, are still in use.

Today the estate comprises an eight-acre wooded knoll. In 1981 it was bought by Carol and John Muir, who had been living in Saudi Arabia. After redecorating the Carpenter Gothic carriage house, they added four third-floor guest rooms in the main house for a total of nine. Instead of duplicating the turn-of-the-century California decor of the lower floors, they chose Portuguese reproductions. Still, the newer rooms are more modern in tone than the original five. The bedroom suite in number 203 is American Victorian Renaissance, with circular mask crests on both the chest and the double bedstead. The only guests who might feel crowded are those in the first-floor room, where more than one visitor has reported seeing a ghost during the night.

Less successful are the accommodations in the outbuildings, which lack the elegance of the original rooms. The Meadow Wood Complex, with its very private bedroom and deck, is headquarters for travelers with children and dogs.

The Garden Suite has recently been redecorated with rattan furniture and a marble fireplace. Because of its seclusion beyond the garden, it is third in popularity only to the veranda rooms. The carriage house, with its massive Nepalese hand-carved rosewood door, houses eight rooms, as well as the new Suite 400, which has contemporary French furnishings and a Grecian marble bathroom. The whirlpool bath has shutters that open onto the sitting room, facing the fireplace.

Herbs and some vegetables from the inn's extensive gardens find their way to the dinner menu at Madrona Manor. Local fish, poultry, and game are often smoked on the premises, and the marmalade at breakfast is made from mandarin oranges picked from several trees on the property.

Address: *1001 Westside Rd., Healdsburg, CA 95448, tel. 707/433-4231 or 800/258-4003.*
Accommodations: *18 double rooms with bath, 3 suites.*
Amenities: *Air-conditioning; fireplace in 18 rooms; restaurant, pool.*
Rates: *$215–$265, suites $265–$290, including full breakfast and, on weekends, dinner. AE, D, MC, V.*
Restrictions: *Smoking outdoors only.*

Beltane Ranch

Beltane Ranch is a century-old farmhouse that commands sweeping views of the Sonoma Valley vineyards. Innkeeper Rosemary Wood, whose family has owned the surrounding ranch for the past 55 years, converted the property into an inn back in 1981.

The two-story wraparound balcony, furnished with hammocks, a wooden swing, and plenty of chairs and tables, is an ideal spot for relaxing after a long day outdoors. Two of the three upstairs rooms extend the entire width of the building, with both front and back access to the porch. Ceiling fans, floral fabrics, comfortable reading chairs, and window shutters remain from the days when this was a cherished family retreat. Some furnishings, including a massive carved-wood marble-top dressing table, are antiques. The somewhat drab bathrooms are offset by cozy dressing areas. Despite a wood-burning stove and plenty of reading material, the public rooms are undistinguished. The inn's greatest glory is its gardens, which are occasionally the scene of various charity fund-raisers.

Address: *11775 Sonoma Hwy., Box 395, Glen Ellen, CA, 95442, tel. 707/996-6501.*
Accommodations: *2 double rooms with bath, 2 suites.*
Amenities: *Private hiking trails, horseshoes, tennis court, off-street parking.*
Rates: *$95–$120; full breakfast. Personal checks accepted.*
Restrictions: *Smoking outside only.*

Brannan Cottage Inn

The town of Calistoga grew up around Samuel Brannan's Calistoga Hot Spring Resort, and this is the last remaining cottage on the original site. Constructed in 1860, the main building has five arches, a wide wraparound porch, and scalloped ridge-cresting.

The four ground-floor rooms feature private entrances off the porch, which fronts a grassy garden. All the rooms have individual hand-painted floral stencil designs on the upper walls; the pastel colors are echoed in the decor, which includes simple pine tables and dressers, wicker chairs, ceiling fans, and lace curtains. The suites, located on the upper floor of a structure in the back, are cramped in comparison but are suitable for romantic getaways.

The white-and-green inn is owned by three single people, former college buddies who moved up in 1991 from Marin County. Mary Jacobson had a travel agency; Earle Mills was in the restaurant and residential-care fields; and Rick Hernandez is a professional pianist.

Address: *100 Wapoo Ave., Calistoga, CA 94515, tel. 707/942-4200.*
Accommodations: *4 double rooms with bath, 2 suites.*
Amenities: *Ceiling fans in rooms; central air-conditioning, extra bed available, afternoon wine and cheese, off-street parking.*
Rates: *$125, suites $145; full breakfast. MC, V.*
Restrictions: *No smoking inside, no pets.*

Campbell Ranch Inn

Although this country property doesn't really feel like a ranch, the Campbell Ranch Inn does deliver all one might expect in terms of fresh air, expansive vistas, and open sky. The 35-acre property is headquartered at a 4,500-square-foot ranch house, built in the late 1960s in typical northern California style. It was bought in 1986 by Jerry and Mary Jane Campbell, who migrated west—separately—meeting in California, marrying in 1958, and raising a family. Now that the kids are grown, Mary Jane spends a lot of time putting up fruit and tending her impressive garden.

The residential-style rooms are nothing really special: clean and pastel with chenille bedcovers and lots of Jerry's excellent photographs prominently displayed. Three rooms are upstairs in the main house; a fourth on a lower level, is more private. Located 4 miles from Lake Sonoma and 3 miles from the Russian River, the ranch is better suited to active people than to those who like to be in the thick of things.

Address: *1475 Canyon Rd., Geyserville, CA 95441, tel. 707/857-3476.*
Accommodations: *4 double rooms with bath, 1 suite.*
Amenities: *Fireplace in 2 rooms; off-street parking, pool, outdoor spa, tennis court, horseshoes, Ping-Pong, bicycles.*
Rates: *$100–$145; full breakfast. MC, V.*
Restrictions: *No smoking indoors; 2-night minimum on weekends.*

Cross Roads Inn

A better view of the area could be found only on a hot-air-balloon tour of the valley. It's no wonder that the most requested accommodations are the Puddle Duck Room, where from the corner whirlpool bath one can take in views of both the valley and the hillside in back. Named for Beatrix Potter characters, all the extra large rooms (such as the one with the king-size, pine four-poster bed Sam and Nancy Scott commissioned for the house) are decorated with pastel colors, lace tablecloths, delicate floral wallpaper, and mahogany, cherry, or pine furniture. The smallest and most private room is the Mrs. Ribby Room, the only guest room that's on the lower floor.

Breakfast can be taken privately or on the spacious decks. Guests can gather later in the living room, where a circular glass fireplace warms the room on chilly evenings.

Address: *6380 Silverado Trail, Napa, CA 94558, tel. 707/944-0646.*
Accommodations: *3 double rooms with bath.*
Amenities: *Whirlpool bath, ceiling fan in 1 room; afternoon and evening refreshments, hiking trails.*
Rates: *$175–$200; full breakfast. MC, V.*
Restrictions: *No smoking; 2-night minimum on weekends and holidays.*

El Dorado Hotel

The pale stucco, white-trimmed adobe El Dorado was built in 1843 by Don Salvador Vallejo, a brother of the legendary Mexican general who laid out the historic Sonoma plaza, but the current interior of this landmark structure bears little resemblance to the original. There is nothing cozy about this inn, which is professionally run by the same company that owns Auberge du Soleil in the Napa Valley.

The open, airy feel of the ground floor—which houses an Italian restaurant and a clothing boutique—is unfortunately lost on the second floor, where most of the rooms are located. Though small, each has a little balcony overlooking either an inner courtyard or the historic town square. Rather than clutter the rooms with knickknacks, the owners have made the most of the limited space by decorating with a light hand. A typical room, done in aqua and peach, has a simple, metal-frame four-poster bed flanked by matching verdigris reading lamps, woven rugs on bare Mexican paver floors, a large willow-framed mirror, and a couple of rattan chairs. The baths and closets are tiny.

Address: *405 1st St. W, Sonoma, CA 95476, tel. 707/996–3030, fax 707/996–3148.*
Accommodations: *27 double rooms with bath.*
Amenities: *Phone, TV, balcony in rooms; restaurant, pool.*
Rates: *$110–$140; Continental breakfast. AE, MC, V.*
Restrictions: *No smoking in rooms.*

The Gaige House

The Gaige House is not the most stunningly furnished bed-and-breakfast in the wine country. Most of the pieces are oak or mahogany reproductions, but what it lacks in luxury the house makes up for in spacious accommodations and an excellent location. Built during the 1890s, the Italianate Queen Anne graces the tree-lined main street of one of Sonoma's most endearing villages. The former estate of author Jack London sits nearby.

After languishing as a boardinghouse and a school, the Gaige House was restored in 1980 by the previous innkeepers. Steve Salvo, a former agricultural researcher in the Central Valley, moved here with his wife, Michol, five years ago. In 1991, they added a room in the Carriage House in the back of the 1.2-acre property, which encompasses a pool and a huge oak-shaded deck overlooking Calabezas Creek. Afternoon wine is served in the parlor amid the Salvos' interesting art collection, which includes a carousel horse carved during the 1920s and a Bakatiara rug.

Address: *13540 Arnold Dr., Glen Ellen, CA 95442, tel. 707/935–0237.*
Accommodations: *9 double rooms with bath.*
Amenities: *Fireplace in 3 rooms; afternoon refreshments, off-street parking, pool, bicycle rentals.*
Rates: *$90–$160; full breakfast. AE, MC, V.*
Restrictions: *Smoking outside only; 2-night minimum Sat. and holidays.*

Healdsburg Inn on the Plaza

Facing Healdsburg Plaza, a mini-version of Sonoma's historic square, the Inn on the Plaza occupies the two upper floors of a turn-of-the-century Victorian that once housed the local Wells Fargo Bank. Natural light streams in from vaulted skylights, delineating a multitude of arches, corbels, and turn-of-the-century chandeliers. In the second-floor all-weather solarium, guests can sip coffee and socialize in an indoor-garden setting. It's one of many idiosyncratic touches provided by innkeeper Ginny Jenkins, who divides her time between this inn and another in Napa.

The rooms, all of which open onto a large zigzag hallway, are larger than average but something of a hodgepodge. Four of them boast Eastlake Victorian antiques, oak rockers and settees, and claw-foot tubs with pedestal sinks in the baths. The color scheme is limited largely to pastels, except in the New Orleans–inspired Romance, which has paisley prints. The most unusual room, Early Light, with a huge slanted window that substitutes for most of one wall on the east side, was originally Healdsburg's first photography studio.

Address: *110 Matheson St., Healdsburg, CA 95448, tel. 707/433-6991.*
Accommodations: *7 double rooms with bath, 1 suite.*
Amenities: *Solarium.*
Rates: *$135–$150, suites $150; full breakfast. MC, V.*
Restrictions: *Smoking on roof garden only, no pets.*

Hope-Merrill House

The north Sonoma town of Geyserville has at least two things going for it: location and this fastidiously restored Eastlake Stick-style manse. Bob and Rosalie Hope had been collecting Victoriana long before they moved here to open a pair of inns—the 1904 Queen Anne cottage (now the Hope-Bosworth House) and the older house across the street, named for J.P. Merrill, the original resident. The latter, built during the 1880s, offered ample space, including a sitting room large enough to accommodate a five-piece Eastlake walnut parlor set.

In a building that has won recognition from the National Trust for Historic Preservation for outstanding restoration, it is not surprising to find the original Lincrusta Walton wainscoting, Bradbury & Bradbury silkscreen wallpapers, striped chaise longues, wicker settees, and other Victorian features. Rosalie and Bob, whose hospitality befits his North Carolina drawl, have recently opened a third inn in Mexico.

Address: *21253 Geyserville Ave., Box 42, Geyserville, CA 95441, tel. 707/857-3356 or 800/825-4233.*
Accommodations: *7 double rooms with bath.*
Amenities: *Fireplace in 3 rooms, whirlpool bath in 2 rooms; outdoor pool, gazebo.*
Rates: *$95–$125; full breakfast. AE, MC, V.*
Restrictions: *Smoking outside only, no pets; 2-night minimum on weekends, 3-night minimum on holidays Apr.–Dec.*

Magnolia Hotel

If the rooms in this inn are on the small side, write it off to authenticity. The three-part inn was built of brick and fieldstone in 1873. Originally a hotel, it served as a bordello, a bastion of bootlegging, and a 4-H Club meeting place before being restored during the late 1960s. Bruce and Bonnie Locken took it over in 1977, abandoning their careers as general manager of San Francisco's Clift Hotel and a professional dietitian, respectively, and bringing aboard their sons Craig and Lars.

The seven rooms in the main building are decorated similarly: Bedstands are brass and/or iron, windows are hung with pink organdy curtains, and occasional tables are topped with marble. The rooms in

the Garden Court and Carriage House, which were remodeled a decade ago, are more spacious, especially Camellia, which has bay windows and a private entrance. Connected by open-air walkways, the ivy-covered buildings are flanked by vineyards and are only a block away from the shops and restaurants of tiny Yountville.

Address: *6529 Yount St., Drawer M, Yountville, CA 94599, tel. 707/944–2056.*
Accommodations: *11 double rooms with bath, 1 suite.*
Amenities: *Air-conditioning; gas-log fireplace in 5 rooms; wine cellar, pool, outdoor hot tub.*
Rates: *$89–$169; full breakfast. Personal checks or cash only.*
Restrictions: *No smoking, no pets.*

Mount View Hotel

Built in 1917 and now a National Historic Landmark, this two-story hotel with its pervasive art-deco motif is the kind of place one either loves or hates. Fans of the sensuous lines of the period will enjoy being surrounded by such matched furnishings as burled veneer chests and pairs of gilded bedside lamps, boudoir chairs, and almost campy ceiling fixtures; some of the pieces, such as a fold-out dressing table with a mirrored surface, are purely decorative. In 1992, the hotel was recarpeted and repainted, and a European-style spa is promised for spring 1993.

The glamour of the 1930s and 1940s is echoed in the suites named for celluloid stars of the period, such as Carole Lombard and Tom Mix. The

Lily Coit Suite, all eggshell-blue walls with lots of fringe and lace surrounding the windows, shares a balcony overlooking the town's main street with the Presidential Suite, a more masculine effort in tones of peach and gray. The ground-floor rooms flanking an inner courtyard are quietest.

Address: *1457 Lincoln Ave., Calistoga, CA 94515, tel. 707/942–6877, fax 707/942–6904.*
Accommodations: *26 double rooms with bath, 8 suites.*
Amenities: *Air-conditioning, phone, TV in rooms; pool, hot tub, restaurant, lounge.*
Rates: *$70–$95, suites $115–$125; Continental breakfast. D, MC, V.*
Restrictions: *Smoking outdoors only, no pets.*

Quail Mountain

The private road off Highway 29 winds up, up, and up through a forest of redwood, Douglas fir, madrona, and oak trees to a site 300 feet above the valley floor. Wild quail scurry about, disappearing into wild lilac, ferns, berry bushes, and wildflowers. Don and Alma Swiers chose this 23-acre parcel in 1980 and opened their inn in 1984, after long careers in education and the oil industry, respectively.

The two smaller accommodations feature small semiprivate decks facing the forested slopes above the inn, but the best choice is the Fern Room, a minisuite with a small sun room facing the valley. The decor is unstudied country-style, with handmade quilts set atop white linen duvets. Furnishings are minimal: an attractive pine bureau, two bedside tables, and a rocking chair.

Afternoon wine and cheese and morning meals are served in the brick-floored solarium. The enormous breakfasts can range from a dish of pureed rhubarb (home-grown) topped with crème fraîche to a colossal apple pancake.

Address: *4455 N. St. Helena Hwy., Calistoga, CA 94515, tel. 707/942–0315 or 707/942–0316.*
Accommodations: *3 double rooms with bath.*
Amenities: *Afternoon wine, pool, hot tub.*
Rates: *$90–$110; full breakfast. MC, V.*
Restrictions: *Smoking outside only; 2-night minimum on weekends.*

Sonoma Hotel

Few American town squares evoke a sense of place and history as well as the plaza in the heart of old Sonoma. Flanked by old adobes and false-front buildings, the square was laid out in 1835 by General Mariano Vallejo. Many of the buildings have been restored and converted into restaurants, shops, and hotels, the most historic of which is the Sonoma Hotel.

An old-fashioned feeling pervades this three-story, century-old adobe structure (the high-gabled top floor was added around 1880). Only when you leave the hotel do you realize that you are in the 1990s, not the 1890s.

There are challenges to furnishing a hotel without a single reproduction—mattresses had to be custommade to fit the oddly shaped beds. Turn-of-the-century English and French bedroom sets furnish most of the accommodations; almost all have such quaint flourishes as lace curtains and chenille bedcovers. The ground-floor lounge is a favorite gathering spot for locals.

Address: *110 W. Spain St., Sonoma, CA 95476, tel. 707/996-2996.*
Accommodations: *5 double rooms with bath, 12 double rooms share 3 baths.*
Amenities: *Restaurant, bar.*
Rates: *$62–$105; Continental breakfast. AE, MC, V.*
Restrictions: *2-night minimum on holidays.*

Thistle Dew Inn

Steps away from historic Sonoma Square, this inn is actually two in one, with accommodations in both the main house, built in 1869, and in a 1905 cottage relocated to these grounds from three blocks away. Most of the Arts and Crafts–style furniture, original to the house, is a suitable match for the relatively simple design of the buildings. The six-leaf dining-room table and matching sideboards, for instance, are Gustav Stickley creations. There are also gallery-quality pieces of Mission furniture, such as the chest of drawers signed by Charles Limbert. In the cottage, where four rooms share a parlor, Navajo rugs and Amish quilts complement the early 1900s decor. The Rose Garden and the Cornflower rooms in the main house have walls that were sponge-painted in their namesake colors vividly enough to keep some guests awake at night.

After Larry and Norma Barnett bought the inn in 1990, Norma, a practicing psychologist, redecorated all of the guest rooms; Larry tends the kitchen and the English-style garden that borders the inn.

Address: *171 W. Spain St., Sonoma, CA 95476, tel. 707/938-2909.*
Accommodations: *6 double rooms with bath.*
Amenities: *Air-conditioning, afternoon refreshments, Jacuzzi, bicycles, access to local health club.*
Rates: *$80–$120; full breakfast. AE, MC, V.*
Restrictions: *Smoking outside only.*

Vintners Inn

In a few years, this 44-room country inn may acquire the patina of an established *auberge* in the south of France. When it opened in 1981, however, it stood out like a cactus in a vineyard. Surrounded by mostly open land, the Vintners Inn consists of four two-story Mediterranean-style villas, topped with red-tiled roofs and set off with arched windows, patios, walkways, and fountains. Clever landscaping makes the nearby freeway much less noticeable.

The decor consists of homey floral-print wallpapers and some antique furnishings, including turn-of-the-century pine chests, desks, and armoires in a French-country style. The suites are huge, and the upstairs corner rooms feature vaulted ceilings and windows on two sides. Instead of closets, there are hanging rods in the dressing room. Buffet breakfast is served in a casual dining room. California cuisine is available at the adjacent John Ash & Co., one of the county's top restaurants.

Address: *4250 Barnes Rd., Santa Rosa, CA 95403, tel. 707/575-7350 or 800/421-2584 in CA; fax 707/575-1426.*
Accommodations: *39 double rooms with bath, 5 suites.*
Amenities: *TV, radio, phone in rooms, fireplace in 18 rooms, refrigerator in suites; conference facilities, outdoor hot tub.*
Rates: *$128–$185; Continental breakfast. DC, MC, V.*
Restrictions: *2-night minimum on weekends Mar. 15–Oct. 31.*

North Coast and Redwood Country

North Coast and Redwood Country
Including Mendocino and Eureka

*The northwestern corner of California lies in splendid
isolation. This land of scenic beauty and serene majesty—
some 400 miles south to north, 50 east to west—has long
lured the independent thinker, the artist, and occasionally
the roadside entrepreneur.*

*California's magical Highway 1 hugs the coast until, about
50 miles north of Mendocino, it turns east, climbs over the
Coast Range, connects with U.S. 101, and meanders
through the redwoods to the Oregon border. Along the way
it passes deep fern-filled gulches where streams and
waterfalls flow, golden rolling hills dotted with oak trees,
farms and sheep ranches, and the quaint fishing villages of
Noyo, Albion, and Elk—century-old hole-in-the-wall ports
where steamers navigated craggy inlets to pick up loads of
lumber.*

*The redwoods, which once covered the hillsides, lured New
Englanders here a century ago. The new settlers built
houses just like the ones they had left back home, hence the
clapboard architecture of most of the towns. They also
brought the region a sense of community that's difficult to
find in other, more urban parts of California. And now the
fiercest protectors of the redwood forests are descendants of
the immigrants who came to fell the trees.*

*It takes time to explore the North Coast, not only because
the roads are narrow, twisty, and slow but also because so
many sights require you to get out of your car and walk.
But the region is worth exploring at leisure. Step up to
a headland above a cove and watch the waves crash over the
rocks. Take in the wildness of the ocean; maybe you'll be
lucky enough to spot a whale in the distance, sounding and
spouting. Take a walk among the redwoods and savor the*

silence, the scent of the flowers, the sweetness of the wood, the near-darkness created by the dense canopy of trees.

The shopkeepers, gallery owners, and restaurateurs along the North Coast are always ready to chat. Ask them what lured them to this isolated part of California, and most will tell you it's the stunning beauty of the coast and the freedom of the isolation, the chance to be part of a community that shares their values. The world they've created is rich for the visitor in both natural beauty and man-made luxuries. Good accommodations in historic bed-and-breakfast inns, outstanding cuisine made from superb local ingredients, and recreation and relaxation await you.

Places to Go, Sights to See

California Western Railroad's Skunk Trains (Fort Bragg, tel. 707/964–6371) offer full- and half-day scenic excursions through the redwood forest to Willits.

Fort Ross State Historic Park (12 mi north of Jenner on Hwy. 1, tel. 707/847–3286) is a reconstruction of the outpost founded in 1812 by Russian seal and otter hunters from Alaska. The visitor center has interpretive exhibits; there is also a Russian chapel, battlements, and picnic facilities.

Kruse Rhododendron State Reserve (10 mi north of Fort Ross on Hwy. 1, tel. 707/847–3221) provides 5 miles of hiking trails among 1,317 acres of wild pink flowering rhododendrons, redwood forest, and bridges over fern-filled canyons. The flowers are at their peak from April through June.

Mendocino, the largest of the villages along the coast, perches on headlands with spectacular ocean views. If the frame buildings of this former lumber port, dating from 1852, look familiar, it's because so many New England–set movies have been shot here. Now a thriving artists' colony, Mendocino hosts galleries, boutiques, and such unusual shops as Wind and Weather (weather instruments) and Out of this World (astronomical items). The Mendocino Arts Center (tel. 707/937–5791) offers classes year-round. The town sponsors a summer arts fair, a music festival, and two performing-arts companies. You get good views (and good picnicking) in Mendocino Headlands State Park, which surrounds the town.

Mendocino Coast Botanical Gardens (south of Fort Bragg, tel. 707/964–4352) covers 47 acres and includes heather, perennials, succulents, ivies, roses, camellias, wildflowers, and dwarf rhododendrons.

Point Arena Lighthouse and Museum (1 mi south of Point Arena, tel. 707/882–2777) is a former whaling station and lumber port. The lighthouse, built in 1870, has been automated; it now contains a museum of lighthouse history.

Redwoods. Redwoods once covered the hillsides above the Pacific from San Francisco all the way north to the Oregon border. Most of the trees have been logged, but a few outstanding groves remain preserved in state parks and in the Redwood National Park. *Armstrong Redwoods State Reserve* (tel. 707/869–2015), near Guerneville, is a 752-acre virgin-redwood grove with hiking trails and picnic facilities. *Humboldt Redwoods State Park* (tel. 707/946–2311), 45 miles south of Eureka on U.S. 101, contains the largest stand of virgin redwoods in the world; Avenue of the Giants, a 33-miles scenic highway; a visitor center and picnic areas; and the Founder's Trail in Rockefeller Forest, which leads to Founder's Tree, one of the tallest of the trees. *Richardson Grove State Park* (tel. 707/247–3318), south of Garberville on U.S. 101, is a 1,000-acre grove of big trees; the favorite scenic walks there are Lookout Trail and Tourney Trail.

Roadside attractions are part of the redwood experience. The *Drive-Thru Tree* at Myers Flat (tel. 707/943–3154) has a base with a diameter of 21 feet, wide enough for a car to drive through. Scotia is the home of *Pacific Lumber Company*, the world's largest redwood lumber mill; a museum displays tools, equipment, and photographs of early logging operations and provides free passes for a tour of the mill. At *Trees of Mystery* (tel. 707/482–5613), near Klamath, a giant statue of Paul Bunyan invites visitors to view unusual redwood formations, as well as a large collection of Native American artifacts in a free museum.

State Parks. Much of the coast up through Sonoma and Mendocino counties belongs to California state parks. Two of the largest are *Sonoma Coast State Beach*, a 10-mile stretch from the mouth of the Russian River south to Bodega Bay, and *Salt Point State Park*, a 6,000-acre beach lover's paradise of wave-sculpted shoreline. Farther north, near Mendocino, *Russian Gulch State Park* offers redwoods, fern glens, and a waterfall; *Westport Union Landing Beach* has beautiful picnic sites.

Victoriana. In *Eureka's Old Town*—an ongoing project to preserve the city's many splendid Victorian buildings, the most striking of which is the Carson Mansion—visitors will find art galleries, boutiques, and antiques and specialty stores, as well as horse-drawn carriage rides. *Ferndale*, an architecturally authentic Victorian village, has been designated a state historic landmark. The town consists of colorful Victorians; the ones along Main Street have been converted into shops, restaurants, and inns. You can get a walking-tour map from the Chamber of Commerce (tel. 707/786–4477).

Restaurants

Several of the inns described here have exceptional restaurants. In addition, the following are recommended: **Cafe Beaujolais** (tel. 707/937–5614) in

Mendocino may be the best restaurant in this part of California. Owner Margaret Fox's innovative breads and confections are famous. **Carter House** (tel. 707/445-1390) in Eureka has gained a reputation for sophisticated cuisine using many ingredients from the hotel's own gardens. The **Samoa Cookhouse** (tel. 707/442-1659), on the Samoa Peninsula, across Humboldt Bay from Eureka, is the last surviving lumber-camp cookhouse in the West and serves up hearty meals family-style at long tables. The two cozy Victorian dining rooms at **The Old Milano Hotel & Restaurant** (tel. 707/884-3256), just north of Gualala on the southern Mendocino coastline, offer creative California cuisine.

Tourist Information

Redwood Empire Association (785 Market St., San Francisco, CA 94103, tel. 415/543-8334); **Eureka/Humboldt County Convention and Visitors Bureau** (1034 2nd St., Eureka, CA 95501, tel. 800/346-3482, 800/338-7352 in CA); **Russian River Visitors Information Center** (14034 Armstrong Woods Rd., Guerneville, CA 95446, tel. 707/869-9009).

Reservation Services

Bed-and-Breakfast Innkeepers of Northern California (Box 7150, Chico, CA 95927, tel. 800/284-4667); **Bed-and-Breakfast International** (Box 282910, San Francisco, CA 94128, tel. 800/872-4500, 415/696-1690 outside the U.S.); **Mendocino Coast Innkeepers Association** (Box 1141, Mendocino, CA 95460, tel. 707/964-0640 or 800/382-7244).

Applewood: An Estate Inn

Jay Gatsby would feel right at home at this country inn surrounded by forests of giant redwoods in the heart of the Russian River resort area. The creation of two refugees from the Bay Area, Jim Caron and Darryl Notter, Applewood occupies a Mission Revival home built in 1922 by the flamboyant financier Ralph Belden. As you sit in the inn's brightly lit solarium sipping wine, it's possible to imagine the flapper-era parties that went on here: beautiful people, enchanting music, bootleg booze.

Jim and Darryl discovered the house while they were visiting the Russian River on vacation. "The area had long been a popular vacation spot for people from the Bay Area, including my family," Jim explains. "But it had become run-down by the 1960s. One of our goals with the Estate is to restore the former elegance."

At the heart of the inn, on the main floor, are the three connecting common rooms. The bright solarium, with windows on three sides and a full-width skylight, makes a natural gathering place for guests, who enjoy curling up on the huge green-and-white rattan sofas. On cold afternoons a fireplace provides a crackling counterpoint to the room's garden ambience. The living room feels more subdued; with burgundy carpet, a heavy-beamed ceiling, and the back of the two-sided

great stone fireplace, it evokes the feeling of a country lodge. Through a set of double doors lies the bright dining room; from here, a pair of French doors open onto the pool area.

Guest rooms—located on the main floor and on a lower level (where there's a small library for guests)—are decorated in easy-to-take pastels and furnished with comfort and understated elegance. They all boast sitting areas and plenty of light and are variously furnished with overstuffed love seats, boudoir chairs, chaise longues, and small desks.

The innkeepers pride themselves on their food. Both are accomplished cooks, Jim having learned "at my mother's knee" and Darryl at a cooking school in Bangkok. The fare tends more toward the hearty than the nouveau—eggs Florentine in the morning, steak or leg of lamb at dinner.

Address: *13555 Hwy. 116 (near Guerneville), Pocket Canyon, CA 95446, tel. 707/869-9093.*
Accommodations: *10 double rooms with bath.*
Amenities: *Phone and cable TV in rooms; heated swimming pool, outdoor hot tub.*
Rates: *$115–$185; full breakfast. AE, D, MC, V. Dinner about $30.*
Restrictions: *No smoking, no pets; 2-night minimum on weekends.*

Gingerbread Mansion

The Gingerbread Mansion is a tourist attraction in and of itself; visitors are constantly making the detour from U.S. 101 to the Victorian village of Ferndale so they can take a picture of its bright-orange-and-yellow exterior and its flower-filled English gardens. The Gingerbread, with its spindle roof ridges and icicled eaves, its bay windows and shingled turret, must be one of the most photographed buildings in California. Pity those who never get inside to enjoy the whimsical fantasy rooms and the warm hospitality of innkeeper Ken Torbert and his staff.

The Gingerbread Mansion has served many different purposes in the years since 1899, when it was built as a doctor's residence. A 1920s expansion converted the Queen Anne–Eastlake mansion into a hospital. Over the years it turned into a rest home and later an American Legion hall; when Ken purchased it in 1981, it had become an apartment house. "Alice's experiences in Wonderland guided my renovating ideas," he explains. Thus the inn is full of surprises—pleasant ones, such as rooms with mirrors for people of all heights, and a pair of claw-foot tubs set toe to toe on a white-fenced platform.

The bathrooms are a special delight. The Fountain Suite bath has side-by-side claw-foot tubs facing a mirrored wall in which the fire in the Franklin stove can be seen flickering. The claw-foot tub on a platform in the Rose Suite bathroom is surrounded by floral wallpaper under a mirrored ceiling; bathing there gives you the feeling of being in a garden. The actual gardens are Ken's pride and joy. Narrow brick paths meander through sculptured boxwood and past blossoming rhododendrons, camellias, and azaleas in winter, and fancy fuchsias throughout the summer and fall.

There are thoughtful surprises, too. Rooms are straightened, the lamps and shades adjusted at turndown each evening. Umbrellas stay at the ready for protection when it rains. Morning coffee is prepared to order for each guest before breakfast, which is served at two large tables in the dining room. This is the time for conversation over a variety of home-baked breads, a selection of unusual local cheeses, and fruit.

Address: *400 Berding St., Box 40, Ferndale, CA 95536, tel. 707/786–4000.*
Accommodations: *9 double rooms with bath.*
Amenities: *Franklin stove in 3 rooms; afternoon refreshments, robes, guest refrigerator, bicycles.*
Rates: *$70–$175; Continental breakfast. AE, MC, V.*
Restrictions: *Smoking outside only, no pets; 2-night minimum on weekends and holidays.*

Harbor House

Some of the guests who arrive at Harbor House never want to leave. Some don't: Innkeepers Helen and Dean Turner fell in love with Harbor House and purchased it in 1985.

Those who love the ever-changing character of the sea find themselves mesmerized by the view from this country inn perched right on the edge of the coast. If you have booked one of the inn's four red-and-white cottages, you'll be able to savor the view from your own furnished deck. In most of the rooms you can warm yourself by a fireplace while studying the sea. If you want to see the ocean close up, you need only descend the steep path to the inn's private beach; although swimming might be dangerous, this is a good place for a picnic.

Harbor House's magnificent setting is just one of its attractions. The rustic-elegant lodge dates from 1916, when it was built as an executive residence for the Goodyear Redwood Lumber Company, which shipped the lumber it logged out of the cove below. The main building—an enlarged version of the Home of Redwood, designed by Louis Christian Mullgardt for the 1915 Panama-Pacific Exposition in San Francisco—was constructed entirely of virgin redwood.

The living room is a stunning example of the carpenter's craft. The floors, walls, and vaulted ceilings are made of old-growth redwood; they were rubbed with beeswax, a natural preservative, to achieve the luster they still have today. This comfortable room beckons you to curl up on one of the overstuffed sofas flanking the enormous stone fireplace.

The guest rooms, also furnished with overstuffed chairs and sofas, are equally comfortable. The Cypress and Harbor rooms, occupying corners on the first and second floors respectively, are both large enough to hold two large beds plus two sitting areas. Both have sea views, as does the Lookout—the smallest room in the inn, on the second floor—which also has its own private deck. Its white cast-iron bed is spread with a wedding-ring quilt.

Breakfast and dinner are served in the dining room. Menus feature fresh local seafood and meats as well as organically grown vegetables.

Address: *5600 S. Hwy. 1, Box 369, Elk, CA 95432, tel. 707/877–3203.*
Accommodations: *6 double rooms with bath, 4 cottages.*
Amenities: *Restaurant; fireplace in 9 rooms; private beach.*
Rates: *$155–$230; MAP. No credit cards.*
Restrictions: *No smoking in restaurant, no pets; 2-night minimum on weekends, 3- or 4-night minimum on some holidays.*

Joshua Grindle Inn

L ike much of Mendocino, the Joshua Grindle Inn looks as if it were imported directly from New England and plunked down on the California coast. And in a way it was. Joshua Grindle, like many of the area's settlers, hailed from Maine. A raftsman for the Mendocino Lumber Company, he built the two-story redwood farmhouse for his bride in 1879; it stayed in the family until 1967.

The inn displays many of Mendocino's best qualities: functional New England architecture, a respect for the land, and a casual, relaxing ambience. It stands on a two-acre hilltop near the turnoff into town from Highway 1. The original farmhouse has five guest rooms, a parlor, and a dining room. Three bedrooms upstairs are bright and airy, with either ocean or treetop views. The guest room called the Library is particularly appealing. A small, cozy room, it has its own seating area, a four-poster queen-size bed, and floor-to-ceiling bookcases flanking a fireplace decorated with hand-painted tiles depicting Aesop's fables. In the late afternoon you'll find guests in the farmhouse parlor, reading or playing backgammon, sipping sherry, or fingering the antique pump organ.

There are two outbuildings. The weathered redwood Watertower has three rooms, including one on the second level with windows on four

sides and, naturally, a splendid view of the ocean and town as well as the mountains to the east. The Cottage, which has two rooms, is shaded by cypress trees that Joshua Grindle planted 100 years ago. Furnishings throughout the inn are simple but comfortable American antiques: Salem rockers, wing chairs, steamertrunk tables, painted pine beds.

Innkeepers Arlene and Jim Moorehead, who purchased the inn in 1989, came to innkeeping after careers with Bechtel in San Francisco. "It was a natural move," Jim said. "We love old houses, good food, and people." At breakfast guests gather around a long, 1830 pine harvest table. Although the table isn't big enough to accommodate everyone when the inn is full, no one seems to mind enjoying a prebreakfast cup of coffee on the veranda. After breakfast, guests frequently take the short walk into town to shop for antiques or explore the art galleries.

Address: *44800 Little Lake Rd., Box 647, Mendocino, CA 95460, tel. 707/937–4143.*
Accommodations: *10 double rooms with bath.*
Amenities: *Fireplace in 6 rooms; guest refrigerator.*
Rates: *$90–$135; full breakfast. MC, V.*
Restrictions: *Smoking outside only, no pets; 2-night minimum on weekends and in Aug., 3-night minimum on holidays.*

St. Orres

This inn is the creation of a man who loves to build. With its copper-plated Russian-style onion domes, it's a landmark along the northern California coast. Eric Black, like many others, moved to Gualala to get back to the earth; he had been a Bay Area master carpenter. Eric purchased a run-down loggers' motel, razed it, and created a hotel that reflects the area's Russian heritage.

St. Orres offers three types of accommodations. The main hotel, which fronts the highway, has eight very small rooms upstairs, beautifully embellished with such woodwork touches as mitered redwood paneling and handcrafted doorless armoires with clothes hooks and shelves. Two groups of cottages offer more comfortable accommodations. The Meadows includes four cottages, ranging from rustic to elegant and offering elevated bedrooms, private decks through French doors, wood-burning stoves, and sun decks. The rustic Wildflower Cabin has an outdoor, but private and protected, shower. The seven Creekside cottages are more luxurious and—scattered on a wooded hillside away from the hotel—quite private. Pine Haven, the largest, has its own skylighted pair of onion domes, one of which holds the blue-and-white tiled bathroom. These cottages share a complex with hot tub, sauna, and sun deck.

The dining room, filling an enormous domed corner of the hotel, has three-story-high leaded-glass windows and rough-hewn open beams. It's a first-class establishment, luring foodies all the way from San Francisco. The fixed-price menu offers quail, rabbit, venison, wild boar, and occasionally wild turkey or raccoon potpie; accompaniments are equally exotic—cream of sorrel or cold strawberry soup, or pâté with sun-dried blueberries. Breakfast is served in the dining room to guests staying in the hotel rooms and delivered in a specially designed wooden box to cottage guests.

Gualala, an 1860s lumbering port, is a lively arts center with plenty of galleries. In addition, the Gualala River is a popular spot for swimming and steelhead fishing.

Address: *36601 S. Hwy. 1, Box 523, Gualala, CA 95445, tel. 707/884–3303.*
Accommodations: *Cottages: 11 double rooms with bath; lodge: 8 double rooms share 3 baths.*
Amenities: *Restaurant, 3 rooms with fireplace, 5 with wood-burning stove; spa complex in Creekside section with hot tub and sauna.*
Rates: *$50–$180; full breakfast. MC, V.*
Restrictions: *No smoking in restaurant, no pets; 2-night minimum on weekends, 3-night minimum on holidays.*

Timberhill Ranch

The two couples who created Timberhill Ranch were seeking a refuge from their harried, urban, corporate lives; they found it on 80 acres of rolling hills in Sonoma County—just a stone's throw from the coast, but worlds apart. Tarran McDaid and Michael Riordan and Barbara Farrell and Frank Watson admit that they created Timberhill mainly for their own pleasure. It has the kind of features they enjoy: privacy, expansive views of rolling hills (green in winter and spring and gold the rest of the year), tennis courts, a swimming pool, miles and miles of trails for quiet strolls in the woods, an excellent dining room, and outstanding and discreet service.

With 15 cottages tucked beneath trees on the hillside above a small pond, the focal point of the ranch is the quietly elegant lodge. The lodge contains an expansive living room with a Sonoma fieldstone fireplace and floor-to-ceiling windows with a view of the pool and the hills beyond.

The dining room is a point of pride. Candlelit and formal in the evenings, it's a marked contrast to the casual atmosphere of the rest of Timberhill. A six-course dinner featuring California cuisine is served nightly. A typical menu features such entrées as ahi tuna with a wasabi beurre blanc and pickled ginger, and New Zealand lamb with cabernet and blackcurrants. There's also a carefully selected wine list, including after-dinner port, sherry, and champagne.

The cottages are identical in design but differ in decor. Small log cabins built of sweet-scented cedar, they have tall windows and decks where many guests enjoy the Continental breakfasts the innkeepers deliver. The beds are dressed with handmade quilts, the walls tastefully decorated with original oils, and the fireplaces stocked up and ready to light. Timberhill provides terry-cloth bathrobes and huge fluffy towels.

This is a ranch, so there are animals: horses in the white-fenced paddock close by; ducks and geese cruising the pond in formation; a pair of llamas; and two dogs—Banger, an Australian shepherd, and Bridgette, a Shih Tzu—who trot behind the innkeepers as they make their daily rounds.

Address: *35755 Hauser Bridge Rd. (Timber Cove Post Office), Cazadero, CA 95421, tel. 707/847-3258, fax 707/847-3342.*
Accommodations: *15 double rooms with bath.*
Amenities: *Fireplace, minibar, refrigerator, and coffee maker in rooms; swimming pool, outdoor hot tub, tennis courts, hiking trails.*
Rates: *$296–$350; MAP; picnic lunches, $15–$25. MC, V.*
Restrictions: *No smoking in dining room, no pets.*

The Whale Watch Inn by the Sea

The Whale Watch isn't really a bed-and-breakfast," says manager Joanna Wuelfing, "it's an illusion." Indeed, everything about this inn—from its location high on a cliff overlooking the Pacific to the attentive and efficient service and the quiet and airy rooms with their fresh flowers and dramatic ocean views—is designed to promote a sense of isolation in which guests can create their own realities.

Started in the mid-'70s, when original owners Irene and Enoch Stewart added a guest house to the original building to accommodate their frequent visitors, the Whale Watch has since added three more buildings, for a total of five. The luxurious modern rooms are decorated in light colors and feature high, angled, skylighted ceilings. Individualized furniture gives each room a different feeling, from Victorian to Asian to art deco. Most rooms have a fireplace, a whirlpool bath, and a private deck. In some, large wall mirrors give one the impression of being surrounded by the ocean vistas; all have been carefully designed to preserve the sense of isolation. Four condolike suites in the Sea Bounty building, equipped with full kitchens, are designed for longer stays.

After a delicious Continental breakfast served in their room, guests may brave the steep stairway down to the beach to explore tidal pools or watch wet-suited abalone fishermen

heading out to sea in rubber boats. Other paths lead visitors on short strolls along the cliffs, through cypress groves and well-tended flower gardens. The Whale Watch building contains a large, comfortable common area. Used for special activities, such as small weddings, it has a sweeping view of the ocean and the annual migration of gray whales along the coast. The nearby town of Gualala has its share of restaurants and tourist attractions, and recreational facilities are within easy reach, but the Whale Watch seems designed less for activity than for relaxation, contemplation, and above all, privacy.

Address: *35100 Hwy. 1, Gualala, CA 95445, tel. 707/884-3667 or 800/942-5342.*
Accommodations: *11 double rooms with private bath, 7 suites, 4 with full kitchen.*
Amenities: *Fireplace, whirlpool bath, icemaker in most rooms; private beach access.*
Rates: *$160–$250; Continental breakfast in room. AE, MC, V.*
Restrictions: *No smoking indoors, no pets; 2-night minimum on weekends, 3-night minimum on holiday weekends.*

Carter House

A deep-brown four-story Victorian, Carter House dominates Eureka's upscaling Victorian Old Town. Though it may look old, Carter House is anything but. The creation of local builder turned innkeeper Mark Carter, the bed-and-breakfast was built in 1982 following a floor plan for a San Francisco mansion. Inside, the inn is as bright and airy as the exterior is dark and brooding. The inn doubles as a gallery for local artists.

The guest rooms on the top floor have the best views, while those on the basement level offer more privacy. The furnishings are simple, mostly antiques, with one dresser dating from the 18th century. There are beds with carved headboards, Victorian settees, and dormer windows with mountain views. Decorations include contemporary art and fresh flowers.

Breakfast is a four-course meal featuring local seafood, fruits, vegetables, and herbs.

Address: *1033 3rd St., Eureka, CA 95501, tel. and fax 707/445–1390.*
Accommodations: *3 double rooms with bath, 3 double rooms share bath, 1 suite.*
Amenities: *Restaurant at adjacent Carter Hotel, fireplace and whirlpool tub in suite, afternoon and evening refreshments.*
Rates: *$75–$185; full breakfast. AE, D, DC, MC, V.*
Restrictions: *Smoking in parlors only, no pets.*

"An Elegant Victorian Mansion"

The 1888 Stick-style Eastlake "An Elegant Victorian Mansion" stands on a quiet street several blocks from downtown Eureka. Hosts Doug and Lily Vieyra, who welcome guests into their home with bright, warm smiles, are likely to be wearing turn-of-the-century costumes. Doug may invite you for a spin in one of his antique Fords.

The four rooms upstairs are smallish but comfortably furnished with antiques; the Senator, for example, contains a bedroom set that Lily used as a child in her native Belgium. Common areas include an enormous double parlor furnished with family heirlooms from Belgium, a games room–library containing an old monk's desk from Lily's school in Belgium, and a comfortable family room with a TV with VCR and a stereo.

Lily, whose cooking has gained an excellent reputation locally, serves a breakfast that features French specialties in the formal dining room.

Address: *1406 C St., Eureka, CA 95501, tel. 707/444–3144 or 707/442–5594.*
Accommodations: *1 double room with bath, 2 double rooms with detached private bath, 1 double room with shared bath.*
Amenities: *Robes, Swedish massage ($45 per hour), afternoon ice-cream sodas, sauna, bicycles.*
Rates: *$65–$105; full breakfast. MC, V.*
Restrictions: *No smoking, no pets.*

Grey Whale Inn

From the outside, the boxy red-wood Grey Whale Inn only hints at what it used to be: the Red-wood Coast Hospital, in the heart of Fort Bragg's commercial district.

The rooms range from small to enormous; the largest contains enough space for two queen-size beds, a sitting area, and a minikitchen. A former delivery room still has the sink in which newborns were bathed. Large windows on all sides let in plenty of light and open out onto some stunning Pacific vistas.

Innkeepers Colette and John Bailey, who opened the inn in 1978, have been sprucing up the decor, some of which dates from the 1960s. Their freshly decorated rooms are definitely of the '90s, with soft, light colors, extensive redwood paneling, and bright, flowered quilts. The larger of the two penthouse rooms has a spacious outdoor deck and a big modern bathroom with a whirlpool tub; the other has a smaller deck and bathroom but a splendid ocean view.

Address: *615 N. Main St., Fort Bragg, CA 95437, tel. 707/964–0640 or 800/382–7244.*
Accommodations: *14 double rooms with bath.*
Amenities: *Phone in rooms, cable TV and kitchenette in some rooms.*
Rates: *$80–$160; full breakfast. D, MC, V.*
Restrictions: *Smoking outdoors only, no pets; 2-night minimum on weekends, 3-night minimum on holidays.*

The Headlands Inn

Although the Headlands Inn offers the best ocean views in town, the gracious hospitality of hosts Rod and Pat Stofle is every bit as big a lure. Their three-story inn is an intriguing blend of New England saltbox with traditional California bay windows.

The hosts greet their guests in a bright parlor furnished with antiques that include a rosewood square piano from the 1860s. Two bedrooms open onto a comfortable antiques-filled parlor that's reserved for guests; its centerpiece is an antique French carousel pig. Two rooms set into the third-floor gables have dormer windows; their bathrooms, though private, open onto a small parlor-landing. There's also a cottage (at one time it was a cook-ie bakery) behind the main house; it comes with a cannonball four-poster, a small refrigerator, and a fireplace. The lavish breakfasts might include Florentine ham rolls, basil-seasoned baked eggs, or Welsh sausage pies.

Address: *Howard and Albion Sts., Box 132, Mendocino, CA 95460, tel. 707/937–4431.*
Accommodations: *5 double rooms with bath.*
Amenities: *Afternoon refreshments, refrigerator available.*
Rates: *$98–$150; full breakfast in room. No credit cards.*
Restrictions: *Smoking outside only, no pets; 2-night minimum on weekends, 3- or 4-night minimum on holidays.*

Rachel's Inn

Although Rachel's Inn stands right on the highway, it's surrounded by more than 80 acres of parkland where you frequently see deer grazing. Rachel Binah greets her guests with an invitation to take a 20-minute stroll to the bluffs above the Pacific. "That way you'll know why I'm passionate about saving this coast from offshore oil development," she explains.

The inn consists of two buildings: a renovated 1860s farmhouse, the Main House, and the new Barn. The Main House has bedrooms and guest parlors on both floors. The Barn has two bedrooms and a parlor downstairs, and two very bright suites upstairs. The furnishings throughout are simple—white wicker, French-country, contemporary, and a few antiques—with sunlight flowing in through the many large windows. A caterer by profession, Rachel serves a hearty full breakfast.

Address: *Hwy. 1 (2 mi south of Mendocino at Little River), Box 134, Mendocino, CA 95460, tel. 707/937–0088.*
Accommodations: *2 triple rooms, 5 double rooms, all with bath, 2 suites.*
Amenities: *Fireplace in 5 rooms, wet bar and refrigerator in suites; beach access.*
Rates: *$96–$165; full breakfast. No credit cards.*
Restrictions: *No pets; 2-night minimum on weekends, 3- or 4-night minimum on holidays.*

Scotia Inn

The Scotia Inn provides an inside look at the world's largest redwood-lumber mill operation. The hotel dates from 1923, when it replaced an earlier structure that had served stagecoach travelers to the Pacific Lumber Company. The inn still provides lodging for people who do business with the company, as well as for visitors who want to find out about the business side of the redwoods.

Although the inn (like the town) is owned by the Pacific Lumber Company, Gerald Carley took over the management of the hotel in 1985. The rooms are fairly Spartan (though the furnishings include carved and canopied beds and art-deco sofas). However, the exceptionally grand dining room and lobby demonstrate how truly beautiful polished redwood paneling, flooring, and woodwork can be. (Guest rooms on the second floor are reached via a gleaming redwood staircase.) The dining room is particularly pleasant, its tables set alongside closely spaced double-hung windows, with huge plants everywhere.

Address: *Main and Mill Sts., Box 248, Scotia, CA 95565, tel. 707/764–5683.*
Accommodations: *10 double rooms with bath, 1 suite.*
Amenities: *Restaurant with banquet facilities, lounge; cable TV in 8 rooms.*
Rates: *$55–$150; Continental breakfast. MC, V.*
Restrictions: *Smoking allowed but discouraged, no pets.*

The Shaw House Inn

Built in 1854 by the founder of the Victorian town of Ferndale, the Shaw House is a spectacular gabled Carpenter Gothic inn listed in the National Register of Historic Places. A half-decade ago, Norma and Ken Bessingpas brought it back to life with their own antiques and a careful eye for old details, such as the original paint they've restored in some rooms and the gazebo in the garden.

Seth Shaw, a justice of the peace, performs small weddings in the parlor, which features an original marble-and-gilt fireplace from Gump's; the upstairs honeymoon suite, with its high coffered ceiling and private deck, is the perfect romantic retreat. The other five guest rooms, library, and parlor are filled with fresh flowers. The place is rich in Victorian details, such as the flowered paper and vintage dresses adorning the walls. Gold-plated plumbing, claw-foot tubs in five of the bathrooms, and guest robes and slippers also help set an elegant but relaxing tone.

Address: *703 Main St., Box 1125, Ferndale, CA 95536, tel. 707/786–9958.*
Accommodations: *5 double rooms with bath, 1 suite.*
Amenities: *Fireplace in library and parlor, guest phone, croquet and bicycles available.*
Rates: *$75–$125; Continental breakfast. MC, V.*
Restrictions: *No smoking indoors; 2-night minimum on weekends, 3-night minimum on holidays.*

The Stanford Inn by the Sea

Innkeepers Joan and Jeff Stanford have presented their guests with only one problem: keeping up with everything that's going on at the Stanford Inn by the Sea. In addition to running the inn itself, they raise llamas and black swans; operate Big River Nurseries, a California-certified organic garden; rent canoes to visitors who want to explore the nearby Big River estuary; and provide mountain and road bikes for tours of the area's scenic biking trails. A spacious indoor swimming pool completes the recreational package.

The comfortable paneled rooms have decks with ocean views, traditional furnishings with four-poster or sleigh beds, fireplaces or wood stoves, and an appealing selection of paintings by local artists. The tourist attractions of Mendocino are only a short walk away.

Address: *Coast Hwy. and Comptche-Ukiah Rd., Box 487, Mendocino, CA 95460, tel. 707/937–5615 or 800/331–8884.*
Accommodations: *23 double rooms with private bath, 3 suites.*
Amenities: *Fireplace, refrigerator, phone, TV with VCR, CD player in rooms; indoor swimming pool, canoes and bicycles available.*
Rates: *$160–$230; Continental breakfast. AE, D, DC, MC, V.*
Restrictions: *No smoking indoors; 2-night minimum on weekends, 3-night minimum on holidays.*

Sacramento and the Central Valley

Sacramento and the Central Valley
Including Stockton and Davis

Sacramento is rarely the first city that leaps to mind when California is mentioned. So it's reasonable to ask why this pleasant if self-effacing metropolis, about 150 miles inland from San Francisco, is the capital of one of the largest and showiest states in the land.

The answer is obvious to anyone familiar with California history: The saga of the state's earliest days is very much the story of Sacramento. In 1848, gold was discovered in the foothills of Coloma, just 30 miles away. Though little more than a modest settlement of farmers and fur trappers then, Sacramento quickly became a bustling supply center.

As the Gold Rush boomed, Sacramento bloomed. With a balanced economy, built on agriculture, shipping, and manufacturing, Sacramento's strength and prosperity were assured for decades to come. When the West Coast was linked to the East Coast by rail, Sacramento was the obvious place to put the station (these days, the site of the old Central Pacific Railroad is a flourishing museum). And in 1854, when Sacramento was selected as the permanent capital of the new state of California, competition wasn't a problem. Los Angeles? Nothing but a dusty dot down south. Even San Francisco was merely a Second City.

This history is worth noting because, aside from rich farmland and an admirable collection of rivers and lakes, history is largely what Sacramento and the tree-lined towns of the vast central valley have to offer these days. It's a lot, of course, particularly in a state where a 1935 bungalow qualifies as a municipal treasure.

Its rip-roaring past is also what makes the area's relative anonymity and laid-back pace so seductive. If Sacramento, an artless metropolitan sprawl with nearly 1.5 million people—and almost as many cars—is a big city now, under its patina of sophistication it remains a small town. People ride bicycles on its busiest streets. Huge trees shade its many parks. Even the big-time business of running this enormous state seems a little slower, a little less impenetrable than it might were it based in Los Angeles, say, or San Francisco. One reason is the pleasingly human scale of the domed State Capitol building, meticulously restored to its 1907 splendor a few years back.

A short drive to the south are the tomato and asparagus farms that have long been the backbone of central California's economy. (This is, after all, some of the richest farmland in the world.) And though the classic valley towns, like Stockton, Lodi, Modesto, and Fresno are not obvious destinations for visitors, they can surprise and delight in subtle ways. Most have a street or two of handsome Victorian houses, nicely restored. This is also superb motoring country if you enjoy a cruise past tranquil acres of cherry trees, grape vines, and almond groves. Best of all, you don't just have to look. Farmer's markets are everywhere, and their offerings, sensibly priced, are inevitably the freshest, sweetest, and juiciest imaginable.

Places to Go, Sights to See

Arco Arena (1 Sports Parkway, Sacramento, tel. 916/928–8499), a $40 million state-of-the-arts multipurpose complex, is home to the Kings, Sacramento's NBA franchise, and regularly hosts music, entertainment, and sports events.

Asparagus Festival. Stockton, the asparagus capital of the world, celebrates this elegant vegetable the fourth weekend in April at Oak Grove Regional Park with live entertainment, an arts-and-crafts show, and food booths (deep-fried asparagus is the favorite edible).

California State Capitol (10th and L Sts., Sacramento, tel. 916/324–0333) was completely gutted in 1972 and rebuilt to look as it did at the turn of the century. The enormous white, gold-domed building in downtown Sacramento houses the governor's offices, both divisions of the California State Legislature, and a museum, with re-creations of early 20th-century government offices. The Senate chamber, where visitors can watch debates from the gallery, is particularly flamboyant, with gilded columns, massive crystal chandeliers, and a magnificent crenellated ceiling.

California State Fair. Held each August in Sacramento, this enormous fair covers 350 acres and offers dancing horses, nightly fireworks, and livestock exhibitions, including a national pot belly pig show.

California State Railroad Museum (2nd and I Sts., Sacramento, tel. 916/445–4029) has a collection of more than two dozen vintage engines and cars, which visitors can walk through and inspect. The Sonoma, a late-19th-century high-tech masterpiece, is widely regarded as the finest restored example of an American Standard locomotive. The Gold Coast private car, with its marble fireplace and swagged curtains, offers a glimpse of how passengers traveled in high style, circa 1895.

Crocker Art Museum (216 O St., Sacramento, tel. 916/264–5423) houses an appealing, if uneven, collection of European and American art in a richly restored Italianate Victorian mansion. The collection is particularly strong in Old Master prints and drawings and in California paintings from the late 19th century and the post-1945 period.

Haggin Museum and Galleries (1201 N. Pershing, Stockton, tel. 209/462–1566), a handsome local history museum, features Indian artifacts, 19th-century French and American paintings, and a room of neatly preserved turn-of-the-century storefronts, including a one-room schoolhouse and a Chinese herb shop.

Leland Stanford Mansion (802 N St., Sacramento, tel. 916/324–0575), built in 1856 by the founder of Stanford University, is the oldest house in Sacramento and is currently being refurbished top to toe. Tours of this work in progress show what's involved in a major historical restoration.

Governor's Mansion of California (1526 H St., Sacramento, tel. 916/324–0539), an opulent white Victorian (and one of California's first homes to have indoor plumbing), was home to the state's governors and their families until 1966, when Ronald Reagan requested a newer residence. The eclectic furnishings include a handsome four-poster bed that was extended to 7 feet to accommodate Governor Earl Warren's height, and an old-fashioned clawfoot bathtub with red fingernail polish on its toenails.

Micke Grove. This handsome, 65-acre grove of oaks trees, located between Stockton and Lodi, is a fine place for picnics, baseball, swimming, and other outdoor activities. The exquisitely maintained two-acre Japanese Garden is graced by waterfalls, arched bridges, and artfully arranged plants and stonework. In addition, the zoo has a strong collection of cats, birds, California sea lions, and primates, including the endangered golden lion tamarin, a rare little monkey from Brazil. The nearby *San Joaquin Historical Society and Museum* (11793 Micke Grove Rd., tel. 209/463–4119), which specializes in agricultural history, features a tractor from 1917, a one-room schoolhouse from 1866, and the largest collection of hand- and foot-powered tools in the west (4,000 in all).

Old Sacramento. Once derelict and slum-ridden, this historic area of Sacramento was transformed in the mid-1960s into a living museum of the gold-rush era, complete with cobbled streets and gaslights. Its frontier-style buildings house more than 100 restaurants, theaters, and shops, as well as the fine *Sacramento History Museum* (101 I St., tel. 916/264–7057) and the *Towe Ford Museum* (2200 Front St., tel. 916/442–6802), with a collection of over 150 vintage Fords.

Sutter's Fort (2701 L St., Sacramento, tel. 916/445–4422), built in 1839, provided free shelter and supplies for pioneers, including surviving members of the ill-fated Donner Party in 1846.

Restaurants

Sacramento's best restaurants are a pleasing blend of sophistication and health consciousness. Adventurous northern Italian food is served with style at **Biba** (tel. 916/455–BIBA), a spacious, white-walled restaurant owned by cookbook author Biba Caggiano. The menu of California–Continental offerings changes each month at **Mitchell's Terrace** (tel. 916/920–3800), where reservations are a must. **Chanterelle** (tel. 916/442–0451), a California French restaurant, is a popular place for catching state legislators tucking into duckling with pear schnapps or quail with truffle sauce. **Caffe Donatello** (tel. 916/973–1800) serves northern Italian dishes and crispy breads in an airy building with a cathedral ceiling. In Stockton, elegant **Le Bistro** (tel. 209/951–0885) specializes in California-French offerings, such as salmon ravioli and stuffed prawns. At **Albert's Restaurant** (tel. 209/476–1763), with its fanciful New Orleans–meets–Northern California decor, specialties include a succulent Portuguese soup, intriguing seafoods, and a spicy house salad. **On Lock Sam** (tel. 209/466–4561), Stockton's best-known Chinese restaurant for nearly a century, offers tasty Cantonese specialties.

Tourist Information

Sacramento Chamber of Commerce (917 7th St., Sacramento, CA 95814, tel. 916/443–3771); **Stockton and San Joaquin County Convention and Visitors Bureau** (46 W. Fremont St., Stockton, CA 95202, tel. 209/943–1987).

Reservation Services

B&B International (Box 282910, San Francisco, CA 94128–2910, tel. 415/696–1690 or 800/872–4500); **Eye Openers B&B Reservations** (Box 694, Altadena, CA 91003, tel. 213/684–4428 or 818/797–2055, fax 818/798–3640).

Amber House

Michael Richardson admits it isn't always easy to run a bed and breakfast inn. "It's like having your mother-in-law for Christmas dinner every day of the year," he says. Still, Michael and his wife, Jane Ramey, former Southern California residents, have no regrets about their decision to move to Sacramento in 1986 to become proprietors of Amber House, a meticulously restored Arts and Crafts house from 1905. Jane, a former merchandise manager for Marriott hotels, redecorated the house's five guest rooms, haunting estate sales for antiques and fashioning each room around a poet. Michael, formerly in real estate, set about buying and restoring the 1913 Mediterranean-style house next door, which now hosts an enormous sitting room with a fireplace and three guest rooms, all named for prominent 19th-century artists.

Though situated on a boring block not far from the State Capitol, Amber House is atmospheric, with lots of nooks and crannies. The main sitting room, with its hardwood floor and wood-beamed ceiling, has plenty of comfortable chairs. And in the late afternoons, guests snack here on cookies, coffee, and mineral water, or retreat to the smaller, front sitting room, with glass-fronted bookshelves and a window seat. Classical music wafts through all the public rooms.

The eight guest rooms are either woody and masculine or floral and romantic. They range from snug (Chaucer) to gloriously spacious (Renoir). The latter has leaded glass windows, a king-size bed, a sofa, and a bathtub built for two. Van Gogh is arguably the most glamorous, with a white wrought-iron bed, white wicker rockers, and a big airy bathroom.

Breakfast is served at a large wood table in the dining room or at little tables in each guest room. Since guests often stay more than one night, it's never the same two days in a row. Quiche and potatoes with bellpeppers is an Amber House specialty, as are waffles and strawberries. As a prelude to the meal, Michael sets early morning coffee or tea on a tiny table outside each room.

Address: *1315 22nd St., Sacramento, CA 95816, tel. 916/444-8085 or 800/755-6526, fax 916/447-1548.*
Accommodations: *8 double rooms with baths.*
Amenities: *Cassette players and clock radios in rooms, phones, cable TV, VCRs in 3 rooms, robes in 4 rooms, whirlpool baths in 4 rooms; air-conditioning, afternoon refreshments, bicycles.*
Rates: *$70–$195; full breakfast. AE, DC, MC, V.*
Restrictions: *Smoking outside only, no pets.*

Hartley House

Boulevard Park is one of Sacramento's less heralded historic treasures. Not far from the State Capitol, the area boasts several blocks of magnificent turn-of-the-century houses. The six little parks in the middle of 21st and 22nd Streets form the district's centerpiece; each is a large, grassy, tree-shaded oval. In the early 1900s, the streets formed a genteel race course; residents in the large houses looked on and cheered as horses ran around the greens.

The original owners of Hartley House, a rambling white 1906 Colonial Revival home, had one of the best views. It's easy to imagine them seated on the expansive front porch, holding cool drinks and watching the races. Guests still sit on the porch, often on the big porch swing, and sip fresh lemonade delivered by Margarita Banda, Hartley House's capable manager.

Randy Hartley, a fourth-generation Sacramentan, turned this one-time boarding house into an inn in 1986, restoring the hardwood floors and stained-glass windows in public rooms to their former glory and outfitting the five guest rooms with a cozy, chintz-free mix of antiques and amenities that evoke the crisp comforts of an Edwardian townhouse. Brighton, set in what was once the sun porch, is arguably the prettiest and certainly the lightest guest room, with three walls of windows, a white wrought-iron bed, ceiling fan, and small TV. Dover flaunts the house's original bathroom fixtures, including a ball-footed tub.

As a guest quickly discovers, Margarita and Michele Bowers (who does the cooking) run a comfortable, down-to-earth inn. The enormous white kitchen, the house's only blatantly 1990s touch, is outfitted with tall stools, where visitors nibble home-made cookies and chat with Michele until she shoos them out. (Guests, if so inclined, are also invited to pitch in when Michele makes ice cream.) Breakfast—blueberry pancakes are the house specialty—is served in the spacious dining room.

Games are piled high on the sitting room shelves and the chess board is always set up on the polished-wood coffee table. But the sitting room is mainly a relaxing place to peruse a good book or the *Sacramento Bee.*

Address: *700 22nd St., Sacramento, CA 95816, tel. 916/447-7829 or 800/831-5806, fax 916/447-1820.*
Accommodations: *5 double rooms with baths.*
Amenities: *Air-conditioning, cable TV, clock radios, robes, phones in rooms, afternoon refreshments, patio.*
Rates: *$79–$125; full breakfast. AE, D, DC, MC, V.*
Restrictions: *Smoking outside only, no pets.*

The Old Victorian Inn

At first glance The Old Victorian Inn has three big strikes against it. It's in hot, dusty Stockton, 49 miles south of Sacramento, a nice enough place to live but hardly a lure for visitors. It's also situated on a busy corner in a charmless old residential district. But although most of the seven rooms share baths, this three-story house, a flamboyant California-style Queen Anne Victorian built in 1890, is enchanting from bottom to top. Meticulously restored in 1985 by owner Rex Buethe, a Stockton native, the inn is like a turn-of-the-century time capsule (with late-20th-century plumbing, fortunately).

The tone is set in the mauve front parlor, where a fire is likely to be flickering in the tile-framed fireplace. On a nearby wall hangs a portrait of Dr. Lester E. Cross, the home's original owner. The parlor's Victorian platform rocker and magnificent carved courting chair are appealing and genuine; like many of the house's antiques, they hail from the Haggin Museum, Stockton's fine museum and art gallery a short drive away. In the hallway near the dining room there's an unusual brass intercom—like the kind seen on old ships—that Mrs. Cross used to converse with her kitchen staff.

Dr. Cross's bourgeois Victorian taste can be seen in the three second-floor bedrooms, all furnished with the house's original armoires, mirrors, and elaborately carved wooden beds. The Canterbury Room, the prettiest, has a wonderful walnut fireplace mantel, an old wicker chair, and lots of satiny pillows. It seems staid, however, compared with the brilliantly colored attic parlor and guest rooms. Papered in Victorian shades of turquoise and rust with lots of gilt swirls, the attic's Grand Gable Room boasts a big brass bed and exquisite oak wainscoting. The bathroom is equally fanciful, with an antique copper tub edged in wood. A candle holder now sits on a nearby table, ever since a guest asked to bathe by candlelight.

Rex, who serves a breakfast of fresh-squeezed orange juice and homemade muffins, is a social worker–turned–antiques addict. He restored the house with an eye to selling it, but once it was done he, understandably, couldn't bear to part with it. Architecture and antiques buffs should be glad he's still in charge.

Address: *207 West Acacia, Stockton, CA 95203, tel. 209/462–1613.*
Accommodations: *1 double room with bath, 2 double rooms share 2 baths, 1 suite.*
Amenities: *Air-conditioning, robes, afternoon refreshments; off-street parking.*
Rates: *$65–$105; Continental breakfast. MC, V.*
Restrictions: *No smoking, no pets.*

Wine & Roses Country Inn

In her high-necked white lace blouse, Kris Cromwell, the personable owner of Wine & Roses Country Inn, looks as though she stepped straight out of *Victoria* magazine. It's no surprise, then, that her inn on three acres of rich farmland in Lodi, a grape-growing, winemaking community south of Sacramento, is unabashedly romantic. The curtains are of white lace, a fire crackles in the sitting room, and fresh, fragrant flowers are everywhere. Ribbons and bows, too, are ubiquitous.

Kris's Victorian touches nicely complement this rambling two-story country house, built in 1903 and a short ride from the Lucas Winery, which offers tours to guests. The sitting room is large and airy, with two walls of windows, rose-colored carpeting, and cushiony sofas. A treadle sewing machine stands in a corner, and family photographs grace the mantel.

Wine & Roses, which opened in 1988, is very much a family affair. Kris, a former real estate agent, runs the place with her son, Del Smith, and his wife, Sherri, whom he met when she was hired as the inn's chef. The couple recently had a baby and there's another on the way, so the Wine & Roses dynasty continues.

Comfort, coziness, and strong colors seem to have been Kris's priorities

while decorating the 10 guest rooms. Eidelweiss, which overlooks the garden, is typical, with deep green walls, pale mauve carpeting, and a green and white floral print duvet on the big brass bed. The bathroom has a claw-foot tub with a shower. A clock radio awakens you if the chickens don't. The attic was recently converted into a suite with cathedral ceilings and French doors. The brass bed sports a chintz comforter with caggage rose print.

Breakfast, Sunday brunch, lunch (Tues.–Fri.), and dinner (Wed.–Sat.) are served in the mauve dining room, overlooking the rosebushes. On warm days and nights, guests can eat outside on big round tables. Or you can sip coffee or wine in the sitting room with Kris, who likes to chat with her guests.

Address: *2505 West Turner Rd., Lodi, CA 95242, tel. 209/334–6988, fax 209/333–0716.*
Accommodations: *9 double rooms with bath, 1 suite.*
Amenities: *Restaurant, afternoon and evening refreshments, air-conditioning, TV, phone, clock radio in rooms; free use of health club, croquet, badminton, horseshoes.*
Rates: *$79 weekdays, $99 weekends, suite $125; full breakfast. AE, MC, V.*
Restrictions: *No smoking, no pets.*

Aunt Abigail's

There's no Aunt Abigail, but Susanne Ventura, who owns this light-filled 1912 Colonial Revival house with her husband, Ken, is as warm and welcoming as a favorite aunt. She leaves her guests homemade cookies on a carved wooden sideboard at night, and the dining-room breakfast table is set with sterling silver flatware and draped with a lacy cloth.

Susanne first visited Aunt Abigail's as a paying guest in 1985. A year later, she quit her job with an insurance company and bought the place, which is situated in what was once one of Sacramento's toniest neighborhoods. Aunt Abigail's six rooms, named for Susanne's and Ken's relatives, include Margaret, in shades of beige and green, with a big photo-graph of Ken's flapperish Aunt Margaret. Uncle Albert boasts Victorian wallpaper. The prettiest, however, is the front parlor, with a big art-deco light fixture from the Alhambra, a much-missed Sacramento movie palace, circa 1927.

Address: *2120 G St., Sacramento, CA 95816, tel. 916/441–5007 or 800/858–1568.*
Accommodations: *4 double rooms with baths, 3 doubles share a bath.*
Amenities: *Afternoon refreshments, air-conditioning in room, TV available; outdoor hot tub, off-street parking.*
Rates: *$75–$135; full breakfast. D, DC, MC, V.*
Restrictions: *No smoking, no pets; 3-night minimum stay holiday weekends.*

Davis Inn

Davis, home to a sprawling campus of the University of California, is a postcard-perfect college town, with tree-shaded streets and students riding bicycles. It's considerably more casual than nearby Sacramento. And appropriately enough, the Davis Inn, the largest bed and breakfast inn in town, is also a good deal more casual than its Sacramento counterparts. Guest rooms are functional, with rag rugs, wood floors, and ancient TVs with rabbit ears. The Balcony Room, one of the largest, is typical, with a king-size bed, a rack of hangers in lieu of a closet, a wall of windows, and access to a pleasing balcony.

Roger and Pat Loomis bought the house, which was built in 1919, nearly 20 years ago and opened it up for business in 1984. The previous owner, a professor at the university, had resided here for 50 years, and the place has a comfortable, lived-in air. The lobby has a high ceiling, hardwood floor, stone fireplace, ceiling fan, and big, well-worn chairs. Pat, wearing an apron, often sits in the rocker, sharing tidbits of the house's history.

Address: *422 A St., Davis, CA 95616, tel. 916/753–9611.*
Accommodations: *18 double rooms with baths.*
Amenities: *Air-conditioning, TVs, phones available, smoking rooms available, off-street parking.*
Rates: *$48–$58; full breakfast. AE, D, DC, MC, V.*
Restrictions: *Smoking allowed on porch and balconies, no pets.*

The Driver Mansion Inn

First things first: The bathrooms in the five largest rooms at the Driver Mansion Inn are fabulous, with whirlpool tubs and stall showers with glass doors and acres of marble. Yet step out of the tub and you're in a three-story turn-of-the-century Colonial Revival house with a sloping lawn and a sprawling wraparound porch, set far back on a busy, semicommercial street near downtown Sacramento. Richard and Sandi Kann, former Los Angelinos, bought the house in 1984.

The guest rooms feel luxurious, with reproduction Queen Anne and Empire furniture and a smattering of new and Victorian pieces. And the enormous pink "penthouse," which occupies the entire top floor, has a marble-top dining table and a big brass and iron bed. Two caveats, however: The rooms can seem a little cold, since they lack the books, fresh flowers, and assorted quirky collectibles found in many inns, and the handsome parlor isn't always open to guests.

Address: *2019 21st St., Sacramento, CA 95818, tel. 916/455-5243 or 800/456-2019, fax 916/455-6102.*
Accommodations: *7 double rooms with baths, 2 suites.*
Amenities: *Afternoon refreshments, air-conditioning, cable TV, phone, clock radio in rooms, fireplace in 4 rooms, whirlpool tub in 5 rooms, refrigerator in 1 suite.*
Rates: *$85–$225; full breakfast. AE, DC, MC, V.*
Restrictions: *No smoking, no pets.*

The Sterling Hotel

It's a nice surprise to find that this classic California Victorian house, with turrets, bay windows, and a graceful, sloping lawn, is actually a small hotel. The California-French offerings of its restaurant, Chanterelle, regularly attract state senators and other politicos from the nearby State Capitol building.

The Sterling Hotel, which opened in 1988, has the size and scale of a bed and breakfast without the intimacy—or the complimentary meals; it's a more businesslike version of the Driver Mansion Inn (*see* above), also owned by Richard and Sandi Kann. Rooms are spacious and often amusingly shaped, with reproduction Queen Anne and Empire furnishings, pale pink carpets, potted palms, and rich, raspberry-color bedspreads. Bathrooms are a feast of pale pink marble, with ample tubs, whirlpool baths, and pedestal sinks.

Address: *1300 H St., Sacramento, CA 95814, tel. 916/448-1300 or 800/365-7660, fax 916/448-8066.*
Accommodations: *12 double rooms with baths.*
Amenities: *Whirlpool baths, air-conditioning, cable TV, phones, clock radios in most rooms, ornamental fireplaces in 3 rooms, laundry service, room service, restaurant, meeting facilities.*
Rates: *$110–$225. AE, DC, MC, V.*
Restrictions: *No smoking, no pets.*

Victorian Manor

A sweet little time-warp town 14 miles north of Sacramento, Newcastle had its heyday at the turn of the century, when Newcastle pears were highly prized in Chicago and New York. These days the town's primary attractions are its sleepy pace, tree-shaded square, and a fine collection of rambling Victorian homes, including Victorian Manor, a proud, white two-story house with gingerbread trim and a garden filled with camellias.

Ed and Cordy Sander, who bought the house in 1984, have tried hard to infuse it with the furnishings, styles, and even sounds of a bygone era. The sitting room features a 90-year-old Ediphone, a scratchy precursor of the phonograph, that Ed cranks up for visitors. And Cordy spent hours poring over history books before making the ruffled pillow shams, fringed lamp shades, and quilts that fill the four carefully furnished guest rooms. (Each has an elaborately carved antique bed.) She also created a vast collection of turn-of-the-century costumes for guests who want to play dress up and have their pictures taken.

Address: *482 Main St., Newcastle, CA 95658, tel. 916/663-3009.*
Accommodations: *1 double room with bath, 3 doubles share 2 baths.*
Amenities: *Afternoon refreshments, air-conditioning, garden, off-street parking.*
Rates: *$60–$65; Continental breakfast. AE, MC, V.*
Restrictions: *Smoking outside only, no pets.*

Gold Country

Gold Country
Along Highway 49

*The reason California is called the Golden State is found
right here, on a long, narrow expanse of land about 150
miles inland from San Francisco, stretching from
Mariposa in the south to Sierra City in the north. The hills
in these parts are often the color of spun gold, but it was
the riches hidden inside that set off the biggest gold rush in
history, endowed California with its buoyant economy—
and earned the state its 18-karat nickname.*

*When gold was discovered on January 24, 1848, at John
Sutter's Sawmill in Coloma, this sleepy town on the banks
of the American River was overrun by frenzied prospectors.
By the next year, some 80,000 treasure seekers had poured
in from every direction to set up mining camps throughout
the western foothills of the Sierra Nevadas. Boomtowns rose
up on the sites of big strikes—and were abandoned as
quickly when the gold ran out.*

*Today the colorful towns along the aptly named Highway
49 (a reference to the year that prospectors flooded the
area) still reflect much of the character of the gold-rush
days, though they are quite different from one another.
Nevada City and Sutter Creek, for example, have become
trendy getaways for city folk, while Columbia and Coloma
have been carefully restored, with wooden sidewalks,
blacksmith shops, and horse-drawn carriages evoking their
heyday.*

*Another tradition has recently been revived here. The roots
of winemaking in the region go back to the gold-rush days,
but the population decline after the closing of the mines,
the devastating phylloxera vine disease, and Prohibition all
caused the wineries to be abandoned over the years. In the
past couple of decades, however, more than two dozen
wineries have sprung up across these rolling Sierra*

foothills, producing zinfandels and cabernets as robust as the region from which they hail. Although Gold Country is becoming an increasingly popular destination for wine lovers, here—in contrast with commercialized Napa Valley—you're still likely to be greeted in the tasting rooms by the winemakers themselves.

The Gold Country is one of the few parts of California that haven't had a population explosion in recent years. The locals like it that way. Up in the foothills of the Mother Lode, Jackson, with around 4,000 inhabitants, is considered big. And although visitors pour into these tiny townlets on hot summer weekends, this is still a splendid place for fleeing the crowds.

The Mother Lode is also a magnificent backdrop for motoring. Driving along Highway 49, you'll see gently rolling hills, sheep and cows, lazy streams—and just when you need some relief from the bucolic, up pops a gold-rush town, such as Drytown, Volcano, or Jackass Hill. Each is outfitted with old wooden buildings, a rustic spot for a picnic, and a pretty little creek. And if that's not enough, the names alone should keep you amused.

Places to Go, Sights to See

Amador County Museum (225 Church St., Jackson, tel. 209/223–6386) offers a glimpse of mining history with a large-scale reconstruction of the famous headframe-hoisting equipment, stamp mill, and wheels used during the 1920s at Jackson's Kennedy Mine, the largest gold mine from the turn of the century until it closed in 1942.

Apple Hill (Apple Hill Visitor Center, 4123 Carson Rd., Camino, tel. 916/644–7692). Orchards of apples, pears, peaches, cherries, plums, persimmons, and pumpkins thrive in the fertile Sierra foothills east of Placerville. Families flock here for events such as the month-long Apple Festival in October, the West Coast Cherry Pit Spitting Championship in June, and outdoor music at the orchards. There are also several good wineries in the vicinity.

California State Capitol (10th and L Sts., Sacramento, tel. 916/324–0333) was completely gutted in 1972 and rebuilt to look as it did at the turn of the century. The enormous white, gold-domed building in downtown Sacramento houses the governor's offices, both divisions of the California State

Legislature, and a museum, with re-creations of early 20th-century government offices. The Senate chamber, where visitors can watch debates from the gallery, is particularly flamboyant, with gilded columns, massive crystal chandeliers, and a magnificent crenellated ceiling.

Coloma. The gold rush, and all the fuss, started on January 24, 1848, in this unassuming town. *Marshall Gold Discovery State Historic Park* (Hwy. 49, tel. 916/622–3470) immortalizes the big event. The town also has a pleasing collection of reconstructed buildings, including an 1850s Chinese store.

Columbia State Park (off Hwy. 49, tel. 209/532–0150). Dozens of the Mother Lode's boomtowns are now ghost towns, but Columbia never became deserted. In 1945, the state of California turned this tiny hamlet into a historic state park where only horses, stagecoaches, and pedestrians are allowed on the unpaved streets. Bartenders and shopkeepers don wild-West attire. And visitors who tire of scouring Main Street's museums and candy stores can try panning for gold at the nearby creek. There's also an excellent nature trail, and the Fallon Theater puts on polished theatrical productions.

Daffodil Hill. In mid-March this 4-acre ranch just north of the tiny town of Volcano, near Jackson, becomes a vibrant display of color with more than 500,000 spring blooms, including, of course, daffodils.

Frog Jumping Jubilee. Held the third weekend in May at the Calavaras County fairgrounds just south of Angels Camp, this much-touted international competition inspired by Mark Twain's story "The Celebrated Jumping Frog of Calavaras County" allows visitors to "rent a frog."

Moaning Cavern (off Rte. 4, on Parrot's Ferry Rd., Vallecito, tel. 209/736–2708) is California's largest public cavern. In addition to taking a guided tour of the main chamber, adorned with minerals and prehistoric bones, visitors who don't mind descending by rope can explore deeper chambers.

Murphys. Known as the Queen of the Sierras, this picturesque gold-rush town has a tree-shaded Main Street lined with rustic wooden buildings. The *Old Timers Museum* (Main St., tel. 209/728–1160), which displays gold-rush and town memorabilia, occupies the old Wells Fargo office built in 1856; it's a miracle building, the locals say, because it has survived three fires and several earthquakes. Across the street, *Murphys Hotel* (457 Main St., tel. 209/728–3444) has a guest book signed by Mark Twain, Black Bart, and Ulysses S. Grant. Upstairs is a reconstruction of the room where Grant stayed in 1880. A few blocks away is *Mercer Caverns* (Sheepranch Rd., tel. 209/728–2101), a collection of unusual natural crystalline formations in wildly varied sizes and textures. Several nearby vineyards are open to the public, including the *Stevenot Winery* (2690 San Domingo Rd., tel. 209/728–3436) and *Milliaire Winery* (276 Main St., tel. 209/728–1658).

Nevada City. This lovely gold-rush town ringed by pine-covered hills is a weekend mecca for city folk looking for R&R, including some top-notch window-shopping, dining, and entertainment. The entire downtown area has been registered as a National Historic Landmark. California's oldest theater,

The Nevada Theatre (401 Broad St., tel. 916/265–6161) once hosted such illustrious patrons as Jack London and Samuel Clemens. *The National Hotel* (211 Broad St., tel. 916/265–4551) is the state's oldest continuously operating hotel. *Firehouse No. 1* (214 Main St., tel. 916/265–5468), often photographed for its Victorian bell tower and gingerbread trim, is now a museum devoted to the Indian and Chinese influence in the area.

Placerville. Nicknamed Hangtown during the gold rush for the punishment given to a gang of gold-thirsty criminals, Placerville is today the pleasant, bustling seat of El Dorado County. A few bargains can still be found in the antiques shops along narrow Main Street. The *El Dorado County Historical Museum* (100 Placerville Dr., tel. 916/626–2250) displays an elegant stagecoach, Indian artifacts, and a Pelton wheel turbine that was used to power a mine. The tiny *Fountain & Tallman Soda Factory Museum* (524 Main St., tel. 916/626–0773) has a great collection of gold rush–era memorabilia. Upstairs is a room fully furnished in Victorian splendor. At *Gold Bug Park* (about 1 mi north of downtown on Bedford Ave.) you can take a self-guided tour of a gold mine.

Sutter Creek. The Mother Lode's classiest little town, this is an ideal place to survey the wooden buildings, narrow streets, and rolling hills that make the Gold Country so appealing. Main Street and Hanford Street boast some of the area's most intriguing antiques and gift shops. The *Stoneridge Winery* (13862 Ridge Rd., tel. 209/223–1761) is also nearby.

Restaurants

In Nevada City, **Cirino's** (tel. 916/265–2246) is a favorite among locals for its unusual pizzas and other Italian specialties. Coloma's **Vineyard House** (tel. 916/622–2217) serves classic American fare, including chicken and dumplings and bread pudding, in several opulent dining rooms. Just east of Placerville on a quiet country road, **Zachary Jacques** (tel. 916/626–8045) offers hearty French-country cuisine. The **Imperial Hotel** in Amador City (tel. 209/267–9172) has a well-earned reputation for its elegant American-style food. But it's getting competition from **Ballads** (tel. 209/267–5403), its new next-door neighbor. In nearby Sutter Creek, **Pelargonium** (tel. 209/267–5008) offers different specials nightly, including a vegetarian entrée. **Teresa's** (tel. 209/223–1786) in Jackson has lots of local color and good standard Italian fare.

Tourist Information

Amador County Chamber of Commerce (Box 596, Jackson, CA 95642, tel. 209/223–0350 or 800/649–4988); **Calaveras Lodging and Visitors Association** (Box 637, Angels Camp, CA 95222, tel. 209/736–0049 or 800/225–3764); **El Dorado County Chamber of Commerce** (542 Main St., Placerville, CA 95667, tel. 916/621–5885); **Nevada County Chamber of Commerce** (248 Mill St., Grass Valley, CA 95945, tel. 916/273–4667 or 800/655–4667); **Tuolumne**

County Visitors Bureau (55 W. Stockton Rd., Sonora, CA 95370, tel. 209/533–4420 or 800/446–1333).

Reservation Services

B&B International (Box 282910, San Francisco, CA 94128–2910, tel. 415/696–1690 or 800/872–4500, fax 415/696–1699); **Eye Openers B&B Reservations** (Box 694, Altadena, CA 91003, tel. 213/684–4428 or 818/797–2055, fax 818/798–3640); **Amador County Innkeepers Association** (tel. 209/296–7778 or 800/726–4667).

The Coloma
Country Inn

It was in Coloma that California's gold-rush fever first erupted in 1848 with the discovery of gold at Sutter's Sawmill. Among the few remaining structures from that period, the Coloma Country Inn, a pretty farmhouse with a wraparound porch and yellow shiplap siding, sits behind a long, white-picket fence in the verdant, 300-acre Gold Discovery State Park.

Cindy and Alan Ehrgott first came to now tranquil Coloma (population 250) in 1983 with the intention of expanding their Los Angeles–based adventure travel business but ended up becoming innkeepers. They still offer rafting trips and hot-air-balloon rides, the latter complete with a full champagne breakfast.

Coloma's history is represented by old photographs along the staircase on the inn's hand-stenciled walls, but the treasures in the house are not restricted to California's gold-rush era: Cindy has a fabulous collection of quilts from the 1880s to 1920s— some folded at the foot of each bed—as well as one of English and German blue-and-white delftware storage jars. An assortment of antique bric-a-brac is displayed in the living room, where you can relax in wingback chairs in front of the fireplace.

The guest-room furnishings are also eclectic, and each room is bright and tasteful. Rose has a bed and dresser made of New Mexico fruitwood; Eastlake boasts an oak Eastlake set with bed, dresser, and washstand; and the roomy, dreamy Cottage has delphinium-blue walls and sage-green trim, as well as a white Jenny Lind–style bed with turned spools. The lovely grounds include a gazebo, crabapple trees, and a small pond; a formal rose garden is being planted.

Guests are wont to gaze out at the pond over breakfast while listening to the ancient strains of Celtic music. Although Coloma is rather isolated, you can have a good dinner at the nearby Vineyard House.

Address: *345 High St., Box 502, Coloma, CA 95613, tel. 916/622–6919.*
Accommodations: *3 double rooms with bath, 2 doubles share a bath.*
Amenities: *Afternoon refreshments, air-conditioning, guest phone; bicycles, canoe; hot-air-balloon and whitewater-rafting packages.*
Rates: *$85–$105; expanded Continental breakfast. No credit cards.*
Restrictions: *No smoking indoors, no pets; advance notice for children under 10.*

Culbert House Inn

aul and Theresa Rinaldi are pure thirtysomething in the nicest way. She's an engineer (mechanical), and he's an engineer (on trains). But when they had their second child, they vowed day care wasn't for them and decided to work at home. After months of hunting in California and Oregon, they found the old Culbert residence in tiny Amador City (population 150), a gold-rush town best known these days for its antiques shops and restaurants.

The sprawling gray Culbert House, owned for years by a prominent Amador City lumber family, was built in stages, the western half in 1860, the eastern half in 1894. Vacant for seven years, it seemed just right for the Rinaldis, with its French windows, lush garden, and mighty trees (the showpiece is a skyscraping sequoia). After months of renovation, the Culbert House Inn opened on Memorial Day weekend in 1990.

The inn is a skillful blend of simplicity and sophistication. Paul and Theresa have kept the best parts of the old two-story house, including the wall moldings, high ceilings, and handsome hardwood floors. They've updated the rest, notably the bathrooms, which have either sizable stall showers or old-fashioned pedestal tubs. The decor is French-country, with swagged window dressings in polished cotton prints,

carved armoires from Belgium, and lots of blue, white, and red.

The Gallic color scheme is particularly appealing in the light-filled sitting room, which has an upright piano, navy blue–and–white checked sofas, and a view of the garden. Each afternoon Theresa sets out her blue-and-white Royal Doulton china and serves fruit, cheese, and drinks, including herbal teas (the Rinaldis are organic-food enthusiasts).

All guest rooms open onto a wraparound porch outfitted with white wicker rockers. The prettiest is probably the Mulberry Suite, a spacious, somewhat formal room with salmon-pink walls, lush flower prints on the bed, Louis XV–style chairs, throw pillows, and a 19th-century love seat covered in red moire beside the glass-fronted fireplace. But the pale pink Magnolia Suite, with an iron and brass bed and adjoining sun room, is a close second.

Address: *10811 Water St., Amador City, CA 95601, tel. 209/267–0750.*
Accommodations: *1 double room with bath, 2 suites.*
Amenities: *Fireplace in 1 room; afternoon refreshments, croquet.*
Rates: *$80–$95 weekdays, $90–$105 weekends; full breakfast. MC, V.*
Restrictions: *Smoking outside only, no pets; 2-night minimum on weekends.*

The Foxes Bed and Breakfast Inn

The simple, pale gray two-story structure that houses the Foxes Bed and Breakfast Inn in Sutter Creek was built during the gold rush, but while its 19th-century origins are intriguing, this elegant six-room inn owes its chief appeal to the late-20th-century pampering of guests. Min Fox, who has owned the inn with her husband, Pete, since 1980, sits down with guests each evening and discusses the next day's breakfast. (There's an airy French toast made with apple juice and egg white for the cholesterol-conscious.) Breakfast is served in your room on an antique wooden table with Queen Anne reproduction chairs, the coffee or tea in an ornate silver pot. The place mats are crocheted, as is the little round doily that is slipped over the base of the stemmed orange-juice glass. And tape decks in each room provide a little background Mozart or, oh well, Mantovani.

For years Pete and Min ran an antiques shop that specialized in Victorian pieces. When they decided to turn the house into an inn, they rearranged the unsold tables, armoires, and carved Victorian beds (one headboard is 9 feet tall) and—voilà—the place was practically furnished. Guest rooms in the inn have grown increasingly romantic over the years, particularly the three newer rooms in the carriage house out back. The big Blue Room, with ice-blue floral-print wallpaper, has a large bed with a carved headboard and a white Marseilles spread. A wooden canopy with pale blue curtains is suspended overhead. The armoire, which looks French-country, was actually made in Argentina more than a century ago. Silk flowers sit in a pot atop a dark wooden pedestal, its base carved in the shape of a griffin. And on the wall there's a print of two baby foxes. (Every room has a foxy touch, such as a fox-head pillow or print, which just misses being twee.)

The house also has a peach-colored front parlor, with a spool-based table and plenty of Rococo Revival love seats for curling up with a good book or flipping through Min and Pete's menu collection (a spicy potpourri sweetens the air). Or you may prefer to sit in the gazebo out back and admire the lush garden, particularly enticing in the spring when the big pink dogwood is in bloom.

Address: *77 Main St., Sutter Creek, CA 95685, tel. 209/267-5882, fax 209/267-0712.*
Accommodations: *6 double rooms with bath.*
Amenities: *Air-conditioning, radio, and tape deck in rooms, fireplace and TV in 3 rooms; off-street parking.*
Rates: *$100–$125 weekdays, $115–$140 weekends; full breakfast. D, MC, V.*
Restrictions: *No smoking, no pets; 2-night minimum on weekends.*

Red Castle Inn

Dubbed the Castle as it rose on Prospect Hill in 1857, this four-story, brick Gothic Revival house still looks majestic. Set in a grove of cedars, chestnuts, and walnuts, the Red Castle Inn has a classic pitched gable roof dripping with icicle-shaped gingerbread and a broad veranda shaded by white sail-canvas curtains tied back with red sashes.

Conley and Mary Louise Weaver, who bought the house in 1985, were the perfect inheritors of this Sierra-foothills treasure: He was an architect in San Francisco, and her specialty was interior design and historic preservation. Between them, the Weavers have transformed the inn into a virtual Vatican of Victoriana. The elegant parlor, its tall French doors draped in lace and framed by satin valances, contains volumes on period furniture and architecture.

Modern baths were installed in the former trunk-storage areas, but the guest rooms are all original to the house. On the first floor, one level below the main entrance, a private door leads to Forest View, where a large mahogany bed has a lighted canopy. On the main floor, the Garden Room's dramatic display of "Victorian clutter" includes a Renaissance Revival hall tree complete with a carved deer's head and real antlers and a reproduction Chinese Chippendale canopy bed. Down the hall in the Gold Room, rust-and-gold drapes hang from a faux-burled cornice. Two diminutive suites on the third floor, formerly the children's quarters, have seven-foot ceilings. Garret East and West, separated by a parlor with a commanding view of the town, feature Gothic arched windows and mid-19th-century sleigh beds.

Mary Louise and Conley's breakfasts, served buffet-style on a sideboard in the main foyer, often include traditional American dishes such as Indian pudding or Dutch babies. Guests can eat in the parlor, outdoors in the terraced garden, or in the seclusion of their private sitting areas and verandas. On Saturday morning, you can hire a horse-drawn carriage to tour the town's historic district.

Address: *109 Prospect St., Nevada City, CA 95959, tel. 916/265–5135.*
Accommodations: *4 double rooms with bath, 2 suites, 1 double suite.*
Amenities: *Afternoon refreshments; air-conditioning in suites.*
Rates: *$95–$110, double suites $140 ($70 each half); full breakfast. MC, V.*
Restrictions: *No smoking indoors, no pets; 2-night minimum on weekends Apr.–Dec. and holiday weekends.*

Camino Hotel

Built at the turn of the century as a boardinghouse for loggers, the Camino Hotel, on the Carson Migrant Wagon Trail, was restored in 1990 by Paula Norbert and John Eddy. There's still a lumber mill in town, but the trail now winds through orchards and wineries.

Because the guests are no longer loggers, the hotel has been gussied up with antiques, most of them local. Paula's hand-sewn curtains complement the rooms' quilts, and such details as a wicker birdcage at the foot of a bed or a hanging sunbonnet with trailing dried flowers help set a country tone, as do the showcase antique sewing machines and quilt stands in the hall. The covered storm porch and large parlor are good spots for reading or chatting with other guests.

After serving a hearty breakfast, Paula and John will point you toward an orchard bakeshop that sells fabulous apple cheesecake and to a hiking trail where you can work it off.

Address: *4103 Carson Rd., Box 1197, Camino, CA 95709, tel. 916/644-7740.*
Accommodations: *3 double rooms with bath, six double rooms share 2 baths, 1 suite.*
Amenities: *Afternoon refreshments, phone in hall.*
Rates: *$55–$85; full breakfast. AE, D, MC, V.*
Restrictions: *No smoking inside, no pets.*

The Chichester House

Doreen Thornhill is filled with historic lore about the 1892 Queen Anne that she and her husband, Bill, bought in 1990: It was the first house in Placerville with built-in plumbing; an entrance to a gold mine lies underneath the dining-room table; and the fireplace in the parlor came from San Francisco's Barbary Coast Hotel. Built by lumber baron D.W. Chichester, the house makes lavish use of redwood inside and out, with a decorative cherry-wood fretwork in the library and parlor. It also has a wonderful tin-floored conservatory.

Rooms are furnished with a mix of antiques and reproductions; each has an armoire draped with an amusing piece of Victorian lingerie. A window seat as well as an Amish oak bed with a handmade fishnet canopy make Yellow Rose the most appealing room, despite the faint traffic sounds.

After Doreen's hearty breakfast, guests can walk a few blocks to downtown Placerville or drive to nearby Apple Hill for a wine tasting.

Address: *800 Spring St., Placerville, CA 95667, tel. 916/626-1882 or 800/831-4008.*
Accommodations: *3 double rooms with half-bath share a bath.*
Amenities: *Air-conditioning, guest phone.*
Rates: *$75–$80; full breakfast. D, MC, V.*
Restrictions: *No smoking indoors, no pets.*

City Hotel

In 1856, when Columbia was all ablaze with gold fever, George Morgan built the City Hotel in the heart of town. Intended as a lodging for gentlemen, this two-story brick storefront was refurbished by the state in 1975 and now welcomes all.

Most of the City Hotel's furnishings predate 1875. All the guest rooms have 14-foot ceilings; the two balcony rooms are the most dramatic, with massive, carved wooden beds and marble-topped dressers. A central sitting parlor scattered with Oriental rugs boasts a felt-topped poker table. After a day of gold-panning, guests can return to sip a cool sasparilla in the hotel's original What Cheer Saloon; in the evening its acclaimed restaurant offers excellent French-American cuisine.

Address: *Main St., Columbia State Park, Box 1870, Columbia, CA 95310, tel. 209/532–1479.*
Accommodations: *10 double rooms with half-bath share 2 showers.*
Amenities: *Afternoon refreshments, air-conditioning, robes, slippers, restaurant, saloon, lobby phone, theater-dinner packages, off-street parking.*
Rates: *$65–$85; expanded Continental breakfast. AE, MC, V.*
Restrictions: *Smoking in lobby and saloon only, no pets; closed Jan. 4–15.*

Combellack-Blair House

This textbook 1895 Queen Anne, with gingerbread, two-story bay windows, stained glass, and even a cupola, stands pink and proud behind twin palm trees and a white-picket fence, one block from busy Main Street Placerville.

Victorianaholics will not be disappointed by the Combellack-Blair House's interior. The front parlor is hung with heavy drapes and has a crystal chandelier. Both the bedrooms have their particular charm. Off the kitchen, the romantic Mazzuchi has a lace bedspread, a clawfoot tub, and French doors opening onto a large porch. Smaller Blair is breathtaking, with its wooden canopy bed inlaid with flowers and burl, window seat, and trompe l'oeil wallpaper. Hosts Al and Rosalie McConnell plan to open up two more bedrooms in the next couple of years.

Having acquired the inn in 1991, after running a home for foster children in Gilroy, the McConnells have enthusiastically entered into the Victorian spirit, serving their guests breakfast by candlelight.

Address: *3059 Cedar Ravine, Placerville, CA 95667, tel. 916/622–3764.*
Accommodations: *2 double rooms with bath.*
Amenities: *Air-conditioning, cable TV, phone in one room.*
Rates: *$89–$99; expanded Continental breakfast. MC, V.*
Restrictions: *No smoking indoors, no pets.*

Cooper House

In 1865, Mark Twain came to Angels Camp and immortalized the food served there: "Beans and dishwater for breakfast, dishwater and beans for dinner, and both articles warmed over for supper." Twain's spirit still resonates through this tiny mining town, but, fortunately, the food's improved. Each morning Chris Sears, who owns Cooper House, cooks something such as meatless eggs Benedict with a honey-mustard and dill sauce, or semi-guilt-free French toast made with homemade whole-wheat bread.

This rambling board-and-batten Craftsman bungalow has a big stone fireplace, polished wood beams, and, like many other foothills homes, a corrugated tin roof. The three carpeted guest rooms all open onto either a porch or veranda. The furnishings are more comfortable than costly, though Chris has a few striking pieces, such as a 19th-century dining table with carved legs, originally owned by Archie Stevenot, an early mine developer.

Address: *1184 Church St., Box 1388, Angels Camp, CA 95222, tel. 209/736-2145.*
Accommodations: *1 double room with bath, 2 suites.*
Amenities: *Afternoon refreshments, air-conditioning, off-street parking.*
Rates: *$85–$95; full breakfast. MC, V.*
Restrictions: *Smoking outside only, no pets; 2-night minimum holiday weekends and 3rd weekend in May.*

The Court Street Inn

The offbeat collectibles—ornate brass cash registers, shoe-shine chair, industrial-size coffee grinder—that Janet and Lee Hammond gathered to decorate the old-fashioned general store they once planned to open are well showcased in the Court Street Inn, which they bought with their daughter and son-in-law, Gia and Scott Anderson. The 1872 yellow clapboard house, with scalloped awnings and embossed-tin ceilings, is a short stroll from sleepy downtown Jackson.

The most enchanting guest room is Muldoon, with its oak-mantel fireplace and delicate Victorian cradle. The Indian House, a two-bedroom cottage overlooking a small rose garden, has a wood-burning stove, a piano, and a huge bath with a claw-foot tub. Guests gather in the formal dining room for a breakfast that may include eggs Benedict with spiced apples. Hors d'oeuvres and dessert are served in the evening.

Address: *215 Court St., Jackson, CA 95642, tel. 209/223-0416.*
Accommodations: *3 double rooms with bath, 2 double rooms share bath, 1 double suite in cottage.*
Amenities: *Fireplace in 1 room; guest phone, TV available, massage available, whirlpool, off-street parking.*
Rates: *$75–$85; double suites $125 (one couple), $170 (two couples); full breakfast. MC, V.*
Restrictions: *No smoking indoors, no pets.*

Dunbar House, 1880

From the jar of marshmallows by the parlor fireplace to the bedtime chocolates and complimentary bottle of wine, innkeepers Barbara and Bob Costa are devoted to details. They have furnished the guest rooms of this 1880 Italianate house with comfortable, newly reupholstered antiques, as well as floral floor-length drapes and matching spreads, wood stoves, down comforters, and antique-replica radios.

This is a great place to perfect the art of lounging: in the spacious parlor, on the wraparound porch, or in the comfortable rooms. The Cedar's sun porch has a view of the white-flowering almond tree; in Sequoia, you can soak in a bubble bath in front of the wood stove while looking out at the garden.

Breakfast is an elegant affair. The Costas whip up dishes they've discovered while attending professional food shows, and Barbara's mother bakes fresh bread and cookies daily.

Address: *271 Jones St., Box 1375, Murphys, CA 95247, tel. 209/728–2897.*
Accommodations: *3 double rooms with bath, 1 suite.*
Amenities: *Evening refreshments; air-conditioning, refrigerator, phone, TV with VCR in rooms, whirlpool in suite.*
Rates: *$95–$140; full breakfast. MC, V.*
Restrictions: *No smoking indoors, no pets; 2-night minimum on weekends.*

Fallon Hotel

From 1850 to 1858, Columbia was a boomtown, with $87 million in gold discovered in its hills. Back then, Owen Fallon's hotel was *the* place to stay. Things calmed down once the gold disappeared.

These days, Columbia is a booming state park, and the state-owned Fallon, sensitively restored to its 1890 appearance, is its shiniest showpiece. The front guest rooms are huge, with reproductions of Arts and Crafts wallpapers, velvet drapes, and headboards in carved wood or iron from the 1890s. The smaller rooms are painted instead of papered. All but number 15 have private bathrooms with chain-pull toilets.

Just as appealing (though the Fallon's bathrooms are better) is the nearby nine-room City Hotel (tel. 209/532–1479), also owned by the state and dating from 1870.

Address: *Washington St., Columbia State Park, Box 1870, Columbia, CA 95310, tel. 209/532–1470.*
Accommodations: *1 double room with wheelchair-accessible bath, 1 double room and 12 double rooms with half-baths share 5 showers.*
Amenities: *Ice cream parlor, air-conditioning; robes, slippers, non-working fireplace in 1 room; off-street parking.*
Rates: *$55–$85; Continental breakfast. AE, MC, V.*
Restrictions: *No smoking, no pets. Closed Mon.–Wed. second week in Jan.–third week in Mar.*

Grandmere's

Doug and Geri Boka left Los Angeles, where he was a police sergeant and she worked for the school district, to run this 1856 Colonial Revival inn near downtown Nevada City. Avid history buffs, they'll tell you all about such colorful past inhabitants of this house as Aaron August Sargent, a forty-niner from Massachusetts who supported women's rights.

Grandmère's is as quaint as its name, with manicured public areas and prim American-country rooms. All similar in decor, the rooms have quilts or floral bedspreads, hand-painted chests at the foot of the beds, and gleaming baths with pedestal sinks and brass fixtures.

You'll be drawn to the rambling back garden, with its stone benches, bird-baths, and footpaths leading through violets, daffodils, and camellias. But sitting on the front veranda, munching Geri's cookies and people-watching, is equally appealing.

Address: *449 Broad St., Nevada City, CA 95959, tel. 916/265–4660.*
Accommodations: *3 double rooms with bath, 2 suites, 1 housekeeping suite.*
Amenities: *Air-conditioning, phone in hall, off-street covered parking.*
Rates: *$100–$145; full breakfast. MC, V.*
Restrictions: *No smoking indoors, no pets.*

The Heirloom

You don't see a lot of homes reminiscent of the Old South in California's Gold Country. But the Heirloom in Ione, a one-street foothills mining town, occupies a gracious two-story house built for a Virginia farmer in about 1863. And it's got columns atop columns, a two-story veranda, wisteria and magnolia—the antebellum works.

The Heirloom is peaceful and old-fashioned. The dining room, where owners Patricia Cross and Melisande Hubbs serve breakfast, is decorated with china plates and copper kettles. The front parlor includes a handsome grand piano once owned by Lola Montez, the Madonna of the gold-rush era. Guest rooms in the main house are snug, with tall windows, lace curtains, and quilts. The biggest has a fireplace, a four-poster bed, and a balcony. Out back, a rustic adobe cottage houses two guest rooms with wood-burning stoves and fragrant cedar, redwood, and pine beams.

Address: *214 Shakeley La., Ione, CA 95640, tel. 209/274–4468.*
Accommodations: *4 double rooms with bath, 2 double rooms share a bath.*
Amenities: *Afternoon refreshments, air-conditioning in rooms, fire-place in 1 room, wood-burning stove in 2 rooms; bicycles, croquet.*
Rates: *$55–$85; full breakfast. No credit cards.*
Restrictions: *No smoking, no pets; 2-night minimum on weekends.*

Indian Creek

Built by Hollywood producer Arthur Hamburger as a weekend residence in 1932, Indian Creek is set on a hillside in 10 acres of meadow, replete with creek and frog pond. It's easy to imagine John Wayne, who was a regular visitor, sitting in front of the two-story fireplace of this two-story log-walled cabin, his voice echoing from the 25-foot cathedral ceiling.

Former Los Angelenos Jay Cusker and Geof Denny have given the public rooms an international look: wooden Adirondack chairs and an 1872 Belgian chamber piano in the living room, Mexican rugs in the reading nook. The guest rooms are just as eclectic: trendy rag-rolled walls and a Civil War–era "sword chair" in one, white-draped ceiling and Sterno fireplace in another.

Jay and Geof's superb breakfasts might feature cream cheese–tarragon French toast or German puff pancakes, which you can devour on the deck overlooking the Japanese garden.

Address: *21950 Hwy. 49, Plymouth, CA 95669, tel. 209/245–4648 or 800/24–CREEK.*
Accommodations: *2 double rooms with bath, 2 double rooms share a bath.*
Amenities: *Evening refreshments, guest phone, pool, hot tub.*
Rates: *$55–$95; full breakfast. D, MC, V.*
Restrictions: *No smoking indoors, no pets.*

The Ryan House

It is said that the Ryan for whom this pale blue Victorian is named fled Ireland in 1855 to escape the potato famine, coming to Sonora to seek his fortune. Later treasure seekers—of natural beauty rather than wealth—Nancy and Guy Hoffman pulled up their corporate roots in the nearby San Francisco Bay Area in 1987 and bought the Ryan House.

This B&B is more modest than some of the flamboyant Gold Country inns, but guests will appreciate the Hoffmans' gentle manner, the few well-chosen antiques, the formal rose garden, and Nancy's zeal for baking (scones and sourdough waffles are her specialty). The prettiest room is May Kelly, with pale aqua walls, a white crocheted popcorn-stitch bedspread, and sun-filled windows overlooking the roses. Guests gather for afternoon tea in front of the wood stove in the library, with its carved grape-pattern Victorian love seat and dusty-rose walls.

Address: *153 S. Shepherd St., Sonora, CA 95370, tel. 209/533–3445 or 800/831–4897.*
Accommodations: *3 double rooms with bath.*
Amenities: *Air-conditioning, TV in pantry, afternoon refreshments, off-street parking, theater-dinner packages.*
Rates: *$80; full breakfast. AE, D, MC, V.*
Restrictions: *No smoking indoors, no pets; advance notice for children under 10; 2-night minimum on holiday weekends.*

Windrose Inn

This romantic house on the outskirts of Jackson, reached by crossing a footbridge over a rushing creek, has a romantic story behind it: Hosts Marv and Sharon Hampton got married after they met at their high school reunion in Long Beach in the mid-1980s.

Their understated pink-and-yellow Queen Anne was furnished in a successful combination of styles. An enormous 1903 wood stove presides over the parlor, with its import-store rattan chairs; a wall of windows looks out onto a gazebo and flowering fruit trees. Two of the guest rooms are decorated in tidy Victorian fashion, and the third has gray-and-black art-deco motifs. Out back, a deceptively rustic cottage houses two comfy rooms with a sleeping loft.

You can dine in the solarium, which overlooks a well hand-dug by Chinese workers from the nearby Kennedy Mine, or on a shaded patio adjoining a goldfish pond.

Address: *1407 Jackson Gate Rd., Jackson, CA 95642, tel. 209/223–3650.*
Accommodations: *3 double rooms with bath, 1 suite in cottage.*
Amenities: *Afternoon refreshments, TV in cottage, guest phone.*
Rates: *$85–$100; full breakfast. MC, V.*
Restrictions: *No smoking indoors, no pets.*

High Sierra

High Sierra
Including Yosemite and Lake Tahoe

*"The Range of Light" is the name the naturalist John Muir
applied to the Sierra Nevada, the mile-high mountains that
form two-thirds of California's eastern border. Stretching
from Lassen Peak in the north past Yosemite, Kings
Canyon, and Sequoia (the site of 14,494-foot Mt.
Whitney) national parks to the Tehachapi range in the south, the
Sierra Nevada contains mile after mile of snowcapped
peaks encircling alpine lakes, flower-filled meadows,
towering waterfalls (including Yosemite Falls, which drops
nearly a half mile), and endless forests, including the giant
sequoias.*

*The mountains have played a significant role in the state's
history. Initially, they formed an all but impenetrable
barrier to explorers and pioneers. (The tragic story of the
Donner party—trapped in the brutal Sierra winter of
1846–47 and driven by starvation to madness and
cannibalism—became engraved in American legend.) To
this day some high passes are closed during the winter, and
snow and ice force others to close intermittently. And the
tracks across Donner Summit still pass through a series of
snowsheds so that the railroad can stay open through the
winter.*

*While much of the gold rush took place at lower elevations,
the forty-niners mined the mountainsides north of Lake
Tahoe as well. Gold Lake Recreation area, in the Lakes
Basin, is said to have gotten its name from nuggets found
strewn on its beaches.*

*During the gold rush and later, when the transcontinental
railroad was built, the mountains yielded up the timber
needed to shore up the mine shafts, brace the hillsides, and
tie tracks together; thus towns like Truckee and Quincy*

sprang up to serve the needs of loggers, miners, and builders.

Today the lures of the Sierra Nevada are gorgeous scenery and endless possibilities for recreation. In the southern portion, the scenic splendor of the three national parks draws millions of visitors each year. Yosemite is the most famous, with its glacier-carved canyon, giant granite monoliths, thundering waterfalls, and pristine acres of alpine wilderness. The Ahwanhee Hotel, with its cathedral ceilings, great stone hearth, and richly decorated Indian rugs, stands in a choice spot, with a stunning view of Half Dome. Sequoia, a strip of rugged natural beauty at 8,000 feet, gets its name from the world's largest living thing, the giant sequoia. This park and the adjacent Kings Canyon National Park offer more than 1,000 miles of high-country trails.

Lake Tahoe—at 12 by 22 miles (and with an average depth of nearly 1,000 feet)—is itself a scenic wonder: The largest alpine lake in North America has water so pure that you can spot a dinner plate 75 feet beneath the surface. Lake Tahoe is a two-season paradise. Winter brings 300–500 inches of snow to the upper elevations, along with some of the finest skiing in the West and some of the best facilities: cross-country trails, snowmobile trails, snow-play areas, and more than 200 lifts and tows. During the summer, the recreation shifts from ice to water: boating, fishing, waterskiing, along with biking and hiking.

North of Lake Tahoe is a largely undiscovered portion of the High Sierra, which includes the Lakes Basin Recreation Area, a gentle wilderness of pristine lakes, trails, and peaks. Historically this is gold country; today it's timber country. Visitors will discover a sparse population and several well-placed bed-and-breakfast inns amid mile upon mile of tranquil, scenic beauty.

Places to Go, Sights to See

Bodie (off Hwy. 395, 7 mi south of Bridgeport, CA, tel. 619/647–6445), an eerily beautiful, noncommercial ghost town, grew to more than 10,000 residents by 1881 during the gold rush and was completely deserted by the 1940s.

Cross-country Ski Centers. *Sorensen's* (Hope Valley, CA, tel. 916/694–2203) provides 20 kilometers of groomed trails and 100 kilometers of marked, unimproved trails, rentals, lessons, and day tours. *Spooner Lake Cross-Country Ski Area* (Glenbrook, NV, tel. 702/749–5349) divides 101 kilometers among 21 groomed trails and offers rentals, lessons, and moonlight tours. *Tahoe Nordic Center* (Hwy. 28, Tahoe City, CA, tel. 916/583–9858) provides 65 kilometers of groomed trails as well as rentals, lessons, races, and full-moon tours. *Royal Gorge Cross-Country Ski Resort* (off I–80 at Donner Summit, Soda Springs, CA, tel. 916/426–3871) has 317 kilometers of groomed track, 77 trails, as well as rentals, lessons, warming huts, trailside cafés, and a ski patrol. *Tahoe Donner Cross-Country* (3½ mi off I–80 at Donner State Park exit, tel. 916/587–9484) has 65 kilometers of track, 32 trails, and offers rentals, lessons, and night skiing (Wed.–Sat.). *Tamarack Cross-Country Ski Center* (Tamarack Lodge, Mammoth Lakes, CA, tel. 619/934–2442 or 800/237–6879) has more than 40 kilometers of groomed trails. *Yosemite Cross-Country Ski School* (Badger Pass, 6 mi east of Chinquapin Junction at Hwy. 41, Yosemite, CA, tel. 209/372–1244) offers 35 kilometers of groomed trails and 80 kilometers of marked trails.

Donner Memorial State Park and Museum (Donner Pass Rd., 2 mi west of Truckee, tel. 916/587–3841) lies beneath the granite wall of Donner Summit, where 22 feet of snow trapped the Donner party during the winter of 1846–47. The *Emigrant Trail Museum* contains exhibits recounting their tragedy and illustrating the history of the Central Pacific Railroad. *Donner Lake*, with 7½ miles of alpine shoreline, offers swimming, fishing, sailing, sunbathing, horseback rentals, and hiking trails.

Genoa, Nevada (Foothill Rd., off Hwy. 207), the first settlement in the state, retains its historic flavor; the town's Victorian Gothic homes are of particular interest. The Carson Valley Chamber of Commerce and Visitors Authority (1524 Hwy. 395, Suite 1, Gardnerville, NV 89410, tel. 702/782–8144) offers tourist information.

Lake Tahoe Cruises. Several companies offer cruises on the lake. The *Tahoe Queen* (Box 14292, South Lake Tahoe, CA 96151, tel. 800/238–2463) is a glass-bottom stern-wheeler that departs on a variety of excursions from Emerald Bay and includes lunch and sunset dinner-dance cruises. *North Tahoe Cruises* (700 N. Lake Blvd., Tahoe City, CA 96145, tel. 916/583–0141) takes visitors on champagne Continental-breakfast cruises, shoreline cruises, and sunset cocktail cruises. *Woodwind Sailing Cruises* (Box 1375, Zephyr Cove, NV 89448, tel. 702/588–3000) operates a 41-foot trimaran on regular excursions (daily Apr. 1–Oct. 31). M.S. *Dixie* (Box 1667, Zephyr Cove, NV

89448, tel. 702/588–3508) offers daily breakfast and dinner cruises to the south and east shores of Emerald Bay.

Lake Tahoe 72-Mile Shoreline Drive (guide from Lake Tahoe Visitors Authority, Box 16299, South Lake Tahoe, CA 96151, tel. 916/544–5050 or 800/288–2463). This stunning scenic drive includes many of Tahoe's high points: deep-green Emerald Bay, the 38-room Scandinavian castle called Vikingsholm, the beautiful beaches at Meeks Bay and D.L. Bliss State Park, and the early 19th-century homes at the Tallac Historic Site.

Laws Railroad Museum and Historical Site (on Rte. 6 off Hwy. 395 at north end of Bishop, CA, tel. 619/873–5950) is a re-creation of a small frontier community, built at the site of the old Laws Railroad Station. *The Slim Princess*, the last narrow-gauge locomotive operating as a public carrier in the West, rests here after 70 years of service. There are also excellent minimuseums displaying rock collections, old bottles, and Indian artifacts.

Mammoth Mountain Bike Park (Mammoth Adventure Connection, Box 353, Mammoth Lakes, CA, tel. 619/934–0606) has 50 miles of mostly single-track trails for advanced-beginner to advanced riders. Ask about the 62 newly marked miles of trails in surrounding areas.

Plumas-Eureka State Park (5 mi west of Blairsden on Hwy. A–14, tel. 916/836–2380), which summons up the gold-mining era in California, contains Johnsville, which verges on being a ghost town, a partially restored stamp mill, and a museum illuminating hard-rock mining and early pioneer life.

Portola Railroad Museum (Box 608, Portola, CA, tel. 916/832–4131) illustrates the history of the Western Pacific Railroad with 25 diesel locomotives as well as freight cars and track and maintenance equipment. You can even drive the train here; one-hour lessons are available.

Sierra County Historical Park and Museum at the Kentucky Mine (Hwy. 49, 1 mi east of Sierra City, CA, tel. 916/862–1310). The mine operated on and off from the 1850s until 1953. The museum contains a collection of local mining memorabilia; tours include a restored stamp mill, tunnel, blacksmith shop, and trestle. Concerts of all kinds are held here on Friday evening in July and August.

Ski Areas. North Lake Tahoe alone has 108 lifts serving 16,500 skiable acres in 12 alpine ski areas. Most areas are served by a single lift ticket, the Ski Tahoe North Interchangeable Lift Ticket. A brief sampling includes *Alpine Meadows* (2600 Alpine Rd., off Hwy. 89, outside Tahoe City, CA, tel. 916/583–4232); *Diamond Peak* (Incline Village, NV, tel. 702/832–1177); *Homewood* (West Shore, Lake Tahoe, CA, tel. 916/525–7256); *Mount Rose* (Mt. Rose Hwy., outside Reno, NV, tel. 702/849–0704); *Northstar-at-Tahoe* (off Hwy. 267, 6 mi from Lake Tahoe, CA, tel. 916/562–1010 or 800/533–6787); and *Squaw Valley USA* (1960 Squaw Valley Rd., off Hwy. 89, Olympic Valley, CA, tel. 916/583–6985). The major resort in South Lake Tahoe is *Heavenly Valley* (½-mile off Hwy. 50, South Lake Tahoe, CA, tel. 800/2–

HEAVEN). Yosemite's skiers resort is *Badger Pass* (6 mi east of Chinquapin Junction at Hwy. 41, Yosemite, CA, tel. 209/372–1330); *Mammoth Mountain* (off Hwy. 395 in Mammoth Lakes, CA, tel. 619/934–2571) is closer to southern California.

Sleigh rides are popular during the winter. Contact *Borges Carriage and Sleigh Rides* (Hwy. 50 and Parkway at Lake Tahoe, NV, tel. 916/541–2953); *Camp Richardson Corral* (Hwy. 89 at Camp Richardson, CA, tel. 916/541–3113); *Kirkwood Ski Resort* (Hwy. 88, 7 mi west of Carson Pass, CA, tel. 209/258–RIDE), or *Northstar* (Hwy. 267 between Truckee and Lake Tahoe, CA, tel. 916/562–1010).

Tahoe Trailways is a network of bicycling and walking paths edging the lake. The trail extends north from Tahoe City along Highway 89 toward Truckee, then east as far as Dollar Point and south along the West Shore to Meeks Bay. Bicycles can be rented from *Olympic Bike Shop* (620 N. Lake Blvd., Tahoe City, CA, tel. 916/581–2500), *Tahoe Gear* (5095 W. Lake Blvd., Homewood, CA, tel. 916/525–5233).

Virginia City, Nevada (Hwy. 341, off Hwy. 50 east of Carson City, tel. 702/847–0177), site of the Comstock Lode, is the nation's most famous mining boomtown. Retaining its century-old rustic flavor, the town contains old-time saloons, Piper's Opera House, a frontier cemetery, shops, museums, mine and mansion tours, gambling, and the offices of the *Territorial Enterprise*, where Mark Twain once worked.

Restaurants

Three of the inns listed below, **Sorensen's** in Hope Valley, **Busch and Heringlake Country Inn** in Sierra City, and **Captain's Alpenhaus** in Tahoma have restaurants. **Le Bistro** (tel. 702/831–0800) in Incline Village has a reasonably priced set menu of rustic French-California dishes. In Tahoe City, **Le Petit Pier** (tel. 916/546–4694) offers lakeside dining and is one of the best French restaurants in the area. **Sunnyside** (tel. 916/583–7200), just south of Tahoe City, has a lakeside dining room with a charming old-boating atmosphere and serves seafood and prime rib. **O.B.'s Pub and Restaurant** (tel. 916/587–4164), in Truckee, is popular for its old-fashioned lace curtains, stained glass, and oldtime atmosphere, and for its California cuisine. The restaurant at the elegant **Ahwahnee Hotel** (Yosemite Valley, tel. 209/372–1489) serves California cuisine in its 135-foot-long dining room, where no jeans or tennis shoes are allowed. Reserve at least two weeks in advance. In Mammoth Lakes, **Anything Goes** (tel. 619/934–2424) offers fresh-baked breads and creative California cuisine in hearty portions.

Tourist Information

Bishop Chamber of Commerce and Visitor Center (690 N. Main St., Bishop, CA, tel. 619/873–8405); **California Highway Information** (tel. 916/445–2820); **Lake Tahoe Visitors Authority** (Box 16299, South Lake Tahoe, CA 96151, tel. 916/544–5050, 800/288–2463 for lodging information, or 900/776–5050 for local entertainment and events information at a $1-per-minute rate); **Mammoth Lakes Visitors Bureau** (Village Center Mall, Main Street, Box 48, Mammoth Lakes, CA 93546, tel. 619/934–2712 or 800/367–6572); **Nevada Highway Information** (tel. 702/289–0250); **North Lake Tahoe Chamber of Commerce** (Box 884, Tahoe City, CA 96145, tel. 916/583–2371); **Plumas County Chamber of Commerce** (500 Jackson St., Box 11018, Quincy, CA 95971, tel. 916/283–6345 or 800/326–2247); **South Lake Tahoe Chamber of Commerce** (3066 Lake Tahoe Blvd., South Lake Tahoe, CA 96150, tel. 916/541–5255); **Yosemite National Park** (Box 577, CA 95389, tel. 209/372–0265).

Reservation Services

Bed-and-Breakfast Innkeepers of Northern California (2715 Porter St., Soquel, CA 95073, tel. 800/284–INNS); **B&B International** (Box 282910, San Francisco, CA 94128, tel. 415/696–1690 or 800/872–4500, fax 415/696–1699).

The Cain House

nnkeeping is in Marachal Goh-
lich's blood. In 1972, when she
was 10, her family fled the Orange County smog to open the Walker River Lodge in Bridgeport.
Seventeen years later, Marachal
came back from southern California,
where she had worked as a hotel operations director, to run an inn of
her own in Bridgeport—the Cain
House. These days she gets help
from her new husband, Chris, a
schoolteacher.

In the late 1920s the descendants of
James Stuart Cain, the principal
landowner in what was once the
boomtown of Bodie, built this clean-
lined two-story structure, painted
burnt-red and white with a gray
slate roof. It's next door to Bridgeport's landmark 1880 courthouse,
whose bell tower plays "Melancholy
Baby" at sunset. In redoing the
house, Marachal devoted a great deal
of attention to stylish detail: The
parlor has a lovely Chinese rug and
carved cherry-wood Kimball couch
with a green velvet seat. Most of the
furnishings are recent acquisitions,
but the rock fireplace, moldings, and
the bathroom of the Candelaria
room, decorated with swirly green
wall tiles and a huge putty-colored
sink, are all original to the house.

Each of the beautifully color-
coordinated guest rooms is decorated
in a different style. Roomy Aurora,
all peaches and pinks, boasts whitewashed pine furniture. Silverado's

pale greens are a cool complement to
its white wicker bedroom set. The
large, deep-blue Masonic room has
two queen-size brass beds and
a library set that belonged to Marachal's grandmother; a matching oak
settee, rocker, and armchair all have
twisted legs, cane backs, and red-
velvet seats.

The dining room is cheerily decorated with antique and reproduction
Swiss posters; at romantic tables for
two, you can savor such delights as
shrimp-and-brie scrambled eggs or
lemon-and-raspberry pancakes. After
breakfast, take the rugged road out
to Bodie, which has been a ghost
town since the 1940s.

Address: *11 Main St., Box 454,
Bridgeport, CA 93517, tel. 619/932–
7040 or 800/433–CAIN, fax 619/932–
7419.*
Accommodations: *7 double rooms
with bath.*
Amenities: *Evening refreshments,
cable TV in rooms; hot tub, off-
street parking, badminton, croquet.*
Rates: *$80–$135; full breakfast. AE,
D, DC, MC, V.*
Restrictions: *No smoking indoors,
no pets; 2-night minimum last
weekend in June and 4th of July
weekend; closed Nov. 1–Apr. 14.*

The Feather Bed

Chuck and Dianna Goubert are innkeeping pioneers. In 1979, when they acquired the Huskinson House in Quincy—the only real city in this corner of California—there were no other bed-and-breakfast inns between Placerville and the Oregon border. Their 1893 Queen Anne–style house, with such Greek Revival touches as Corinthian columns, is a pale peach charmer with turquoise and brick-red trim.

The Gouberts have decorated their spacious rooms with vintage wallpapers and a few well-chosen Victorian antiques; well suited for business travelers, most of the accommodations have desks. The secluded Sweetheart Cottage, as romantic as its name, has a brass and white-iron bed, delicate floral wallpaper, and a claw-foot tub in the carpeted bathroom; French doors open onto a private garden. The more masculine Barrett features an oak drop-leaf desk with leather inlay and an antique fireplace mantel used as a headboard.

The gardens at the Feather Bed are spectacular in spring. Tulips, daffodils, Oriental poppies, and phlox surround the stone fountain in the formal Victorian garden. A rose garden, cheerful border plantings, and a lush green lawn complete the idyllic picture.

Guests often find themselves chatting with the gregarious innkeepers on the porch or in the parlor. Chuck will direct you to such local sights as the Plumas County Museum, devoted to gold rush–era history, to nearby Plumas–Eureka State Park, or Lassen Volcanic Park, an hour's drive away. Ardent theater lovers—Dianna is an actress and singer as well as director of the local high school plays—the Gouberts often put on summer-evening melodramas in their converted red barn.

They're also good cooks. Breakfast starts with the inn's trademark smoothie, followed by a bowl of fresh fruit and—if you're really lucky—buttermilk pancakes with oatmeal, walnuts, and blueberries. Dining on the flower-bedecked front porch in summer is a real treat.

Address: *542 Jackson St., Box 3200, Quincy, CA 95971, tel. 916/283-0102.*
Accommodations: *6 double rooms with bath, 1 suite.*
Amenities: *Phone, radio in rooms, air-conditioning in 4 rooms; TV in sitting room, afternoon refreshments, bicycles, airport pickup, off-street parking.*
Rates: *$65–$95; full breakfast. AE, DC, MC, V.*
Restrictions: *No smoking indoors, no pets.*

High Country Inn

With the craggy Sierra buttes in the background, High Country Inn offers arguably the most stunning view to be had at any lodging in the area. The inn is located in the remote Lakes Basin Recreation Area, where more than 30 jewellike lakes nestle against the jagged mountains.

High Country Inn is the creation of Marlene and Cal Cartwright. Cal, whose roots in this region date from the 1850s, when his ancestors traveled from Maine around Cape Horn to reach the fields and hillsides of the gold rush, wanted to settle here upon retirement. When he and Marlene found a ranch-style mountain house on a 2½-acre corner, they snapped it up.

The house was built in 1961; a new section, added in 1981, offers the best room, the second-floor Sierra Buttes Suite. Tall cathedral windows across one wall frame the buttes; you can laze in bed and watch the morning sun creep down them. There's a wood-burning stove in one corner, a modern bath–dressing room with a 6½-foot tub, a good collection of books, and contemporary art on the walls. The furnishings reflect Calvin's and Marlene's family history. The cane-seat chairs in the Golden Pond Room came from the East with Calvin's family in 1852. Marlene, a midwesterner, has decorated the rooms with the quilts her mother made.

The heart of the inn is a big, open space that serves as living room, dining room, and kitchen. Guests gather here in front of a huge stone fireplace to curl up with a book (the Cartwrights' library is especially good on local history) or just admire the view.

The inn has a special brand of entertainment in its trout pond. Marlene invites guests to feed the fish—more than 300 nibblers come right up to shore to get a bite.

You can expect a delicious breakfast here. Marlene sets up places at a long table fronting the window wall, so everyone has breakfast with a view; in good weather she serves on the deck. She collects unusual recipes, so corn bread and quiche might come spiced up southwestern-style. Despite its remote location, the inn is close to some good dining spots, such as the lodges at nearby Sardine Lake and Packer Lake.

Address: *Hwy. 49 at Bassets, HCR 2, Box 7, Sierra City, CA 96125, tel. 916/862–1530.*
Accommodations: *2 double rooms with bath, 2 double rooms share a bath.*
Amenities: *TV with VCR in living room; trout pond, river.*
Rates: *$75–$125; full breakfast. MC, V.*
Restrictions: *Smoking outside only, no pets; 2-night minimum on holiday weekends.*

New England Ranch

hree miles outside of Quincy on 88 acres of pasture land sits a little white house that was built in the 1850s. It had fallen into disrepair by the time Barbara Scott bought it, but she spent three years restoring the New England Ranch—which looks like an East Coast cottage. In 1991 she opened a strikingly lovely and intimate inn, decidedly English-country in tone with its beautiful family heirloom antiques and polished wood floors.

Both of the light-filled upstairs guest rooms have an expansive view of the countryside. The pale apricot Vincent, with a lace-covered, brass step-up bed, shares a cozy sitting room with Chandler, which has a chenille bedspread and delicately patterned wallpaper. The bathrooms are especially cheery, with white-painted wood floors and bright floral wallpaper; one has an old English commode with a built-in sink, and the other features a large pedestal sink and claw-foot tub. When the two guest rooms are occupied, Barbara rents out her own large room and spends the night in her deluxe trailer.

The exquisite pair of gold-leaf Czechoslovakian plates on the dining table are just for show, but Barbara does bring out her china and silver to serve the fresh ranch eggs, blintzes, and scones that she cooks

on the house's original wood stove. The fresh herbs, vegetables, and fruits are all from her newly planted garden. In winter, you might retire after breakfast to the dusty-rose parlor, lounge on the cream-colored camelback couch, and look out the lace-curtained bay window or gaze into a blazing fire.

But in fine weather, you'll want to go out and explore the grounds. The outbuildings include an old creamery, a chicken coop, a machine shop, and a blacksmith shop. Some of the land is leased to neighboring ranchers, so cattle and horses graze the grounds. You can ride out into the rolling green hills on one of Barbara's mountain bikes or take a dip in one of the creeks that run through the property. And if you've never met a llama, ask Barbara to introduce you to her pal, Pierre, who might nibble alfalfa from your hand.

Address: *2571 Quincy Junction Rd., Quincy, CA 95971, tel. 916/283–2223.*
Accommodations: *3 double rooms with bath.*
Amenities: *Portable phone, creeks, mountain bicycles, horse stables and corrals, off-street parking, airport pickup.*
Rates: *$70–$95; full breakfast. MC, V.*
Restrictions: *No smoking indoors, no pets (horses allowed).*

Sorensen's

If you ever wanted to go camping in the High Sierra and couldn't take the idea of sleeping on the ground, Sorensen's is a good alternative. A historic mountain resort lying alongside the Carson River, at the 7,000-foot level just east of Carson Pass, open year-round, Sorensen's offers access to 600 square miles of public land: mountain scenery, hiking trails, fishing streams, star-laden nighttime skies, and fields of summer wildflowers. The inn provides comfortable accommodations, ranging from the fairly primitive to the classy, in bed-and-breakfast units and housekeeping cabins. Some of the latter date from the turn of the century, when Martin Sorensen, an immigrant Danish shepherd, and his wife, Irene, began camping here. For more than 50 years, the place was a summer hangout for wilderness folk, fishing people, and family friends. In 1970, the family sold the business, beginning a decade of decline during which the Sorensen's came to be known locally as the Last Resort.

Enter John and Patty Brissenden, community activists from Santa Cruz, who purchased the Last Resort for 1,000 ounces of gold and set about to revitalize it, renovating some of the cabins and building others from scratch.

The result is an eclectic collection of accommodations connected by a net-work of trails: log cabins in the woods, rustic cedar-sided cabins, even a replica of a 13th-century Norwegian house. Most of the cabins have kitchens; many have separate sitting areas and sleeping lofts. Cabins are offered on a housekeeping basis, but there are small, simply furnished bed-and-breakfast rooms as well. Guests select breakfast from the menu at the Country Café, housed in a log cabin and open for all three meals.

Not only do John and Patty offer accommodations for outdoor lovers; they also try to enhance your understanding of it all with classes in fishing and fly-tying. Guests can hike along the historic Emigrant Trail (which passes through the property), study the stars, and cross-country ski throughout the winter.

Address: *14255 Hwy. 88, Hope Valley, CA 96120, tel. 916/694–2203 or 800/423–9949.*
Accommodations: *1 double room with bath, 2 double rooms share a bath, 28 housekeeping cabins, each accommodating 2–8 persons.*
Amenities: *Restaurant, woodburning stoves, pets permitted in 2 cabins; convenience store, sauna, trout pond, picnic tables, barbecues, children's play area.*
Rates: *$70–$110, cabins $55–$275; full breakfast. MC, V.*
Restrictions: *No smoking; 2-night minimum on weekends, 3- or 4-night minimum on holidays.*

White Sulphur Springs

Travelers have been stopping at the big white farmhouse called White Sulphur Springs since the 1850s, when it was built as an overnight lodge for the Quincy Mohawk Stage Line. But today's visitors will have a tough time picturing the thousands of prospectors who once ranged over the tree-covered hillsides and gentle valleys that surround this inn. For this is now a quiet place. On a still summer night you can hear a car coming down the highway long before its headlights become visible.

Although the surrounding countryside has turned calm, the ambience of the inn remains much the way it was when George McLear operated it as a stagecoach stop. Many of the furnishings are original to the inn: a pump organ in the parlor, an antique piano, brocade-covered Victorian settees, a pine bedroom set handcrafted by McLear himself. Other pieces, including crystal chandeliers and an extra large dining room table, came later.

The inn also contains an ancient wood stove (today it sits in an upstairs bathroom) with the name "Clio" on the door. "Originally the bustling town nearby was called Wash, but people kept confusing it with Washington a few miles away," explains Linda Vanella, whose family has long owned the property. "The folks who gathered at the store in town were trying to come up with a new name when someone spotted the stove and said, 'That's it! Clio.' They named the town after the wood stove."

There are guest rooms in the main house and in two cottages, the Dairy House and the Hen House (the original chicken coop). All are bright and airy, with expansive views of meadows and mountains; a balcony across the front of the main house extends the view for guests on the second floor. The Victorian furnishings include a fainting couch, antique washstands, dry sinks, and rocking chairs.

The inn has a warm spring-fed, Olympic-size swimming pool. With four championship courses in the area, golf is popular with visitors, too.

Address: *Hwy. 89, Box 136, Clio, CA 96106, tel. 916/836–2387 or 800/854–1797.*
Accommodations: *1 double room with bath, 5 double rooms share 2 baths, 1 housekeeping and 1 double housekeeping suite.*
Amenities: *Terry-cloth robes; outdoor pool, picnic area, barbecue, facilities for horses.*
Rates: *$70–$140; full breakfast. D, MC, V.*
Restrictions: *Smoking outside only, no pets (except horses); 2-night minimum on summer and holiday weekends.*

Busch and Heringlake Country Inn

Like many other High Sierra and Gold Country inns, the Busch and Heringlake Country Inn was originally a stagecoach stop. Guests will find reminders of the building's history in the 2-foot-thick walls, the exposed-stone wall behind the bar, and the brick facade, as well as in the antique safe and old boiler in a corner.

But the accommodations on the second floor are thoroughly modern, with four guest rooms comfortably furnished to reflect an earlier era: brass and four-poster beds, exposed woodwork, and original art on the walls. The inn is the creation of the engaging Carlo Giuffre, who bought the long-neglected property in 1986. Carlo is full of information about the exploits of local adventurers and of-fers plenty of advice on where to see what they discovered.

Carlo has turned the ground floor of the inn into a gold rush–era saloon and restaurant serving moderately priced Italian food. A new, well-seasoned chef has recently taken over the kitchen, which now operates year-round.

Address: *Main St., Box 68, Sierra City, CA 96125, tel. 916/862-1501.*
Accommodations: *4 double rooms with bath.*
Amenities: *Restaurant and bar (seasonal), whirlpool tub in 2 rooms, fireplace in 1 room.*
Rates: *$85–$110; full breakfast. MC, V.*
Restrictions: *No smoking, no pets.*

The Captain's Alpenhaus

The Captain's Alpenhaus on Lake Tahoe is an international experience. This 1944 inn, with its dormer windows and long balcony, is reminiscent of a Swiss chalet, but there's plenty of Old Tahoe–style knotty-pine paneling inside. And in a rustic dining room with a roaring fire, excellent Italian-German food is prepared by Irish chef Kerry Evans.

Retired Navy captain Joel Butler and his wife, Phyllis, have decorated their homey rooms with antique brass or wood beds with floral spreads. The suites, with their somewhat discordant patterns, don't quite measure up in charm, but there are attractive cottages out back among the Douglas fir and ponderosa pines.

Address: *6941 W. lake Blvd., Box 262, Tahoma, CA 96142, tel. 916/525-5000.*
Accommodations: *5 double rooms with bath, 2 doubles share a bath, 2 suites, 4 double housekeeping cottages.*
Amenities: *Phone in rooms, TV in some rooms, fireplace in cottages; restaurant, pool, spa, badminton, volleyball, horseshoes, Ping-Pong.*
Rates: *$65–$135; full breakfast (except for cottages). AE, D, MC, V.*
Restrictions: *No smoking indoors, pets in cottages only; 3-night minimum on holiday weekends, 2-night minimum on weekends in cottages.*

Chalfant House

This simple wood house in the heart of Bishop was built in 1898 by P. A. Chalfant, editor and publisher of the first Owens Valley newspaper, and converted in the 1940s into a hotel for silver miners. When Sally and Fred Manecke acquired it, they painstakingly restored such details as the dark-wood trim and the etched glass in the doorway transoms.

A few antique pieces are well complemented by new country-style quilts and comforters in the guest rooms. The most attractive has a princess dresser, navy-and-white wallpaper, and a grandmother's-flower-garden quilt; another boasts an impressive three-piece Eastlake set. In the dining room, with its fireplace and bay window, the Maneckes serve a breakfast that might include Dutch babies with hot cinnamon peaches, homemade bread, and their homemade grape juice.

Address: *213 Academy St., Bishop, CA 93514, tel. 619/872–1790.*
Accommodations: *5 double rooms with bath, 1 suite.*
Amenities: *TV in parlor and suite, guest phone, air-conditioning, afternoon ice-cream sundaes, off-street parking, airport pickup, antiques shop.*
Rates: *$60–$75; full breakfast. AE.*
Restrictions: *No smoking indoors, no pets; 3-night minimum Memorial Day weekend.*

Clover Valley Mill House

The Clover Valley Mill House is intimately connected with the history of the tiny sawmill town of Loyalton, abutted by the Tahoe National Forest on one side and the flat Sierra Valley on the other. A cream-colored Colonial Revival structure that sits on an acre of manicured lawn, it was built for the town's mill owner in 1906, and Leslie Hernandez bought it in 1986 from the mill's last supervisor.

Leslie has lavished the house with antiques and family heirlooms. In the sprawling living room, a beautiful oak sideboard displays a collection of Waterford crystal. The Sugarpine suite is the most alluring of the four lovely guest rooms, with a lacy daybed in the sitting room and, in the bedroom, a four-poster pine bed and matching armoire on a sky-blue dhurrie rug. After breakfast in the sunny dining nook or on the deck, you can play lawn games or just relax on the porch.

Address: *Railroad Ave. and S. 1st St., Box 928, Loyalton, CA 96118, tel. 916/993–4819.*
Accommodations: *3 double rooms (one with half-bath) share 1 full bath; 1 suite.*
Amenities: *Phone in rooms; TV with VCR in living room, horseshoes, volleyball, tetherball.*
Rates: *$75–$105; full breakfast. MC, V.*
Restrictions: *No smoking indoors, no pets.*

Cottage Inn at Lake Tahoe

hese lakeside cottages have lured visitors to Tahoe for more than 50 years. The Old Tahoe-style cottages and the main lodge, called the Pomin House, are sun-spotted under a canopy of trees and surrounded by walkways and sitting areas. Inside, guests find stream-lined pine furnishings, traditional Tahoe knotty-pine walls, and bright Scandinavian color schemes. The rooms are generally small, but the suites—two to each cottage—all have separate sitting rooms. The Family Suite is well named: A separate housekeeping unit that can be rented with or without the upstairs, it has a brass trundle bed in the parlor, a queen-size brass bed in a separate bedroom, and a TV.

The inn stands on a busy highway and is convenient to all the Tahoe attractions.

Address: *1690 W. Lake Blvd., Box 66, Tahoe City, CA 96145, tel. 916/581-4073.*
Accommodations: *6 double rooms with bath, 8 suites, 1 housekeeping suite.*
Amenities: *Afternoon refreshments, wood stoves in 2 cottages, fireplace in 1 cottage; beach access, docks, sauna, barbecues, shuffleboard, croquet, ski lockers.*
Rates: *$95–$105 weekdays, $105–$115 weekends; full breakfast. Family suite $120–$220; no breakfast. DC, MC, V.*
Restrictions: *No smoking, no pets; 2-night minimum on weekends, 3- or 4-night minimum on holidays.*

Haus Bavaria

he first bed-and-breakfast in Incline Village, built by a German couple in 1980, the two-level, stucco-and-wood Haus Bavaria is still the only B&B at the north end of the lake. It's now owned by cheerful Bick Hewitt, who left an airline job in San Diego to run the inn in 1990. Haus Bavaria is a good place for those who want quiet and convenience.

After a strenuous day on the slopes—or a lazy one on the beach—guests can relax on the leather sling-chairs in the living room, where a wood stove blazes in the corner. The simple guest rooms have Danish-style dressers and headboards and sliding glass doors that open onto private decks.

Breakfast, served in the knotty-pine dining room, might include the terrific cornmeal pancakes that Bick makes from his Texan grandmother's recipe. Ask him to recommend one of the area's several good French restaurants for dinner.

Address: *593 N. Dyer Circle, Box 3308, Incline Village, NV 89450, tel. 702/831-6122.*
Accommodations: *5 double rooms with bath.*
Amenities: *TV in living room, guest phone, mudroom, off-street parking.*
Rates: *$90; full breakfast. AE, MC, V.*
Restrictions: *No smoking indoors, no pets.*

The Matlick House

About 50 yards off Highway 395 and sheltered by a row of towering trees, the Matlick House is a good stopover for those touring the eastern side of the Sierras. This stately, three-story, gray-and-pink house with a double veranda was built in 1906 by Alan Matlick, one of the pioneers of the Owens Valley. It was restored in 1987 by Nanette Robidart, who formerly worked as a controller for a Long Beach trucking company.

The dark woods with which Nanette has furnished the spacious parlor—a claw-foot settee with massive curved arms, an antique recliner, and a European burled-wood armoire—complement the original cherry-wood fireplace. Nanette and her mother made the quilts in all of the bedrooms. The prettiest room, Lenna, has a white-iron bed, an Eastlake chair, and a pink quilted settee. A traditional American breakfast of scrambled eggs, bacon, and homemade biscuits is served in the cheery dining room.

Address: *1313 Rowan La., Bishop, CA 93514, tel. 619/873-3133.*
Accommodations: *4 double rooms with bath.*
Amenities: *Afternoon refreshments, TV in common area; air-conditioning in rooms; off-street parking.*
Rates: *$65–$75; full breakfast. No credit cards.*
Restrictions: *No smoking indoors, no pets.*

Mayfield House

Norman Mayfield, Lake Tahoe's pioneer contractor, built this classic Old Tahoe–style stone-and-shingle house in 1932 as his home and office. Converted into an inn in 1979, it was purchased in 1989 by southern California exiles Cynthia and Bruce Knauss. Close to the restaurants and shops of central Tahoe, it's separated from the commercial hub by a pine grove.

This comfortable, eclectically furnished inn, with its many sloping ceilings, has well-stocked bookshelves and fresh flowers everywhere (Cynthia and Bruce also own a flower shop). The guest rooms have cozy down comforters and pillows. Guests who eat their puffed Finnish pancakes or Portuguese French toast in the breakfast nook have a view of an English garden. They can also dine beside the stone fireplace in the living room or on the back patio.

Address: *236 Grove St., Box 5999, Tahoe City, CA 95730, tel. 916/583-1001.*
Accommodations: *5 double rooms share 3 baths.*
Amenities: *Afternoon refreshments, hall phone, TV in one room, mudroom, off-street parking.*
Rates: *$75–$125; full breakfast. MC, V.*
Restrictions: *No smoking indoors, no pets; 2-night minimum on weekends in summer and winter; 3-night minimum on holiday weekends.*

Rainbow Tarns

This rustic 1920s log house is tucked up against a hillside of enormous granite boulders that seem to defy gravity; it's fronted by three tranquil ponds where trout from nearby Crawley Lake come to spawn. In 1988, Lois Miles, a tanned outdoorswoman with a salt-and-pepper braid, bought the 3-acre property and opened a bed-and-breakfast. She renovated Rainbow Tarns in 1992, adding skylights, two deluxe bathrooms, a new kitchen, and a loft for herself.

The Victorian-style bedrooms have down comforters, lace curtains, dainty wallpaper, and hand-painted glass lamps. A Winthrop drop-front desk in the log-walled Great Room dates back to Colonial days.

Lois's breakfast feasts usually include eggs from her chicken coop. Once you're good and fed, she'll recommend the best spots for outdoors activities.

Address: *Crowley Lake Dr., Box 1097, Crowley Lake, CA 93546, tel. 619/935-4556.*
Accommodations: *3 double rooms with bath.*
Amenities: *Afternoon refreshments, TV available, 2 baths with whirlpool, trout ponds, horse stables and corral.*
Rates: *$95–$125; full breakfast. No credit cards.*
Restrictions: *No smoking indoors, no pets (horses allowed); 2-night minimum on weekends, 3-night minimum on holiday weekends.*

Rockwood Lodge

When you step inside the Rockwood Lodge, innkeepers Lou Reinkens and Connie Stevens ask you to remove your shoes—"in the Dutch tradition." Actually, the request may have more to do with the white carpet, which sets the tone for this quietly elegant, antiques-filled inn on the west shore of Lake Tahoe. The beautiful stone building—one of the last to be constructed in the Old Tahoe style, with knotty-pine paneling—was built in 1939 by Bay Area dairyman Carlos Rookwood with winnings from the Irish Sweepstakes. The adornments are as lovely as the architecture: original Dalí and Boulanger prints, an 18th-century cobbler's bench in the Rubicon Bay Room, and a 7-foot soaking tub and shower for two in the shared bathroom. The inn makes

a good headquarters for a Tahoe visit. It stands across the street from a public beach and marina, where boats can be rented, and is a short distance from ski lifts and bicycle and cross-country trails.

Address: *5295 W. Lake Blvd., Box 226, Homewood, CA 96141, tel. 916/525-5273, fax 916/525-5949.*
Accommodations: *2 double rooms with bath, 2 double rooms share a bath.*
Amenities: *Terry-cloth robes, afternoon refreshments, mudroom with ski storage, barbecue.*
Rates: *$100–$150; full breakfast. No credit cards.*
Restrictions: *Smoking outside only, no pets; 2-night minimum on weekends, 3-night minimum on holidays.*

White Horse Inn

nterior designer Diann Lloyd and her builder husband, Russ, recently moved from Palm Desert to open a B&B in Mammoth Lake. Their 1970s wooden ski house is rather nondescript, but Diann drew on the acquisitions of her extensive travels to decorate the guest rooms in a delightfully fanciful style.

The most dramatic room evokes Mammoth's Chinese Quarter from the gold-rush days: It has a Chinese wedding bed with a carved canopy, emerald-green carpeting and shoji screen, and a huge black-lace umbrella. Everything in the Blizzard Room is white: the snow-textured walls, the English featherbed, and the moire swag drapery. The Tribal Room features a twin bed draped with an old Amish buggy blanket and walls covered in camel suede. Guests meet on contemporary American territory in the billiard room, where they gather for wine and cheese, a game of darts, or an après-ski video.

Address: *2180 Old Mammoth Rd., Box 2326, Mammoth Lakes, CA 93546, tel. 619/924-3656.*
Accommodations: *3 double rooms with bath.*
Amenities: *Afternoon refreshments, air-conditioning, laundry facilities; billiard room with fireplace, kitchen, and TV with VCR; mudroom, whirlpool.*
Rates: *$125-$200; full breakfast. No credit cards.*
Restrictions: *No smoking indoors, no pets.*

Wildassin House

n contrast to the generic hotels of Main Street and the cloned condos that crowd the hillsides, this pale-blue wood cabin is an oasis of country charm. Wildassin House—built in 1949, before the first chair lift was installed at Mammoth Lake—is directly across the street from the shuttle to the ski resort, and innkeepers Roxanne and Tony Romo provide a cozy setting for year-round outdoor enthusiasts.

If they're not soaking in the hot tub under the pines, guests are usually lounging in the parlor, where a stone fireplace takes the chill off a winter evening. When the last embers die, they retire to charming rooms decorated with an eclectic variety of antique pieces and pretty bedspreads. Country Manor is the most elegant, with its canopy bed, moire-covered settee, and gold-framed portraits. The Attic Hideaway, nestled among the pines that surround the inn, feels like a tiny tree house.

Address: *26 Lupin St., Box 8026, Mammoth Lakes, CA 93546, tel. 619/934-3851.*
Accommodations: *5 double rooms with sink share 2 baths.*
Amenities: *Evening wine, TV in parlor, guest phone, mudroom, hot tub.*
Rates: *$75-$85; Continental breakfast. No credit cards.*
Restrictions: *No smoking indoors, no pets.*

Winters Creek Ranch

T he Winters Creek Ranch, situated on 10 acres on the eastern slope of the Sierra Nevada, midway between Reno and Carson City, offers an Old West, ranch-style experience with the comforts of a bed-and-breakfast inn. Built in 1980, it provides four accommodations with Victorian furnishings—a cherry-wood sleigh bed, an 1865 carved bed and nightstand, and a collection of 19th-century clothing. Innkeepers Michael and Patty Stockwell encourage guests to hike, ride horses, or mountain-bike on the many trails around the inn. Horses are a big attraction; the inn's stable includes eight for riding, plus a pair of wild mustangs. Winter guests have an equally wide selection of pursuits: ice-skating on the pond, sleigh riding, cross-country skiing, sledding down the hillside.

Because of the inn's rural location, many guests opt to order dinner from a local caterer and sup in their rooms.

Address: *1201 Hwy. 395, Washoe Valley, NV 89704, tel. 702/849–1020.*
Accommodations: *1 double room with bath, 2 suites, 1 housekeeping cottage.*
Amenities: *Fireplace in 1 room; afternoon refreshments, picnic lunches and catered dinners available, rental horses, trout pond, sleigh rides, barbecues, special events.*
Rates: *$75–$105; full breakfast. AE, MC, V.*
Restrictions: *Smoking outside only, no pets; 2-night minimum on holiday weekends.*

The Yosemite Peregrine

F inding a place to spend the night in Yosemite can seem as difficult as climbing the face of Half Dome, and if you do manage to get lodging in the valley, you've got to contend with crowds and auto fumes. A much better option has just been provided by Yosemite's federal magistrate Don Pitts and his artist wife, Kay, who opened a bed-and-breakfast on the southern edge of the national park.

Picture windows afford stunning views, and fireplaces made of local rock in each guest room are subtly patterned to reflect the room's theme. Kay has painted murals for two of the rooms and put up attractive batik curtains in all of them.

You can have a private breakfast in your room or eat in the cathedral-ceilinged dining-living area. If you're itching to head outdoors, Don and Kay will send you off for a nearby hike or a cross-country ski trip with breakfast packed to go.

Address: *7509 Hennes Circle, Box 306, Yosemite, CA 95389, tel. 209/372–8517.*
Accommodations: *3 double rooms with bath.*
Amenities: *Fireplace in rooms, spa in 1 room; TV room, off-street parking.*
Rates: *$100–$150; full breakfast. MC, V.*
Restrictions: *No smoking indoors, no pets.*

Directory 1
Alphabetical

Directory 2
Geographical

California

Please help us evaluate B&Bs and country inns for the next edition of this guide. Mail your response to Fodor's Travel Publications, Inc., 201 E. 50th St., New York, NY 10022.

B&B or Inn

City/State

Comments

B&B or Inn

City/state

Comments

General Comments

Your Name *(Optional)*

Number/Street

City/State/Zip

Fodor's Travel Guides

U.S. Guides

Alaska

Arizona

Boston

California

Cape Cod, Martha's
Vineyard, Nantucket

The Carolinas & the
Georgia Coast

Chicago

Disney World & the
Orlando Area

Florida

Hawaii

Las Vegas, Reno,
Tahoe

Los Angeles

Maine, Vermont,
New Hampshire

Maui

Miami & the Keys

New England

New Orleans

New York City

Pacific North Coast

Philadelphia & the
Pennsylvania Dutch
Country

San Diego

San Francisco

Santa Fe, Taos,
Albuquerque

Seattle & Vancouver

The South

The U.S. & British
Virgin Islands

The Upper Great
Lakes Region

USA

Vacations in New York
State

Vacations on the
Jersey Shore

Virginia & Maryland

Waikiki

Washington, D.C.

Foreign Guides

Acapulco, Ixtapa,
Zihuatanejo

Australia & New
Zealand

Austria

The Bahamas

Baja & Mexico's
Pacific Coast Resorts

Barbados

Berlin

Bermuda

Brazil

Budapest

Budget Europe

Canada

Cancun, Cozumel,
Yucatan Peninsula

Caribbean

Central America

China

Costa Rica, Belize,
Guatemala

Czechoslovakia

Eastern Europe

Egypt

Euro Disney

Europe

Europe's Great Cities

France

Germany

Great Britain

Greece

The Himalayan
Countries

Hong Kong

India

Ireland

Israel

Italy

Italy's Great Cities

Japan

Kenya & Tanzania

Korea

London

Madrid & Barcelona

Mexico

Montreal &
Quebec City

Morocco

The Netherlands
Belgium &
Luxembourg

New Zealand

Norway

Nova Scotia, Prince
Edward Island &
New Brunswick

Paris

Portugal

Rome

Russia & the Baltic
Countries

Scandinavia

Scotland

Singapore

South America

Southeast Asia

South Pacific

Spain

Sweden

Switzerland

Thailand

Tokyo

Toronto

Turkey

Vienna & the Danube
Valley

Yugoslavia

Fodor's Travel Guides

Special Series

Fodor's Affordables

Affordable Europe

Affordable France

Affordable Germany

Affordable Great
Britain

Affordable Italy

**Fodor's Bed &
Breakfast and
Country Inns Guides**

California

Mid-Atlantic Region

New England

The Pacific Northwest

The South

The West Coast

The Upper Great
Lakes Region

Canada's Great
Country Inns

Cottages, B&Bs and
Country Inns of
England and Wales

The Berkeley Guides

On the Loose in
California

On the Loose in
Eastern Europe

On the Loose in
Mexico

On the Loose in the
Pacific Northwest &
Alaska

**Fodor's Exploring
Guides**

Exploring California

Exploring Florida

Exploring France

Exploring Germany

Exploring Paris

Exploring Rome

Exploring Spain

Exploring Thailand

Fodor's Flashmaps

New York

Washington, D.C.

Fodor's Pocket Guides

Pocket Bahamas

Pocket Jamaica

Pocket London

Pocket New York
City

Pocket Paris

Pocket Puerto Rico

Pocket San Francisco

Pocket Washington,
D.C.

Fodor's Sports

Cycling

Hiking

Running

Sailing

The Insider's Guide
to the Best Canadian
Skiing

**Fodor's Three-In-Ones
(guidebook, language
cassette, and phrase
book)**

France

Germany

Italy

Mexico

Spain

**Fodor's
Special-Interest
Guides**

Cruises and Ports
of Call

Disney World & the
Orlando Area

Euro Disney

Healthy Escapes

London Companion

Skiing in the USA
& Canada

Sunday in New York

**Fodor's Touring
Guides**

Touring Europe

Touring USA:
Eastern Edition

Touring USA:
Western Edition

**Fodor's Vacation
Planners**

Great American
Vacations

National Parks of the
West

**The Wall Street
Journal Guides to
Business Travel**

Europe

International Cities

Pacific Rim

USA & Canada